Paul's Epistle

to the

Ephesians

IN GRATEFUL APPRECIATION

To my family and staff who were more than patient with me when I was *preoccupied* with the manuscript. Surely a great recompense of reward awaits them at the Lord's appearing.

Once again, to my dear wife, Vicki, who has always encouraged me in the work. She spent many hours smoothing out the original manuscript and putting together the Scripture Index that appears in the back of the volume.

To my son and faithful co-laborer, Kevin, who laid out and typeset the entire manuscript. Since I tend to be a *perfectionist*, his job was not an easy one, but I am most thankful for his patience and understanding.

Many, many thanks to Pastor David Havard, Linda Bedore, Fred Wisniewski, and Wesley Baum, all of whom painstakingly proofread the whole manuscript and offered many *helpful* suggestions. Since authors tend to run rough-shod over their errors, if you find a mistake I'm sure *they* would love to hear from you!!! A challenge some are sure to take seriously, especially since they're like needles in a haystack.

We also want to convey our appreciation to all those who contributed to this project that it might become a reality. Mere words fail to convey my *appreciation* for your prayers and support.

Finally, thanks be unto God for supplying the opportunity and the strength to complete this work. It is the author's earnest prayer that God will be *glorified* in this labor of love.

—The Author

PREFACE

The ministries of the *Berean Bible Society* are an outgrowth of Pastor C. R. Stam's first pastorate in 1940. Since that time BBS has grown into an international organization reaching millions with the gospel of the grace of God. The purpose of the *Berean Bible Society* is to help believers understand and enjoy the Word of God, rightly divided. In 1987 I had the privilege of joining Mr. Stam in the work. He was becoming increasingly concerned that failing health would soon force him to hang up the spikes, as it were. Thus, to insure that his legacy would continue, I was called upon to oversee his writings. But Pastor Stam also understood that *new* works would need to be written to address current issues in the Church. This commentary is one such work.

The *Book of Ephesians* has been called the Alps of the Pauline Epistles. It most assuredly brings us to the pinnacle of Body truth where the doctrines of *grace* might be viewed in their fullest sense. I asked Pastor Stam, over dinner one evening, why he had never written a commentary on *Ephesians*. He explained that years ago *Ephesians* was so frequently preached in our churches that he felt most Grace believers had a fairly good understanding of the epistle. Thus, when Brother Stam began his writing ministry, he directed his attention to those areas of Paul's revelation that weren't dealt with as extensively from the pulpit.

I guess it seemed to me that *Ephesians* was the logical place to begin, although I could see Pastor Stam's point having gone through the latter part of the era he was speaking of. But times *change*! Today, the Grace message has spread around the world from its humble beginnings in this country. Furthermore only a small percentage of believers have the unique privilege of attending a Grace assembly. Consequently, a large number are dependent upon our Grace

11

organizations for sound literature that they might grow in the grace and knowledge of our Lord Jesus Christ according to the *Mystery*.

If the Lord tarries, we pray this volume will be used of God to bring many into a fuller knowledge of His will. "That ye might walk worthy of the Lord unto all pleasing, being fruitful in every good work, and increasing in the knowledge of God" (Col. 1:10).

—Pastor Paul M. Sadler

INTRODUCTION

The *Berean Bible Society* is a conservative Christian organization dedicated to the proclamation of Christ and Him crucified. We hold to all the fundamentals of the faith, therefore, we believe:

The verbal inspiration and plenary authority of the Word of God in its original writings—the eternal trinity of the Godhead—the eternal deity and spotless humanity of the Lord Jesus Christ—mankind by nature is sinful and under the condemnation of God—personal salvation is by God's grace through faith in the crucified, risen, glorified Lord—the eternal security of all the saved—the personality and deity of the Holy Spirit—the communion of the Lord's Supper—the resurrection of the body—the Pretribulational Rapture of the Church—the personal, Premillennial return of Christ to reign on earth, and the eternal punishment of the unsaved.

We also acknowledge the *distinct* apostleship and message of Paul, which sets us apart from the traditional Acts 2 dispensationalists. As we shall see in the pages that follow, all Scripture is for us, but it is not all written to us, nor is it all about us. According to II Timothy 2:15, we must rightly divide the Word of truth to ascertain what God's will is for the Church with regard to the Mystery. The Mystery "hid in God" was the *divine* purpose to make Jew and Gentile a whole new entity, that is, the Church, which is Christ's Body.

The revelation of this truth was committed to the Apostle Paul and as Dr. C. I. Scofield stated: "In his writings alone we find the doctrine, position, walk, and destiny of the Church."[1] This symphony of God's wonderful *grace* is revealed in its fullness in *Ephesians*. Not even the angels of heaven had any knowledge of this *hidden* revelation until the conversion

13

of Paul on the road to Damascus. "O the depth of the riches both of the wisdom and knowledge of God! How unsearchable are His judgments, and His ways past finding out!"

Our family has taken a number of guided tours over the years. They normally give you insight into things you may have never thought of before. With God's help, we would like to serve as your tour guide through Paul's letter to the *Ephesians*. Always keep us in sight on the tour so Satan doesn't mislead you with the traditions and commandments of men. May this feeble effort bring honor to His name and extol the riches of His grace.

—Pastor Paul M. Sadler

Milwaukee, Wisconsin
August 12, 1999

1

A Clear View From Mt. Everest

"Paul, an apostle of Jesus Christ by the will of God,
to the saints which are at Ephesus, and to the faithful
in Christ Jesus."

—Ephesians 1:1

The city of Ephesus was a teeming metropolis that served
as the capital of proconsular Asia. Located on the Cayster
River, which flowed into the Aegean Sea, Ephesus was a
commercial mecca of the ancient world. Like Chicago, all
roads passed through this *opulent* Gentile city as it formed
a natural bridge between the East and the West. Pliny, the
Roman naturalist and writer, called Ephesus the "ornament
of Asia." Travelers were awestruck by the Greek architec-
ture that graced the landscape, not to mention being intoxi-
cated by the Greek games and philosophy.

In the eyes of the Ephesians, however, the crown jewel of
the city was the temple of Diana, considered to be one of the
seven wonders of the ancient world. Historians tell us that
the temple was 425 feet in length and 220 feet in breadth.
On the outer perimeter stood 127 magnificent pillars, each of
which towered 60 feet in height. Within this edifice stood the
goddess Diana, whose name was revered throughout the then
known world. In addition, archeologists have discovered that
her image was quite common on Greek coins in Asia, which
included cities such as Ephesus, Hierapolis, Perga, and Samos.
It could be said, what Chase-Manhattan Bank is to New York,
Diana's temple treasury was to the Ephesians.

Diana was served by hundreds of priestesses who were nothing more than temple prostitutes. These morally bankrupt liaisons most likely drew many unsuspecting worshippers of the goddess into the magical arts (Acts 19:11-19). Luke records these enlightening words for us in his journal on the life and times of the apostles:

> "So that not only this our craft [the silversmiths who made idols] is in danger to be set at nought; but also that the temple of the great goddess Diana should be despised, and her magnificence should be destroyed, *whom all Asia and the world worshippeth"* (Acts 19:27).

> "All with one voice about the space of two hours cried out, Great is Diana of the Ephesians. And when the town clerk had appeased the people, he said, Ye men of Ephesus, what man is there that knoweth not how that the city of the Ephesians is a worshipper of the great goddess Diana, and of the image which fell down from Jupiter?" (Acts 19:34,35).

Into this den of debauchery came the Apostle Paul to preach the gospel of the grace of God. Although the apostle only stopped briefly at Ephesus during the end of his second apostolic journey, he returned about two years later for an extended visit (Acts 18:19-21 cf. 19:1,9,10).

Customarily the apostle entered the area synagogue when he arrived at his destination. The purpose for this was twofold: First, the synagogue was the meeting place where the Jews gathered to worship. It would be the natural place to begin to preach Christ. Furthermore, the Gentiles who desired to know more about the true and living God would often gather outside, which gave the apostle an audience among *both* the Jews and the Gentiles (Acts 13:16,42). Second, this platform also gave Paul the opportunity he needed to announce to Israel that she was being set aside in unbelief.

When the religious leaders of the synagogue at Ephesus hardened their hearts against the gospel, Paul moved his base of operations to the School of Tyrannus, from where all Asia heard the Word of God. This should be a solemn lesson to religious leaders today. If they continue in their unbelief God will send the message of His redeeming love to those who will receive it.

For the better part of two years the apostle boldly proclaimed there are "no gods, which are made with hands" (Acts 19:26). Of course, this didn't sit well with the craftsmen who made silver shrines for the goddess Diana—their livelihood was being placed in jeopardy. Consequently, they literally dragged Paul's companions into the open-air theater and would have beaten them to death had it not been for the intervention of the town clerk. Nevertheless, without regard for his life the apostle continued to preach the Cross in the midst of this intense opposition. As a result, many turned from their idol worship to serve the living and true God.

From this turbulent beginning sprang one of the more spiritual assemblies Paul established. Having been tried in the furnace of affliction, these saints were now prepared to ascend to the summit of God's will for the Church, which is His Body. Thus, the Book of Ephesians brings us to the very *pinnacle* of Body truth. Those who have visited the Rocky Mountains know something of their majesty. But this is not to be compared with the ever-abounding majesty of God's grace found here in Ephesians.

Perhaps we should pause for a moment to point out that the saints addressed here by the Apostle Paul should never be confused with the church of Ephesus found in the Apocalypse. According to Ussher, the Apostle John penned the Book of Revelation from the Isle of Patmos around 96 A.D.

Of course, by this date the temple at Jerusalem had been destroyed, most of the kingdom saints had passed from the scene, and the dispensation of Grace was in full bloom. With this in mind, we believe that the Book of Revelation is entirely *futuristic*.

> "I John, who also am your brother, and companion in tribulation, and in the kingdom and patience of Jesus Christ, was in the isle that is called Patmos, for the Word of God, and for the testimony of Jesus Christ" (Rev. 1:9).

The phrase "companion in tribulation" has the definite article before the term *tribulation* in the original. In other words, John was their companion through the events of *the* Tribulation, and in the kingdom (millennial reign of Christ). But how could this be possible inasmuch as these events are yet future? The solution to the problem is found in verse 10: "I was in the Spirit on the Lord's day, and heard behind me a great voice, as of a trumpet."

The Spirit of God supernaturally transported John to the future *day of the Lord*.[1] While there, he was instructed to record what he had witnessed and "*send* it unto the seven churches which are in Asia; unto *Ephesus*, and unto Smyrna, and unto Pergamos, and unto Thyatira, and unto Sardis, and unto Philadelphia, and unto Laodicea" (Rev 1:11). Essentially this was accomplished when this message was included in the canon of Holy Scripture. Therefore, the church at Ephesus referred to by John is a future *Jewish* assembly clearly associated with the Kingdom Program (Rev. 2:1-7,9,14,26, etc.). On the other hand, the church at Ephesus that Paul addresses was a *Gentile* assembly that had been raised up to make all men see what is the fellowship of the Mystery (Eph. 3:1-3,8,9).

DATE AND THEME OF THE EPISTLE

Ephesians was written from Rome in 64 A.D. by the Apostle Paul. Due to the apostle's failing eyesight, he normally dictated his letters to a personal secretary. In this particular case Tychicus was apparently called upon for the task at hand. We do know for certain that he carried the epistle to its final destination (Eph. 1:1 cf. 6:21). This letter is the first of Paul's prison epistles, which marks the division between the apostle's early and latter ministries. To help you place when the Book of Ephesians was written, we would suggest the following chronological order of Paul's epistles:[2]

Pre-Prison Epistles: *I & II Thessalonians* were written during Paul's visit at Corinth—54 A.D. (Acts 18:1,5,11 cf. I Thes. 3:1-13).

I & II Corinthians were penned at Ephesus where the apostle resided for a period of two years—59-60 A.D. (Acts 19:1,8-10 cf. I Cor. 15:30-34).

Romans and Galatians were the fruits of Paul's stay at Corinth for three months—60 A.D. (Acts 20:1-3).

Prison Epistles*: Ephesians, Philippians, Colossians, Philemon, I Timothy, and Hebrews* were the product of the apostle's labors during his first Roman imprisonment—64 A.D. (Acts 28:16,29,30 cf. Eph. 6:20; Phil. 1:12-19; Col. 4:7-10; Philemon 1:1; I Tim. 3:14; Phil. 2:17-24 cf. Heb. 13:23-25).

Liberty Epistle: *Titus* was probably written during Paul's brief release from prison while he resided at Nicopolis awaiting the return of Titus from Crete—65 A.D. (Titus 3:12).

Second Roman Imprisonment Epistle: *II Timothy* was the last epistle that Paul wrote just prior to his death at Rome—66 A.D. (II Tim. 1:8; 4:6-9).

The theme of Ephesians is clearly *God's Eternal Purpose for the Church, the Body of Christ* (Eph. 3:11,12). In this epistle, Paul fully develops the doctrines of grace which distinguish this dispensation from all others. Within the guidelines of our theme the book is divided into two parts—*Standing* (chapters 1-3), and *State* (chapters 4-6).

The believer's standing has to do with his position in Christ. It is a perfect, unchangeable work that has been accomplished by God. Positionally, we are blessed with all spiritual blessings in the heavenlies. In regard to redemption for example, the moment we believe the gospel our sins (past, present, and future) are *forgiven* according to the riches of His grace (Eph. 1:7). That's our position; it's like the water flowing over Niagara Falls—constant!

The state of the believer, however, is *imperfect* and often changes from moment to moment. This is the practical side of the Christian life or as some have called it, "divine training and development." Every January the President of the United States gives what is known as the *State of the Union* address. It's sort of a barometer of the nation's condition. Interestingly, different themes emerge every year. The believer's state is much the same way—always changing! Thus, our experiences, which are many and varied, are to be brought into conformity with our standing.

A believer may understand he is forgiven in Christ, but have difficulty forgiving others who have wronged him. But God says: "And be ye kind one to another, tenderhearted, forgiving one another, even as God for Christ's sake hath forgiven you" (Eph. 4:32). The following illustrates the above:

"Years after her concentration camp experiences in Nazi Germany, Corrie ten Boom met face to face one of the most cruel and heartless German guards that she had ever contacted. He had humiliated and degraded her and her sister. He had jeered and visually raped them as they stood in the tells us of the exceeding riches of His grace in kindness towards us through Christ Jesus. But even this definition does not tell half of all the Glory this wonderful document contains. It is God's highest and God's best. Even God cannot say more than what He has said in this filling full of His Word."[4]

If you are called to help others, then be innovative, coming up with new ways to minister to the brethren. You might take a dear saint aside who is bewildered and give him a few words of godly counsel. In our former ministry, we used to place a rose on the pulpit which announced the arrival of a newborn in our midst. Sometimes our thoughtfulness of others will go a long way in opening new doors to minister to them in spiritual things.

If God has called you to be a *pastor* then fulfill your ministry, don't be half-hearted, but preach in the power of the Spirit. Put your heart and soul into the work; however, be careful not to neglect your family. If you're a Sunday School teacher strive for excellence by developing new illustrations to make the Scriptures come alive to those young, impressionable minds.

May God give us the strength to serve Him with fervor of the Spirit as if it were our last day on the face of the earth. After all, it just might be! Why not consider becoming more involved in the Lord's work by rededicating yourself to some area of His service? There is nothing more satisfying to the soul than to further the cause of Christ and the blessed message of Grace. We must always remember, only those things which are done for Christ are going to endure throughout eternity! To think that He has chosen to use unworthy sinners, such as you and me, to carry out His will. It is an honor, indeed!

You can be sure that failures and setbacks are going to occur. These are inevitable due to the fall of man and Satanic attacks. Problems are going to arise from places we thought there were no problems. But take heart, Paul didn't quit, nor should we. He was determined, as we should be, to press toward the mark and rest in the hope that one day soon the Lord will return and resurrect us from among the dead, that is, "out from among" the dead prophetic saints and the unsaved, at which time He will catch us out to take us home to forever be with Him.

DISPENSATIONAL DISTINCTIONS

"To the saints which are at Ephesus, and to the faithful in Christ Jesus" (vs. 1).

As we have seen, the scope of Paul's words here extend far beyond Ephesus. The apostle is addressing the Church in general. Dispensationally, the saints and faithful in Christ Jesus should not be confused with the prophetic saints. The saints to whom Paul was writing were members of the Body of Christ.

Today, many have the misconception that sainthood is only conferred upon those who performed at least two miracles and lived exemplary lives during their pilgrimage here on earth. Normally, the act of canonization is not bestowed until centuries after the death of the one being venerated. According to the encyclopedia, "Canonization is a proclamation...by which a person famous for holiness is understood to be in heaven. That person is given the title of saint. Respect is shown for a saint through prayers, festivals, and art connected with the individual, and the church encourages imitation of the saint's life.

"The church conducts a strict examination and inquiry into the person's life and virtue before issuing the proclamation of canonization. The examination may require several miracles attributed to the person. The individual can then be proposed as an example of how to live a dedicated spiritual life. Only certain people are declared saints through canonization."[1]

While religion may sing the virtues of this position, it is a flat contradiction of the Word of God. According to the

Scriptures, the moment a sinner places his faith in the finished work of Christ, he is a *saint*. The Greek word *hagios* was used by the pagans to describe a temple that was set apart for a particular Greek god. In the biblical sense it has the idea to be "separated from sin and therefore consecrated [set apart] to God" for some area of service.[2] In short, we have been taken out of Adam and placed into Christ. In Christ, every saint is justified, sanctified, and glorified.

Interestingly, Paul addresses both the *saints* at Ephesus and the *faithful* in Christ Jesus. While all the "faithful" are saints, it cannot be said that all the "saints" are necessarily faithful. The apostle, for example, commended Timothy for his faithfulness to the cause of Christ. But this could not be said of all his coworkers. It was with a heavy heart that Paul had to inform the brethren that Demas had forsaken the things of the Lord, having loved this present world. Both were saints, but the conduct of Demas grieved the heart of God. There's an old saying that goes something like this: "To live with the saints above, oh, that will be glory; but to dwell here below with the ones that we know, well, that's another story."

We should note that Paul was the *first* to call our Lord *Christ Jesus* in contrast to Jesus Christ. While the name "Jesus Christ" is closely associated with the Lord's humiliation, the name "Christ Jesus" has to do with His *exaltation* as the glorified Lord of heaven. Thus, those who are "in Christ" dispensationally share in His exaltation.

> "Grace be to you, and peace, from God our Father, and from the Lord Jesus Christ" (vs. 2).

Most commentators conclude that the opening words of Paul's epistles are merely his salutation to the churches. But a closer reading is revealing—you may want to read the passage a second time. Notice that this is not a salutation from the pen of Paul, but a *declaration* from God the Father and God the Son. A declaration, we might add, that is dispensationally significant.

Have you ever been asked why God hasn't poured out His wrath on this evil world system and established the kingdom of His dear Son? This is a legitimate question, one that we believe deserves an honest answer. What is hindering the fulfillment of these prophetic events? Simple! With the nation Israel *derailed* due to the rejection of her Messiah, God has temporarily left her on a remote siding. This means that the prophetic freight is sitting idle on the rails. Today, God is operating non-stop service to the Rapture on the *GraceXpress.* Once the members of the Body of Christ reach their heavenly destination, Israel and the prophetic freight will again be permitted to return to the mainline.

Hence, today God is declaring "grace" and "peace" to an undeserving world. The opposite of grace is "works" while the opposite of peace is "war." Of course, "works" and "war" characterized the Prophetic Program. Under that program, faith expressed itself by *works.* If an Israelite lived under the law, if he believed Christ was his Messiah, he expressed his faith by being water baptized. Failure to do so was an indication of *unbelief* (Mk. 16:16 cf. Luke 7:28-30). In addition, the chosen nation always looked forward with anticipation to the day when Jehovah would declare war on her enemies and deliver her from the hand of the oppressor. That day will indeed come—it's called the *day of the Lord!* (Psa. 2:1-12 cf. Zeph. 1:14-18).

But now, God is lavishing the world with the riches of His grace. Thus, we are saved by grace through faith alone apart from works. Paul plainly says: "But to him that **worketh not**, but believeth on Him that justifieth the ungodly, his faith is counted for righteousness" (Rom. 4:5). Those who are the recipients of His grace will be delivered from the wrath to come. Brethren, we should humbly thank God that we are living under God's declaration of peace (Eph. 1:2 cf. I Thes. 5:9-11).[3]

3

The Charter of the Church

"Blessed be the God and Father of our Lord Jesus
Christ, who hath blessed us with all spiritual blessings
in heavenly places in Christ."

—*Ephesians 1:3*

Paul could have written a novel about the glories of the
Roman Empire. He had heard the roar of the crowds at the
coliseum, walked along the Appian Way, experienced the
forum, and stood in the ivory palace of Caesar. But the
apostle knew it was all a *fading* glory. Like the morning
dew, it would soon be swept away. The believer is not to
look "at the things which are seen, but at the things which
are not seen: for the things which are seen are temporal;
but the things which are not seen are eternal" (II Cor.
4:18).

Although Paul was a prisoner of Rome at the time of this
writing, he never allowed the experience to rob him of his
joy. But trials will do just that if we fail to keep our eyes
upon the Lord. The apostle had learned the importance of
setting his affections on things above. Consequently, as the
wonders of God's matchless grace filled the apostle's mind,
he delivered perhaps the most significant doxology found in
his epistles.

"Blessed be the God and Father of our Lord Jesus
Christ, who hath blessed us with all spiritual blessings
in heavenly *places* in Christ" (vs. 3).

THE BELIEVER'S POSITION IN CHRIST

God is worthy of our worship by virtue of who He is—the Creator and Sustainer of all things. But we also lift our voices in praise and thanksgiving before the throne because He has blessed us beyond measure. And it was to the Apostle Paul that God chose to reveal His *eternal purpose* for the Church, the Body of Christ. Namely, that we are blessed with all spiritual blessings in heavenly places. The translators supplied the word "places" here to show that it doesn't appear in the original language. The actual Greek construction is *en tois epouranios* or "in the heavenlies." The phrase is a reference to the sphere from where our blessings emanate, for we only enjoy our position and blessings in the heavenlies according to the measure of our faith.

We would venture to say that most believers would probably be hard-pressed to name seven spiritual blessings we enjoy in Christ. Now be honest; can you? Some claim there are well over a hundred to be found in Paul's epistles. While this may be true, we do know that there are at least seven blessings presented to us here in verses 3 through 14. Before commenting on these riches, we need to understand that there has been a shift in emphasis from that which was revealed in time past.

Those who lived prior to the dispensation of Grace were given an *earthly* hope and calling. In accordance with their program, God primarily blessed them with *physical blessings*. This is another important dispensational distinction which must not be overlooked. It clearly shows that God is doing something entirely new and different today among the Gentiles. If you will bear with me for a moment, I would like to contrast Israel's blessings under the *law* with those that we possess under *grace*.

BLESSINGS IN THE LAND

> "And it shall come to pass, if thou shalt hearken diligently unto the voice of the LORD thy God, to observe and to do all His commandments which I command thee this day, that the LORD thy God will set thee on high above all nations of the earth: And all these blessings shall come on thee, and overtake thee, if thou shalt hearken unto the voice of the LORD thy God" (Deut. 28:1,2).

Notice that Israel's blessings were *conditional*. "**If** thou shalt hearken diligently unto the voice of the LORD thy God, to observe and to do all His commandments...." In other words, her blessings were contingent upon obedience to the law. While Israel was promised spiritual blessings according to the law and the prophets, her primary blessings were physical in nature. For example:

1. *"Blessed shalt thou be in the city..."* (vs. 3). What do people normally do when they travel to the city? They buy, sell or trade. God promised Israel that He would richly bless her business dealings at the marketplace. She would never be left holding the short end of the stick, as they say!

2. *"Blessed shalt thou be in the field"* (vs. 3). When the Israelite put his hand to plow, the earth yielded her fullness. Seedtime and harvest would be celebrations throughout the land. According to the law, those who tilled the ground were never permitted to harvest the corners of the fields or glean the vineyards. This was reserved for the poor. Thus, God looked favorably upon even the least among them (Lev. 19:9,10 cf. Ruth 2:4-7).

3. *"Blessed shall be the fruit of thy body, and the fruit of thy ground, and the fruit of thy cattle, the increase of thy kine, and the flocks of thy sheep"* (vs. 4). Sadly, many families today consider conception a curse. In the days of Israel just the opposite was true; it was a curse to be barren. Thus,

God promised the nation that throughout her generations, they would hear the pitter-patter of little footsteps in their homes. This blessing even extended to the chosen nation's herds and flocks, which in biblical times was always a measure of wealth and prosperity.

4. *"Blessed shall be thy basket and thy store"* (vs. 5). The term "store" used here by Moses is the Hebrew word *mishereth* or kneading-trough. In short, there would always be *bread* upon the Hebrew's table. Even through the wilderness wanderings, God faithfully provided manna from heaven.

5. *"Blessed shalt thou be when thou comest in, and blessed shalt thou be when thou goest out"* (vs. 6). The Israelites were also promised a blessing on their family life. This included their devotions and the instruction of their children and everything in between. In addition, He gave them *rest* from their labors. In the event that they traveled outside the camp where thieves and robbers often lurked, God granted them journey's mercies.

6. *"The LORD shall cause thine enemies that rise up against thee to be smitten before thy face: they shall come out against thee one way, and flee before thee seven ways"* (vs. 7). Every Israeli found comfort in the fact that God had put a protective hedge around the congregation of Israel. Essentially, He promised to go before them like a mighty man of war. Thus, when the chosen nation was in the center of God's will, her enemies were scattered to the four winds. Of course, it wasn't long before the nations of the world came to fear the God of Israel.

7. *"The LORD shall command the blessing upon thee in thy storehouses, and in all that thou settest thine hand unto; and He shall bless thee in the land which the LORD thy God giveth thee"* (vs. 8). Even her storehouses would be protected

from infestations and adverse weather conditions. We should also note that these blessings were closely associated with Israel's occupation of the land. This, of course, is the Land of Promise that was deeded to Abraham, Isaac, and Jacob (Gen. 12:1-4; 26:1-5; 28:10-15). Consequently, Israel's hope and blessings were inseparably tied to the earth.

These blessings and many, many more would be generously bestowed upon Israel *if* she met God's demands. Once again, the key word here is "if." Israel's blessings were conditional; that is, she had to obey the Law of Moses to receive the full benefit of them. Failure to do so brought her under the curse of God, as promised in Deuteronomy 27:26: "Cursed be he that confirmeth not all the words of this law to do them. And all the people shall say, Amen."

BLESSINGS IN THE HEAVENLIES

If we rightly divide the Word of truth consistently, it will lift the fog from our understanding. Once we begin to see Paul's gospel clearly, it immediately becomes apparent that God has changed His dealings with mankind in a wonderful way.

> "Blessed be the God and Father of our Lord Jesus Christ, who hath blessed us with all spiritual blessings in heavenly *places* in Christ."

Notice the absence of the supposition "if." There are no conditions to be met under grace. We have received the full benefit of our blessings in Christ—they are a present possession! We simply need to lay hold of them by *faith*. In addition to the spiritual blessings we enjoy, God has promised to meet our needs according to His good pleasure. Therefore, any physical blessings God may bestow upon us today are merely icing on the cake.

With God's help, we would now like to share the seven spiritual blessings we enjoy in Christ that are found here in Ephesians 1:4-14:

1. *"According as He hath chosen us in Him before the foundation of the world, that we should be holy and without blame before Him in love"* (vs. 4). Clearly we have been chosen in Him before the world began. The key phrase here is "in Him." Christ is the source of our salvation and spiritual blessings. He is the Author and Finisher of our faith.

Here we learn that the Body of Christ wasn't an afterthought of God, but a *forethought*. With the world ripe for judgment following the stoning of Stephen, God interrupted the Prophetic Program to make known the Mystery, which He had hidden from ages and generations past.

In eternity past, God had planned and purposed that there would be the *corporate* entity known as the Church, the Body of Christ, and that it would be composed of Jews and Gentiles without distinction. We were chosen for the praise of His glory, that in the ages to come He might present us to Himself "a glorious Church, not having spot, or wrinkle, or any such thing."

The *doctrine of election* has long been a bone of contention among the brethren. It almost always produces more heat than light! This is undoubtedly one of the reasons why there is so little understood about it. The following are the most popular views on the doctrine of divine election. Unfortunately, each of them leaves us with more *questions* than answers.

1. God elected some to be saved while passing by others. This view is called individual election unto salvation.

2. Free will: On the basis that God foreknew who would believe, He simply chose them to comprise the Church, the Body of Christ.

3. The antinomy position—both "election" and "whosoever will may come" are equally true.

4. Election is merely unto service.

What we are about to present is by no means the final word on the matter. In fact, we hold those in high regard who defend other positions knowing that they, too, have sincerely sought to offer a plausible explanation to an extremely complex subject.

May we suggest that *both* "election" and "whosoever will may come" are taught in the Word of God. A proper understanding of these two doctrines will deepen our appreciation for the goodness of God.

> **Election:** "But we are bound to give thanks always to God for you, brethren beloved of the Lord, because God hath from the beginning *chosen* you to *salvation* through sanctification of the Spirit and belief of the truth: Whereunto he called you by our *gospel*, to the obtaining of the glory of our Lord Jesus Christ" (II Thes. 2:13,14 cf. I Tim. 6:12).

> **Whosoever will:** "For there is no difference between the Jew and the Greek: for the same Lord over all is rich unto all that *call* upon him. For *whosoever* shall call upon the name of the Lord shall be *saved*" (Rom. 10:12,13 cf. Acts 13:26).

> **Election:** "For so hath the Lord commanded us, saying, I have set thee to be a light of the Gentiles, that thou shouldest be for *salvation* unto the ends of the earth. And when the Gentiles heard this, they were glad, and glorified the Word of the Lord: and as many as were *ordained* to eternal life *believed*" (Acts 13:47,48 cf. Rom. 8:30-33).

> **Whosoever will:** "For I am not ashamed of the gospel of Christ: for it is the power of God unto *salvation* to *every one* that believeth; to the Jew first, and also to the Greek" (Rom. 1:16 cf. Titus 2:11).

Election: "Remember that Jesus Christ of the seed of David was raised from the dead according to my *gospel*: Wherein I suffer trouble, as an evil doer, even unto bonds; but the Word of God is not bound. Therefore I endure all things for the *elect's* sakes, that they may also obtain the *salvation* which is in Christ Jesus with eternal glory" (II Tim. 2:8-10 cf. Rom. 11:5).

Whosoever will: "For this is good and acceptable in the sight of God our Savior; who will have *all* men to be *saved*, and to come unto the knowledge of the truth" (I Tim. 2:3,4 cf. Rom. 3:22).

While this may seem to be a contradiction to our finite minds, it is nevertheless a clear line of teaching throughout the Scriptures. Through the years many have sought unsuccessfully to reconcile these two doctrines. But most agree that they will probably remain unreconcilable until eternity. It could be God never intended them to be reconciled. Perhaps they are meant to remain independent of one another?

We merely have an *antinomy*, that is, "a contradiction between two apparently equally valid principles."[1] Beloved, which statement is true: Christ is *wholly God*, or Christ is *wholly man*?[2] "For in Him [Christ] dwelleth all the fulness of the Godhead bodily" (Col. 2:9). Even though we cannot reconcile these two statements, we accept by faith that *both* are true. May we suggest that the same consideration be given to the doctrines before us.

Consider for a moment the *elect* in Israel. They were called His sheep, but interestingly the good Shepherd also spoke of *other* sheep which must be brought into the fold. "As the Father knoweth me, even so know I the Father: and I lay down my life for the sheep. And *other* sheep I have, which are not of this fold: them also I must bring, and they shall hear my voice; and there shall be *one fold*, and one shepherd" (John 10:15-16 cf. Acts 2:21).

Brethren, the subjects of the *sovereignty of God* and *human responsibility* have been hotly debated for centuries by some of the greatest scholars that have ever graced the Church. But when it was all said and done, most of them had to humbly confess that the issue went far beyond their comprehension. However, this doesn't imply that we shouldn't continue to study the matter.

Our inability to plumb the depths of God's grace doesn't mean that election is untrue. Nor does it give us the liberty to eradicate the doctrine from the Scriptures. Let us be careful not to minimize the glory of His grace by calling into question the good pleasure of His will. It is far better to wait upon the Lord for further light.

It is questionable that we will fully comprehend these wonderful truths on this side of glory, simply because God has not seen fit to fully reveal the counsel of His will on the matter. Therefore, we should respect one another's convictions on the subject and never allow the discussion to deteriorate to the point where it disrupts our fellowship. But there is one thing that all sides can and should agree upon— we can all uphold our *God-given responsibility* to preach the gospel and leave the end result with the Lord. In regard to lost souls, may the desire of our heart be that of Paul's, "I am made all things to all men, that I might by all means save some" (I Cor. 9:22).

"According as he hath chosen us in him before the foundation of the world, that we should be holy and without blame before him in love" (vs. 4). Clearly God the Father conceived our spiritual blessings before the foundation of the world. Some have drawn the conclusion from Paul's usage of the Greek word *katabole* (foundation) that the apostle is making a veiled reference to the Ruin and Reconstruction Theory. That is, God destroyed the original creation due to

sin leaving millions, perhaps billions, of years before He created the present heavens and earth recorded in Genesis chapter one. According to Strong the term *katabole* denotes "a deposition, i.e. founding," or "a casting down" as W. E. Vine defines it.[3] Those who hold to the Gap Theory conclude that it was before God cast down the original creation in judgment that He chose us in Christ.

However, we do not believe that *katabole* is to be understood here in the sense of judgment. For example, Paul states that he was "cast down" (*katabole*), but *not destroyed* (II Cor. 4:9). Rather the term has the idea of laying down or founding, similar to the foundation that a house is built upon. The classical Greek also corroborates this definition. Thus, *before* He laid the foundation of the earth, God chose us in Christ and blessed us with all spiritual blessings in the heavenlies. The Ruin and Reconstruction Theory self-destructs in view of Genesis 1:31:

> "And God saw every thing that He had made, and, behold, it was very good. And the evening and the morning were the sixth day."

After God surveyed His creative handiwork in heaven and earth, He pronounced it very good. This pronouncement could not have been made had sin and death been present anywhere in God's creation. Apparently, Lucifer fell sometime between Genesis 1:31 and Genesis 3:1 when he appeared in the garden to tempt our first parents. Interestingly, God never again calls His creation good, much less very good, after this point.

The fact that *"we should be holy and without blame before Him in love"* has to do with our *character*. This is a reference to our positional sanctification. In Christ, we are holy. God has set us apart from sin unto Himself that we might worship and serve Him. Furthermore, we are *without* blame or blemish before Him in love. However, what we enjoy positionally in Christ must translate to our everyday lives—while we are in the world, we are not of the world. In short, you want the boat in the water, but not the water in the boat. In a practical sense, to be without blame means that our conduct is above reproach.

2. *"Having predestinated us unto the adoption of children by Jesus Christ to Himself, according to the good pleasure of His will"* (Eph. 1:5). The doctrine of predestination has suffered greatly at the hands of misguided theologians. Theologically, there are those who teach that God has predestined some men to the lake of fire. But quite the contrary is true! God loved the world and gave His only begotten Son to die for our sins. Thus, it is imperative to understand that the plan of redemption is *unlimited*—Christ died for *all* so that whosoever shall call upon the name of the Lord shall not perish, but have everlasting life (Acts 16:31; Rom. 5:8; 6:23; 10:11,12; II Cor. 5:14,15).

Paul's use of the term "predestinate" is always in direct connection with the household of faith. "Having predestinated *us*," that is, the members of the Body of Christ. Predestination merely means to "determine beforehand." It has been said that what God foreknew was not merely what man would do, but rather what He would do for man. By the grace of God, I travel extensively throughout the year to preach the gospel. Prior to these trips, which take me from one end of the country to the other, my secretary prearranges my travel itinerary months in advance.

In like fashion, God has foreordained us "unto the adoption of children by Jesus Christ to Himself, according to the good pleasure of His will." The translators' use of the phrase "adoption of children" here is somewhat misleading. The Greek word Paul used was *huiothesia* or the *placing as sons*.

49

In biblical times adoption had to do with *position*—taking those who were *already* children and making them full-grown sons. Normally, there was a special gathering of friends and family at which time the father would declare his child to be his *son*, with all the rights and privileges that went along with this blessing. As the heir, he now held a position of esteem.

Imagine, Gentiles who were once aliens and strangers are now the *sons of God*. We are the heirs of His grace, not by works, but according to His good pleasure. That's grace! Just as the United States Constitution guarantees that every American has inalienable rights, which other governments can never take away, we, too, have rights and privileges as the citizens of heaven. In addition to being seated with Christ in the heavenlies, we are going to rule and reign with Him. In fact, as the sons of God, we are destined to judge men and angels at the Great White Throne Judgment.

> "Do ye not know that the saints shall judge the world? and if the world shall be judged by you, are ye unworthy to judge the smallest matters? Know ye not that we shall judge angels? how much more things that pertain to this life?" (I Cor. 6:2,3).

3. *"To the praise of the glory of His grace, wherein He hath made us accepted in the Beloved"* (Eph. 1:6). The world places a great deal of prominence upon acceptance. Rejection isn't an option in the minds of most people. Whatever it takes to be a part of the crowd; drinking, smoking, drugs, swearing, dress, hairstyle, they are more than willing to make the accommodation. But, the very One whose approval they do need, they have forsaken. Why? because they must come to Him on His terms, by way of the *Cross*.

In Adam, we are unacceptable to a holy and righteous God. The natural man is a sinner in word, thought, and deed— rotten to the core. Thus, it is God's holiness that must be satisfied. It is His standard of righteousness which must be met. In short, we must be *perfect* to enter into His presence. In the Old Testament, the sinner was required to bring a sacrifice to the door of the tabernacle. God made the determination whether or not it was acceptable in His sight (Lev. 4:1-8). As the plan of redemption unfolded, the day Christ shed His precious blood, God declared it to be the acceptable sacrifice for sin. This, of course, was manifested in due time through Paul's gospel (I Tim. 2:3-7). Today, then, the sinner must place his faith in the finished work of Christ. He is the once-for-all sacrifice (Heb. 10:10-12).

God has made those who have received the riches of His grace accepted in the Beloved. We are the objects of His *favor*. Therefore, we have full access day or night to come boldly before the throne of grace to make our requests known. This is remarkable when we consider that God's people in time past approached Him in fear and trembling. "And all the people saw the thunderings, and the lightnings, and the noise of the trumpet, and the mountain smoking: and when the people saw it, they removed, and stood *afar off*. And they said unto Moses, Speak thou with us, and we will hear: but let not God speak with us, lest we die" (Ex. 20:18,19). When death casts its shadow over us, we need not fear, for we will instantaneously step into the glory of His presence. We are accepted in the Beloved!

4. *"In whom we have redemption through His blood, the forgiveness of sins, according to the riches of His grace; wherein He hath abounded toward us in all wisdom and prudence"* (Eph. 1:7,8).

In 1913 George Bennard penned the famous hymn *The Old Rugged Cross*, which beautifully portrays the suffering and death of our Savior. But as is the case with most hymns, it falls far short of being Scripturally accurate. The chorus reads as follows:

"So I'll cherish the old rugged Cross,
Till my trophies at last I lay down;
I will cling to the old rugged Cross,
And exchange it some day for a crown."

Forgive me, but we shall *never* exchange the Cross or what was accomplished there for a crown. Throughout eternity those nail prints in our Savior's hands and feet will serve as a constant reminder that Christ is our Redeemer, to the glory of God (John 20:24-29 cf. Rev. 5:6).

The "old rugged Cross" is more than a mere instrument of death. Christ and Him crucified is a glorious message which extols God's love for a world of lost and undeserving sinners. Accordingly, the Holy Spirit has carefully selected certain words such as *redemption* and *forgiveness* to convey what God has accomplished for us at Calvary.

Most of us are familiar with the term *redemption*. I doubt if there is a woman alive in America who has not used a coupon to redeem a grocery item. I will never forget the time that I stopped by the supermarket to pick up a few things for my wife on my way home from the office. As I made my way to the checkout counter I noticed that everyone had overlooked the end counter, or so I thought. Lo, and behold, there stood a little gray-haired Grandmother. It soon became apparent that these seasoned shoppers knew something I didn't—Grandma had a large box of coupons. Before the ordeal was over the checkout girl was in a frazzle, everyone in the other lines was gone and I was late for dinner! Grandma was tickled pink though because she had *redeemed* half of her groceries with a handful of coupons.

In biblical times the term *redemption* was closely associated with slavery. Back in Paul's day there were approximately

6 million slaves in the Roman Empire who were bought and sold like mere pieces of merchandise. Slave owners frequently came to the slave-market where they paid large sums of money to make a purchase. Sometimes a master would happen upon a slave who was a friend or loved one, at which time he may well have paid the ransom price that the slave might be set free.

When Adam disobeyed God by eating of the forbidden fruit, the entire human race was catapulted into the slave-market of sin. Henceforth, sin has become a cruel taskmaster that subjects its captives hopelessly to a lifetime of bondage and fear of death. Thankfully, God sent forth His Son who stepped into the slave-market of sin that He might purchase us unto Himself.

Since God's holiness was violated at the Fall, only the Holy One of heaven, to whom the payment must be made, could determine the required ransom price for such a transaction. Thus, we are not redeemed with corruptible things such as silver and gold, but by the "precious Blood of Christ" (Rom. 3:25; Heb. 9:11-14). But what has Christ redeemed us from?

1. The curse of the Law (Gal. 3:13).
2. The slavery of sin (Rom. 6:18).
3. The fear of death (Heb. 2:15).
4. The power of Satan (Heb. 2:14).

The "Blood of Christ" is the spiritual *coupon* that redeems us back to God and gives us full access into the heavenlies. Dear friend, if you are reading these lines and have never received your free coupon, simply trust Christ, who died for your sins (personally), and believe that He was buried and that He rose again the third day. Our freedom from bondage has come to us at a great cost. Therefore, may we never be guilty of using our liberty for an occasion to the flesh.

Another wonderful theme of the message of the Cross is *forgiveness*. God's forgiveness, unlike ours, is total and *complete*. Suppose for a moment that a sinner was to write on a chalkboard all of the sins he had ever committed. Each sin, whether it be lying, pride, or impure thoughts is another nail in his eternal coffin that will eventually condemn him. However, this man suddenly comes to his senses and casts himself at the foot of Calvary's Cross. The instant that he believes on the Lord Jesus Christ, his slate is wiped completely clean. In the place where those sins once appeared is now written the word "FORGIVEN"!

Often the question is asked, "But what about the future sins that one may commit?" Judicial forgiveness is past, present and future. Stop and think: were not all of our sins *future* when Christ died on the Cross? Furthermore, those who lived before the Cross are said to be forgiven *"through the forebearance of God"* on the basis of the shed blood of Christ (Rom. 3:25).

Positionally then, no accusation can stand against us, although many may be brought by our archenemy. We're sure that Satan still takes gratification in appearing before the Throne of God to accuse the brethren (see Job 1:1-12). "You call him a saint? This so-called believer who has bitterness in his heart toward another; who won't give his brother another chance; who hates and won't forgive others?" Surely, the heart of God is grieved at such times, but it is comforting to know that our blessed Lord intercedes on our behalf in the following manner: "These accusations may be true, but he is forgiven!"

If we understand what was involved to secure forgiveness in the Old Testament, it will give us a greater appreciation of being *forgiven* in Christ. According to the law, a sinner was required to offer a sacrifice that was without spot or blemish. Usually, the animal was observed over a four-day period to insure it was free of disease. He then brought the animal to the door of the tabernacle. This was undoubtedly one of life's embarrassing moments as he walked through the camp with his sacrifice trailing behind. Everyone he passed by was thinking the same thing, "Uh-huh! I wonder what sin he committed?"

Once at the door of the tabernacle, the sinner laid his hand on the head of the animal and confessed his sin. With his sin now symbolically transferred to the animal, the throat of the sacrifice was slit and its blood drained into a bowl. The priest was then instructed to sprinkle the blood before the veil seven times, dab blood on the horns of the altar of incense, and pour the remainder at the *base* of the brazen altar. This foreshadowed the blood of the Savior, which dripped to the *foot* of the Cross (Lev. 4:1-7).

In order to ensure that nothing was ever overlooked, God instituted a national Day of Atonement in which an additional sacrifice was offered yearly for the sins of the nation. For fifteen hundred years the blood of bulls and goats ran like a river. Amazingly, all those sacrifices only *atoned* for or covered their sins. "For it is not possible that the blood of bulls and of goats should take away sins" (Heb. 10:4). Thus, the sacrificial system has been correctly called the Levitical drudges.

Today, we are forgiven *in Him*. Christ was lifted up once for all that we might enjoy a knowledge of sins forgiven. He has removed our sins as far as the east is from the west (Psa. 103:12). We find it interesting that while north and south eventually meet one another, east and west never meet. If you travel east you will never meet the west—it's *endless*. Our sins have been washed away forevermore by His precious blood. As the hymn writer appropriately says:

"What can wash away my sin?
Nothing but the blood of Jesus.
What can make me whole again?
Nothing but the blood of Jesus."

—Robert Lowry

Paul adds, *"wherein He hath abounded toward us in all wisdom and prudence"* (vs. 8). The Cross is a demonstration of the *wisdom* of God. Unfortunately, some believe that if the doctrine of forgiveness is taught in this manner it will give the believer a license to sin. However, once we have received the grace of God and understand that Christ has redeemed us from the slave market of sin, we won't desire to sin. Our aim should be to *please* Him. Thus, the grace of God teaches "…us that, denying ungodliness and worldly lusts, we should live soberly, righteously, and godly, in this present world" (Titus 2:12).

5. *"Having made known unto us the mystery of His will, according to His good pleasure which He hath purposed in Himself: that in the dispensation of the fulness of times He might gather together in one all things in Christ, both which are in heaven, and which are on earth; even in Him: in whom also we have obtained an inheritance, being predestinated according to the purpose of Him who worketh all things after the counsel of His own will: that we should be to the praise of His glory, who first trusted in Christ"* (Eph. 1:9-12).

The Mystery of His will has to do with God's *eternal purpose* for the heavens and the earth. We should add that God hid a principal part of this purpose from past generations; not even the elect angels had any knowledge of it. With both the Jews and Gentiles set aside in *unbelief*, God was free to make known the counsel of His will, which He foreordained before the foundation of the world. God changed the course of history by unfolding a new *program* known as the Mystery (Rom. 16:25; Eph. 3:1-3; Col. 1:25,26).

The Mystery is God's *secret* purpose for the Church, the Body of Christ. And it was foreordained that this truth would exclusively be revealed through Paul's apostleship. Paul was given the revelation regarding the *heavenly* ministry of Christ, which introduces us to a new creation. The Body of Christ, with its heavenly position, is the focal point of God's plan and purposes for the dispensation of Grace. Therefore, it is our responsibility to make known the exceeding riches of His grace. In addition to being blessed with all spiritual blessings in the heavenlies, we have a heavenly hope and calling.

"That in the dispensation of the fulness of times He might gather together in one all things in Christ, both which are in heaven, and which are on earth." The dispensation of the fulness of times is the counsel of His will regarding the eternal state. In eternity God is planning to sum up *all things* in Christ, both in heaven and on earth. Notice that the distinction will remain between heaven and the earth throughout eternity.[4] But there's also an ominous omission here.

> "Wherefore God also hath highly exalted Him, and given Him a name which is above every name: that at the name of Jesus every knee should bow, of things in heaven, and things in earth, and things under the earth; And that every tongue should confess that Jesus Christ is Lord, to the glory of God the Father" (Phil. 2:9-11).

Here, as in Ephesians, the "things in heaven" is clearly the Body of Christ that will be seated with Christ in glory. And the "things in earth" is a reference to the redeemed prophetic saints who will rule and reign with Christ upon the new earth. However, it is a solemn thought that those "things under the earth," the unsaved of all ages, aren't included in God's plans and purposes for eternity. When the unbelieving world is cast into the lake of fire, they are *forever* removed from God's presence and the glory of His power (II Thes. 1:9). May God help us to have a greater burden for lost souls.

According to the exceeding riches of His grace, *reservations* have been made in the name of Christ for every member of His Body. "In whom...we have obtained an inheritance, being predestinated according to the purpose of Him who worketh all things after the counsel of His own will: that we should be to the praise of His glory, who first trusted in Christ" (Eph. 1:11,12). Pastor Edward Drew, the prince of illustrators, has this to say about our heavenly inheritance and the glory we will have with Christ:

"When a saved soul goes to heaven surpassing all the angels, archangels, and principalities and powers, and takes a place ahead of them all, I don't doubt they wonder at it all. There is a story that came from the Civil War that illustrates what I mean. The story of a poor soldier after the Civil War, when they were not very well taken care of. He wandered about for months not knowing what to do, his clothes were worn, he was tired and sick. But he had a letter in his pocket from a friend that had died on the battlefield. The letter was written to his friend's father just before he died. The boy who was dying said to his pal, if he was ever in trouble to take this letter to his father.

"So when he was at the end of everything and didn't know what to do, he went to find the father of the boy who died. He found the man, who as it turned out, was the head of a prosperous business. The man had been helping soldiers, and had come to the place where he felt it was interfering with his business. Therefore, he decided not to do it any longer. When he was told that a soldier wanted to see him, he said, 'No!' So the soldier sent the note to the man. He was admitted at once. The note said, 'Dear Father: this is John, my pal. He is sitting here with me and I'm dying. He has promised to sit with me until I go. Anything you can do for him, do it for *my* sake.' And he signed his name.

"That soldier was taken to the man's home; he soon recovered and was taken into the business. He quickly learned the business, and became a real businessman. The father showed him everything, taught him everything, and then placed him with himself as one of the owners of the company. You might imagine the astonishment of the superintendent and the managers of different departments, when they saw this boy rising past them. He passed them all, until he sat with the owner of the company.

"That's what is going to happen to you and to me. We are going to take our places beyond all the angels and pass them all by. I recently read a hymn written several hundred years ago, trying to picture us all going to be with the Lord, it said: 'Past the cities of angels,' and I wondered if there are cities of angels. Heaven is *populated*. It must be, there are millions and millions of angels and they all have rulers over them. The moment a soul saved from sin, who's washed in the blood, departs this earth he goes past all the cities of the angels, and past all created beings, until he takes a place with Christ in the heavenlies, above all."

6. *"In whom ye also trusted, after that ye heard the Word of truth, the gospel of your salvation: in whom also after that ye believed, ye were sealed with that Holy Spirit of promise"* (Eph. 1:13).

This passage is confirmation that the Holy Spirit plays an essential role in the *eternal security* of every believer. The moment we have taken Christ as our personal Savior, the Holy Spirit baptizes us into the Body of Christ, *sealing* us there for eternity. We are not sealed with a mere circular impression as on a legal document. Rather the Scriptures clearly teach that the Holy Spirit Himself is the seal that secures us in the Body of Christ. Years ago my grandmother sealed jars of jelly with wax—the jellies were sealed by her, but with wax. *The wax was the seal.* Thus, according to Ephesians 1:13, believers are sealed *"with* that Holy Spirit of promise," the Holy Spirit *Himself* keeping us safe forever.

During biblical times when a ruler would fix a seal to an object it was done to *secure* his decree, thus making it irrevocable. After the other two presidents persuaded King Darius to make a declaration against petitioning any God, the King was forced to place Daniel in the lion's den, sealing it with his own signet. The record informs us that the sealing with the King's signet was done, "that the purpose might not be changed concerning Daniel" (Dan. 6:16,17). If this is true in the affairs of men, how much more so in the affairs of God. Every believer has been sealed with the Holy Spirit, and this proclamation of God can never be reversed—we are safe and secure in the everlasting arms.

7. *"Which is the earnest of our inheritance until the redemption of the purchased possession, unto the praise of His glory"* (Eph. 1:14).

God has left no stone unturned, for here we learn that the *earnest* of the Spirit is the pledge or the down payment until the transaction is completed. To place earnest money down in Paul's day, as well as in our day, meant three things:

1. It was a down payment which made a contract binding.
2. It represented an obligation to purchase.
3. It was a foretaste of what was to come.

When purchasing property it is a common practice to place a certain amount of earnest money down. This makes the deal binding and obligates the buyer to purchase the piece of land according to the terms of the contract. So it is with God. He has given us the earnest of the Spirit (the indwelling Spirit) as a down payment, which means He now has the obligation to honor His Word to complete the transaction. Thus, when the trump sounds God will claim His purchased possession, ushering us home to be forever with Him (I Thes. 4:17).

The world can fall apart around us, but "if God be for us who can be against us?" In a world of uncertainty and chaos, the believer can rest assured that he belongs to the Lord, who is able to *keep* him until the day of redemption.

One of the many benefits of understanding the doctrine of eternal security is that it removes the fear of ever losing our salvation. Instead of finding ourselves twisting in the wind, wondering if we have gone too far in sinful behavior, we can rest in the truth that, by His grace, we are still safe and secure. With the distraction of ever losing our salvation removed, we can devote all of our time and energy to carrying out the commands of Christ to the praise of His glory!

These are only seven of the spiritual blessings we enjoy in Christ. As we shall see, the unsearchable riches of Christ are found throughout the Ephesian letter.

4

In God We Trust

"Wherefore I also, after I heard of your faith in the Lord Jesus, and love unto all the saints, cease not to give thanks for you, making mention of you in my prayers."

—Ephesians 1:15,16

"The story is told of the famous violinist who consented to perform at a concert. It was announced that at the performance he would play a *twenty thousand dollar* Stradivarius violin. Music lovers and violin greats came from near and far to hear the maestro play. To the delight of the audience, as he came out on stage, he played the number flawlessly.

"However, before he departed he threw the violin to the floor and trampled it into a hundred pieces. The audience was *horrified!* Just then the conductor stepped up to say that the violin the master just finished playing and smashing was only worth twenty dollars and that now he would play the twenty thousand dollar Stradivarius!"

The author went on to add, "The point was of course—it was not the instrument, but the master who made the beautiful music. Sometimes we are like that twenty dollar violin—far from what we should be, inadequate and out of tune, but the *Master* is able to bring beautiful music from us if we would only be willing instruments."[1]

Of course, this not only applies to our willingness to serve the Lord, but should also filter down to our *prayer life*. God would have us to be instruments of praise and thanksgiving. Although the subject of prayer is woven throughout the Scriptures, it must be studied *dispensationally* to ascertain God's will. Sometime back, a Christian brother dropped us a note to express his displeasure concerning our dispensational approach. He stated: "I don't chop up the Bible like you folks are guilty of—I believe all the promises in the Book are mine!!" I graciously responded: "If that's true, beloved, then don't forget to apply all the curses in the Book when you disobey the Word of the Lord."

Theologically, a knowledge of dispensationalism saves us from feeling that the Scriptures contradict themselves. It guards against doctrinal errors, shows where we are in the history of the world, and protects us against fears and false hopes. While many clamor these days that doctrine is dead and should be buried alongside its counterpart, dispensationalism, without a proper understanding of both, one will quickly find himself out of the will of God.

PRAYER, DISPENSATIONALLY CONSIDERED

Which of the two following statements are *true* of your prayer life:

> "And all things, whatsoever ye shall ask in prayer, believing, ye shall receive" (Matt. 21:22).

> "Likewise the Spirit also helpeth our infirmities: for we know not what we should pray for as we ought: but the Spirit itself maketh intercession for us with groanings which cannot be uttered" (Rom. 8:26).

Under the former dispensation of the Law, God spoke to Israel through miraculous manifestations, which were often reflected in her prayer life during the earthly ministry of Christ. She walked by faith and by *sight*. Thus, when our Lord said to His disciples, "If ye shall say unto this mountain,

Be thou removed, and be thou cast into the sea; it shall be done," their prayer would have been answered, if they truly believed (Matt. 21:21-22). That mountain would have literally disappeared into the depths of the sea.

Shortly after the day of Pentecost, the disciples were persecuted and their lives threatened for preaching that Christ was the Messiah of Israel. Unshaken by these threats, this company of believers prayed the Lord would give them *boldness*. They besought the Lord to stretch forth His hand to heal, and that signs and wonders would be done. "And when they had prayed, the place was shaken where they were assembled together; and they were all filled with the Holy Spirit, and they spoke the Word of God with boldness" (Acts 4:29-31).

Why are the above responses unheard of today, and who would dare say otherwise? Why is it wrong to claim these promises today? Simple! God has changed His dealings with mankind. We are living in the dispensation of Grace. Today, the heavens are *silent* in regard to outward miraculous manifestations associated with prophecy. Our prayer life reflects the grace of God. Consequently, "we walk by *faith*, not by sight" (II Cor. 5:7).

On the one hand, the saints on the day of Pentecost were under the complete control of the Holy Spirit, therefore, they knew the will of God and prayed accordingly. On the other hand, we are admonished "to be filled with the Spirit," which is a *goal* to be attained through Bible study and prayer. Since the members of the Body of Christ are not under the total control of the Spirit, "we know not what we should pray for as we ought." For example, is it God's will to spare the life of an ill loved one? We have no way of knowing with any certainty. Thus, our prayer for them must close with, "as it is according to Thy will, Lord" (Rom. 8:27).

PAUL'S PRAYER LIFE

"Wherefore I also, after I heard of your faith in the Lord Jesus, and love unto all the saints, cease not to give thanks for you, making mention of you in my prayers" (Eph. 1:15,16).

The prayers of the Apostle Paul, two of which are found here in Ephesians, serve as lighthouses for the Church, the Body of Christ. Their beacons of light help guide us through the treacherous water of life's uncertainties. Prayer is merely *communication* with God. It's the channel through which the finite has *access* to the infinite. If we desire to have an effective prayer life, we must follow Paul's example. Unlike most believers today, Paul never underestimated the importance of prayer. He clearly understood that it was the source of our spiritual power in Christ. Those who shook the foundations since the apostle echoed the same through the centuries by their actions. It is said that Martin Luther prayed for two hours every morning before beginning his day. If he was facing a particular busy day, he prayed for three hours!

As we have seen, Paul had established the church at Ephesus on his third apostolic journey. Some years later, during his Roman imprisonment, he was encouraged to find that they were still standing for the truth. Thus, he commends them for their *faith* in the Lord Jesus Christ and acknowledges the sincerity of their *love* for all the saints. Usually believers turn this around. They tend to place their trust in men, and then speak of loving the Lord, which of course we should. The problem with trusting men is, if they fall from grace, those who are following them often become disillusioned with the Lord's work. A missionary once said: "The more I have dealings with men, the more I trust the Lord." We cannot overemphasize the importance of keeping our eyes upon the Lord. The wheels may fall off the buggy of life, but if you have your eyes upon Him, it will remain upright.

The Apostle Paul was a model of *thankfulness*. As Paul wrote to the saints at Ephesus, he was genuinely grateful that they were saved by grace and living for the Lord. "Wherefore I also...cease not to give thanks for you, making mention of you in my prayers" (Eph. 1:15,16). The apostle did not selfishly feel he was the only one who could effectively serve Christ. He thanked God that others were standing for the truth as well. Perhaps we should pause here for a moment to ask, when was the last time we thanked the Lord for someone else's faithfulness?

If there is one things God *abhors*, it's ingratitude. In fact, "when they [the Gentiles in time past] knew God, [i.e. about Him] they glorified Him not as God, neither were thankful" (Rom. 1:21). Rather than being grateful that God had revealed Himself to them, and blessed them beyond measure, they turned their backs on the Creator, which brought His judgment.

As believers in Christ we should be the most grateful people on the face of the earth. The apostle not only instructs us to pray and be thankful for all things, we are also to watch in prayer. "Continue in prayer, and watch in the same with thanksgiving" (Col. 4:2). We are to "continue in prayer," that is, cling hard to it, persevere in taking *all things* to the throne of grace. Paul's primary intercession for the saints usually centered around spiritual things. However, he also placed a great deal of emphasis upon their *physical* needs, as seen in his prayers for earthly rulers (I Tim. 2:1-2); gratitude for daily meals (I Tim. 4:3-5); healing of physical infirmities (Phil. 2:24-30); deliverance from prison (Phil. 1:19,20); journeys' mercies (Rom. 1:7-10); etc.

Then we are to *watch* in the same with thanksgiving. The word "watch" in Colossians 4:2 is the Gr. *gregoreuo*, which means to be alert, stay awake, be vigilant. We need to stay alert, lest we find our minds wandering off to fleshly things. Furthermore, it is essential to watch to avoid becoming careless or neglectful of the privilege of communicating with God. As we pray with thanksgiving, we are giving thanks to our heavenly Father for past evidences of His goodness and mercy, knowing that, even now, He can again supply our *needs* according to the riches of His grace.

> "That the God of our Lord Jesus Christ, the Father of glory, may give unto you the spirit of wisdom and revelation in the knowledge of Him" (Eph. 1:17).

Our doctrinal statement reads: "Jesus Christ was begotten of the Holy Spirit and born of the virgin Mary, and is true God and true man." We teach without apology that Jesus Christ is *God*—He is co-equal and co-eternal. What then is the apostle speaking of when he says: "The God of our Lord Jesus Christ?" This phrase must be interpreted in light of the *humanity* of Christ. Our Lord emptied Himself of the outward manifestation of His attributes and glory. He laid them aside for the great work of redemption that was set before Him. Thus, as a *man*, who took on the form of a servant, it is correct to say "the God of our Lord Jesus Christ" (Phil. 2:5-8). As the *eternal Son*, the apostle emphasizes His relationship with the Father: "Blessed be God, even the Father of our Lord Jesus Christ" (II Cor. 1:3 cf. Isa. 9:6).

Paul prays for the Ephesians that the Father would give them "the spirit of wisdom and revelation in the knowledge of Him." Notice that the apostle doesn't pray that they would receive a direct revelation from the Lord; this was reserved for the *inspired* apostle of Grace (Eph. 3:2,3). Rather, he prays that the Holy Spirit would give them wisdom and illuminate them to the revelation already given in his epistles.

If you have a knowledge of the preaching of Jesus Christ according to the revelation of the Mystery, it affirms two things. First, you were searching for the truth. Second, the Spirit of God enlightened you to this blessed message through your study of the Scriptures. He delights in teaching us the things of God. Pastor C. R. Stam used to say, "It's like the man who was searching for the sun one morning—then, it dawned on him!"

The apostle's prayer for these dear saints was that they might have a *fuller* knowledge of Christ. Incredibly, after thirty years of service, Paul says: "That I might know Him, and the power of His resurrection, and the fellowship of His sufferings." I always like to tell young couples who are planning to marry that they really won't know one another until after the first year of marriage. They usually look at one another in disbelief. But that young lady has no way of knowing that her husband-to-be is miserable to be around when he first wakes up in the morning. Probably most reading these lines know the Lord, but our desire for you is that you may know Him more deeply, more intimately. This is accomplished by acknowledging and prayerfully studying the revelation committed to Paul.

GOD'S INHERITANCE

"The eyes of your understanding being enlightened; that ye may know what is the hope of His calling, and what the riches of the glory of His inheritance in the saints" (Eph. 1:18).

Once we come to a knowledge of the Mystery, the Lord would have us understand "what is the hope of His calling." There are various callings in the Scriptures, but this particular calling has to do with our *future state*. The storms of life may rage, the enemy may ruthlessly attack, despair may seem like a close friend, but the beacon of light that shines on the horizon gives us hope of arriving at a safe harbor. That light is the glorious *appearing* of our great God and Savior Jesus Christ. The *Rapture* is the hope of His calling. We can survive most anything as long as we have hope. Our hope is to be caught up together to meet the Lord in the air! Some golden daybreak we are going to be delivered from this body of death.

Those who have believed the gospel have experientially tasted of the "riches of His grace." We have a knowledge of sins forgiven, new life in Christ, and understand that we will be delivered from the wrath to come. However, we have yet to experience the "riches of His glory." Not until we step into His presence, and see Him face to face, and behold the wonders of heaven itself, will we fully comprehend the *riches of His glory*. Our finite comprehension of His glory is so inadequate that every believer in Christ will be completely awestruck on that day.

Paul carefully distinguishes here between "our inheritance" in verse 11, and "His inheritance" in verse 18. An inheritance is when property or possessions pass from one party to another. Normally, it is never fully realized until *death*. For example, if your father names you in his estate as the sole beneficiary of one hundred acres, that's your inheritance. It will be titled in your name. Insofar as God is the sovereign Creator of heaven and earth, He has every right to give them to whom He will. Since Christ is carrying out His heavenly ministry during this present parenthetical period of grace, the Father has chosen to sign over the rights of the heavenly realm to us. Thus, the members of the Body of Christ have a *heavenly* inheritance (Phil. 3:20 cf. Col. 1:5).

But what is "His inheritance in the saints"? We believe this is another distinct aspect of Paul's revelation. According to Ephesians 5:27, the *Body of Christ* is His inheritance. "That He might present it [the Body of Christ] to Himself a glorious Church, not having spot, or wrinkle, or any such thing; but that it should be holy and without blemish." Think of it, unworthy sinners like us occupying a place in the heart of God! That's grace!! As the recipients of His secret purpose, we are His prized possession on the basis of the shed blood of Christ. He who made the universe is going to showcase us as the trophies of His grace. Through *us* God will receive honor, glory, and worship in the ages to come. Our prayer is that He will grant us the opportunity to be instruments of praise and thanksgiving as we await the sound of the trump.

Before we ascend into the heavenlies to survey the glory of His exaltation, perhaps we should acquaint ourselves more fully with the *Deity of Christ*. As we shall see, Christ is all He claimed to be, and more!

THE PREEMINENCE OF CHRIST

When we open the treasure chest of God's Word there is one spiritual gem that outshines all others. I am referring, of course, to the *preeminence* of Christ. Looking through the telephoto lens of prophecy we observe that Christ was raised to ascend to the throne of David as the King of Israel. Change to the wide angle lens of the Mystery and He holds an exalted position in the heavenlies as the Lord of glory far above all principalities and powers. Focusing on the plan of redemption, which encompasses both programs of God, He holds a preeminent position here as well.

Those who were present on the day of the crucifixion were dealt a crushing blow when they witnessed their Messiah suffering on that cruel tree. Moreover, to them it seemed to be a chain of untimely circumstances, which abruptly ended the Lord's ministry among them. But now, as we look down from the mountaintop of Paul's epistles, we understand that God was in Christ, reconciling the world unto Himself. God the Father had sent His Son to become the Redeemer of mankind, which bestowed upon Him the *exalted* position of being seated at the right hand of the Majesty on high (Heb. 1:3).

All this, of course, implies that the Lord Jesus Christ is indeed God. But probably the most conclusive body of evidence establishing the Deity of Christ is found in Paul's letter to the Colossians. The apostle confirms this by presenting Christ in relation to the Father, to creation and to the Church.

a. God the Father

"Who is the image of the invisible God" (Col. 1:15).

I am strongly inclined to believe that there is a twofold purpose in all of the epistles of Saint Paul. First, and foremost, is the imparting of the Mystery. But the apostle also takes occasion to deal with certain problems and unsound doctrine which threatened the spiritual welfare of the saints. Watch how with one turn of the wheel he accomplishes both purposes. In Colossians 1:9 Paul encourages the saints at Colosse by revealing that he had been praying for them and desired that they *"might be filled with the knowledge [full knowledge] of His [God's] will in all wisdom and spiritual understanding."* His words of consolation, however, change quickly to words of warning in Colossians 2:18, where he says, *"Let no man beguile you of your reward in a voluntary humility and worshipping of angels."* The cause for concern in this particular case was the insidious teaching of Gnosticism (knowledge), which *denied* the Deity of Christ, teaching that Christ was merely a created being of the highest order of the angels.

The instigators of this system boasted of having superior knowledge, that is, human knowledge, with all its vain imaginations. Sir Robert Anderson was correct in his observation that "Satan still camps under the tree of knowledge." Beloved, beware because gnosticism still exists today in some of the modern cults. Paul's refutation of this heresy can be effectively applied even at this hour to those well-groomed visitors who go door to door to prey on the unsuspecting. When they visit your door be sure to be armed with "the gospel of the grace of God."

The apostle sets out to confirm the Deity of Christ, under the watchful eye of the Holy Spirit, by first establishing the *unity* of God. *"Who [Christ] is the image of the invisible God."* The term "image" found here can be used either in the sense of likeness, or exact likeness (cf. Heb. 1:3). Years ago it was not uncommon to hear someone say, "That boy is the 'spit'n' image' of his father." They meant, of course, that the father and son resembled one another. But the word "image" can also express exact likeness, such as in the case of seeing my own reflection in a pond. You might step up and even say, "I see your image in the water." The water is reflecting my *true* features because it is actually *me* standing there on the shore.

This latter sense is precisely how Paul uses our term in relation to Christ in Colossians 1:15. He is the *exact image* of the invisible God because *He is God.* But how can we know for certain that this was the intended meaning of the Holy Spirit? Such an important matter as this is not left open to speculation, but dealt with in a very precise manner. Who in prophecy is called Wonderful, Counsellor and the Prince of Peace? I'm sure we would agree wholeheartedly that it is none other than Christ Himself. Thus we must also acknowledge that He is the *Everlasting Father* in light of Isaiah's words, which we now present in their entirety:

> "For unto us a child is born, unto us a Son is given: *and the government shall be upon His shoulder: and His name shall be called Wonderful, Counsellor, The mighty God, THE EVERLASTING FATHER, The Prince of Peace"* (Isa. 9:6).

Everyone knows about doubting Thomas; but few, it seems, know that Philip was worthy of this title as well. Philip, Bartholomew and Thomas must have all been born doubters because their inquiring minds seemed to give the Lord numerous opportunities to strengthen their faith. This is a clear indication that they were not gullible men who would believe anything. They wanted the truth, the whole truth, and nothing but the truth. During the upper room discourse it was Philip who asked, *"Lord, show us the Father, and it sufficeth us."* The answer he received was probably not what he expected, but it does substantiate once and for all that Jesus Christ is God.

> "Jesus saith unto him, have I been so long time with you, and yet hast thou not known Me, Philip? he that hath seen Me hath seen the Father; and how sayest thou then, show us the Father?" (John 14:9).

b. The Firstborn

> "the firstborn of every creature" (Col. 1:15).

Next, the apostle turns to Christ's relationship to *creation* as further confirmation of His Deity. Most believers are woefully ignorant of the Old Testament, which is oftentimes a real hindrance in their quest to have a fuller knowledge of God's Word. A case in point centers around the word "firstborn." To most this term is commonly understood to mean, "the one born first into the family." However, in the Old Testament the *firstborn* was not necessarily the first to be born. In other words, the term is not exclusively associated

74

with origin, sometimes it was used as a title of honor and dignity to denote a position of priority.

For example, was Israel the first nation of civilization? History bears out that there were numerous nations in existence long before Israel. But consider these words of the Lord, *"And thou shalt say unto Pharaoh, Thus saith the Lord, Israel is My son, even My firstborn."* Firstborn, that is, in the sense of a position and standing above all other nations. Furthermore, God channeled His choicest blessings through His chosen nation, which meant they enjoyed certain rights and privileges that were denied others.

Who does not know that Ishmael was the first of the sons of Abraham? However, the blessing was conferred upon Isaac. God's words to Abraham are very clear, *"In Isaac shall thy seed be called"* (Gen. 21:12). The same can be said of Esau and Jacob in like manner. You will recall that when Jacob was stricken in years Joseph brought Manasseh, his firstborn son, along with Ephraim, to his father's side to be blessed. It is interesting to note that when Jacob placed his right hand on the head of the younger Ephraim, Joseph sought to correct his father's error, but carefully observe the patriarch's response:

> "And his father [Jacob] refused, and said, I know it, my son [Joseph], I know it: he [Manasseh] also shall become a people, and he [Manasseh] shall also be great: but truly his younger brother [Ephraim] shall be greater then he [Manasseh], and his seed shall become a multitude of nations" (Gen. 48:19).

These examples from the Old Testament serve as solemn reminders that the term *firstborn* must never be limited to *first in time*. Paul's reference to Christ in Colossians 1:15 as "the firstborn of every creature" surely is not to be understood in the sense that He was the first created being; this would be out of harmony with the context. Quite the contrary, for Christ holds a *position of priority* over His creation, because He is the Creator. Therefore, Christ is indeed God, for only God has the power to create *ex nihilo* or out of nothing.

"For by Him were all things created." Who filled the heavens with stars which cannot be numbered, and calls them all by their names?—Christ. Who designed the eggshell? And how is it possible for a baby chick to grow inside a closed shell without oxygen? Scientists have discovered, to their amazement, that the eggshell has thousands of microscopic pores which allow oxygen in and carbon dioxide out. It is unbelievable that evolutionists have the audacity to deny the existence of God with their theory of evolution. If we acknowledge there is design in creation then there must be a designer! *"O the depth of the riches both of the wisdom and knowledge of God! how unsearchable are His judgments, and His ways past finding out!"*

"And He is before all things, and by Him all things consist" (Col. 1:17). Christ is also the Preserver of His creation as exhibited by the words, "and by Him all things consist," or are held together. I was taught years ago in general science that atoms, which make up the physical universe, each have positively charged protons that repel each other. I can still see my instructor pacing across the front of the room shaking his head saying, "We just do not know what holds the atom together. For all intents and purposes everything should be blown into oblivion." Should you ever desire to arouse the attention of a physicist simply tell him you know who holds the physical universe together. The One who holds all things together by the power of His might is the same One who offers eternal life to all who will come unto Him.

76

All things have been created by Christ and for Him, thus man's purpose in life is to honor and glorify God. Unfortunately sin has brought death and condemnation, separating man from God. To remedy this condition, he must believe on the Lord Jesus Christ, who is the only one who can liberate him from his sins. Then and only then can he truly glorify God.

c. The Church

"And He is the head of the Body, the Church: who is the beginning, the firstborn from the dead; that in all things He might have the preeminence" (Col. 1:18).

The biblical record documents various reversals of death, but Christ holds the distinct honor of being the firstborn from the dead. He was not merely raised from the dead. He *arose* from the dead! He is the firstfruits of them which slept, indicating that only He has a glorified body. According to Paul's gospel one of the purposes of Christ's resurrection from the dead was to assume the headship of the Body of Christ. Here again He holds a position of priority.

The headship of Christ supplies each member of the Body with an endless source of life, both spiritually and eternally. Since only God can impart life this gives us further verification of the Deity of Christ. *"For in Him we live, and move, and have our being."* Headship also implies authority. Therefore, Christ brought this new creation into existence and has already predetermined when the Body will be complete.

Who can possibly deny the Deity of Christ in the presence of such weighty evidence set forth by the Apostle Paul? We should all take great comfort in the truth that Jesus Christ is God! He is the sovereign One who created all things in heaven and in earth by the word of His power. Christ is preeminent in *all* things! The question is, does He hold a preeminent position in your life?

THE EXALTATION OF CHRIST

"And what is the exceeding greatness of His power to us-ward who believe, according to the working of His mighty power, which He wrought in Christ, when He raised Him from the dead" (Eph. 1:19,20).

Often believers find themselves so caught up in the grind of everyday life that their prayer life begins to center around their circumstances. While God would have us to bring everything before the throne of grace, it is interesting to examine the prayers of the Apostle Paul. He prayed that the saints would have a fuller knowledge of Christ according to the revelation of the *Mystery*. And that the eyes of their understanding might be opened to what is the hope of our calling.

Those who level the criticism that doctrine is unimportant should prayerfully consider Paul's words here in Ephesians. The apostle understood the importance of the saints being *established* in the faith. This would enable them to walk worthy of their calling and to be unshaken by unforeseen circumstances. Thus, Paul prayed that we might comprehend "what is the exceeding greatness of His power to us-ward who believe according to the working of His mighty power, which He wrought in Christ, when He raised Him from the dead." A knowledge of the "greatness of His power" and a proper application of it are essential to live a godly life in Christ Jesus. As the old saying goes: You can take the farmer out of the country, but you can't take the country out of the farmer. Thankfully, the two are inseparable. The same is true of standing and state.

When God desired to demonstrate His power in the Old Testament He always appealed to the parting of the Red Sea.

The Psalmist writes: "Nevertheless He saved them for His name's sake, that He might make His **mighty power** to be known. He rebuked the Red Sea also, and it was dried up: so He led them through the depths, as through the wilderness...And the waters covered their enemies: there was not one of them left" (Psa. 106:8-11).

Imagine standing at the shore of the Rea Sea, watching the waters part before you and stand upright on the right and on the left. The walls of water would have towered high above as you watched over one million Israelites pass through the sea on dry ground. Before you could recover from that breathtaking experience the Lord of hosts drew the enemy into the jaws of death, where they perished in a watery grave. What a scene! These unbelievable sights, the deafening sound, the raging fury, were all a demonstration of God's *mighty power*. It would be a timeless story told again and again through the generations.

Today God has revealed His power in a much different way. Paul shifts the emphasis from time past to an even more glorious miraculous manifestation—the *resurrection of Jesus Christ*. We are inclined to view the resurrection of Christ through the eyes of faith without giving much thought to the actual event. But when we ponder what actually took place in that cold, dark tomb, the resurrection casts a long shadow over the miracle that took place at the Rea Sea.

For the first four thousand years of human history men lived in fear of *death*, and were in bondage their entire lifetime (Heb. 2:15). Death reigned as *king*. The very thought of the great unknown struck terror into the heart of every man. Those who were restored to life only lived to die another day, including Lazarus. The grim reaper unmercifully cut down his victims like the mighty combine that harvests the winter wheat. He then cast his subjects into a place called, in the Hebrew tongue, *Sheol*—"the unknown."

As our Lord prepared to redeem mankind from the bondage of death, He came to the Garden of Gethsemane. It was there that He prayed what might seem at first an unusual prayer. "O my Father, if it be possible, let this cup pass from Me: nevertheless not as I will, but as Thou wilt...if this cup may not pass away from Me, except I drink it, Thy will be done" (Matt. 26:39,42).

This *cup* contained more than physical sufferings; it held the sins of the world, the righteous judgment of God, and death. Christ was staring into the very face of a formidable foe. Death had conquered completely, sealing its subjects hopelessly in the grave. And every evil force in the universe was intent on keeping it that way. Christ's prayer doesn't imply that there was a reluctance on His part to redeem us. Rather, He shrunk from the thought of being *forsaken* of the Father. This was the bitter ingredient in the cup that He dreaded the most.

"Father, if it be possible, let this cup pass from Me." In other words, Father if there is any other way that redemption can be secured without being forsaken of Thee, let it be so. But there was no other way. Christ would voluntarily bear the sins of the world *alone*. Thus, when the Savior cried out on the Cross "My God, My God, why hast Thou forsaken Me?" He found solace in the fact, "But Thou art *holy*, O Thou that inhabitest the praises of Israel" (Psa. 22:3).

The Father had to draw away from the Son when He was made sin for us.[2] The Scriptures emphatically state, "Thou art of purer eyes than to behold evil, and canst not look on iniquity" (Hab. 1:13). Those who believe that God will merely overlook the sins of the unsaved in eternity fail to understand the holiness of God. His holiness always demands justice.

80

Between the Lord's death and His bodily resurrection stood *the power of sin*, the *power of death*, the *power of Hades,* the *power of darkness* and the prince of the *power of the air* in whom resided the control of these dominions. The day Christ died the powers of darkness were convinced they had overthrown the plans and purposes of God in regard to redemption. These dreadful words may have well echoed throughout the spiritual realm: "He's dead! He's dead! We have conquered the Son of God." The conflict of the ages had ended in a resounding victory, or so they thought.

We must concede that from all outward appearances it was the darkest day this world has ever known. The Father had forsaken Him, Judas betrayed Him, Peter denied Him, and the other disciples were in hiding for fear of losing their own lives. If the angels of God weep, there probably wasn't a dry eye in heaven. For three days and three nights heaven and earth mourned. But just when all hope seemed to be lost, Christ *arose!* The bars of death could not hold Him. The one indisputable fact that Christ triumphed over sin and death is His bodily resurrection. That's *power!*

When Christ ascended to the Father after His resurrection the Scriptures declare: "And having spoiled principalities and powers, He made a show of them openly, triumphing over them in it" (Col. 2:15). The fallen host of heaven was confident that they had put the final nail in His coffin. Wouldn't it have been wonderful to see the expression on their faces as Christ ascended through the spiritual realm, making a show of them openly! They knew that it spelled their *doom.*

Armed with a knowledge of "the exceeding greatness of His power to us-ward who believe," we are equipped to *triumph* over sin and death. For example, the day Saul of Tarsus saw the glorified resurrected Christ on the road to

Damascus his stony heart of flesh melted within him. He could not deny his senses; he could only humble himself before the Savior. The gospel *transforms* lives, "it is the power of God unto salvation to every one that believeth." Every conversion is a demonstration of His mighty power.

In regard to temptation, it should never be said that I was merely a helpless victim. The tempter's influence may indeed be intense to sin against God, but the power of His resurrection is even greater to triumph over it to the glory of God. The believer need not be held in sin's dread sway.

But is it possible to withstand the workers of darkness that oppose us? Those who attempt to do so in their own strength will find themselves casualties of the battle. The key is to remember our position in Christ. He has already conquered the powers of darkness; we merely need to keep this in mind when engaged in the conflict. We must *surrender* ourselves to Christ, allowing Him to live His life through us. Here's how it's accomplished. The apostle had learned to make his position in Christ a *practical* reality: "I am [old sin nature—self] crucified with Christ: nevertheless I live [new nature, raised from the dead, walking in newness of life]; yet not I, but Christ liveth in me: and the life which I now live in the flesh I live by the faith of the Son of God, who loved me, and gave Himself for me" (Gal. 2:20).

Christ has also given us *victory* over death. One day a farmer took his two sons to visit the family beehive. While he was attending to the hive one of the boys was stung by a honeybee. As the poor little guy began to scream and roll on the ground in pain, the same bee began to buzz around the head of his brother who was standing nearby. Needless to say, he immediately became hysterical! The wise old father picked up his son and said, "That bee can't hurt you. It can only sting *once* and he already stung your brother."[3]

When death tries to scare the wits out of you, simply remember the power of death no longer holds sway over the believer. Even though the time of our homegoing may be unknown to us, the sting of death has been removed at the Cross; therefore, it is merely a passageway for the believer into eternal life. Death has been swallowed up in victory, thus the grave will one day surrender to the future resurrection (I Cor. 15:51-57).

THREE DOMINIONS OF CHRIST'S EXALTATION

"Which He wrought in Christ, when He raised Him from the dead, and set Him at His own right hand in the heavenly places" (Eph. 1:20).

As we study the Word of God rightly divided, we are to understand that God has arranged His dealings with mankind into two programs. We have His *prophesied purpose* and His *secret purpose.* Prophecy has to do with the earth and Christ's reign upon it during the millennial kingdom, while the Mystery concerns our exaltation with Christ in the heavenlies. Consequently, there is a *twofold* purpose in regard to the resurrection of Christ. According to prophecy Christ was raised to be seated on the throne of David (Acts 2:29,30). Since God's Prophetic Program has been temporarily suspended, this promise that was originally made with David is yet to be fulfilled.

With the introduction of the dispensation of Grace, God has given us a new revelation regarding His Son. Paul says: "Consider what I say; and the Lord give thee understanding in all things. Remember that Jesus Christ of the seed of David was raised from the dead according to *my gospel*" (II Tim. 2:7,8). The passage before us has long been a stumbling block to many. This must have also been the case in Paul's day. Thus, he challenged Timothy to "consider what I say" calling upon his God-given authority as the inspired apostle of Grace. And then he prays that the Lord would give him wisdom.

This type of emphasis should cause us to pay careful attention to what is about to be stated: "Remember that Jesus Christ of the seed of David was raised from the dead according to my gospel." Paul makes it very clear that he wasn't proclaiming "another Jesus." Rather it was the *same* person—Jesus Christ of the seed of David. What the apostle wanted Timothy, and us, to understand was that he preached the resurrection of Christ in a completely different light. Today the terms of salvation include belief in the resurrection of Christ (Rom. 10:9 cf. I Cor. 15:1-4). We also learn through Paul's gospel that we are identified with Christ's death, burial, and resurrection (Rom. 6:1-4).

Years ago C. H. Mackintosh made this insightful observation: "Empty Cross, empty tomb, the throne of heaven occupied." According to Paul's epistles, the resurrected Christ is presently seated at the right hand of the Father as the God of grace. "Wherefore henceforth...though we have known Christ after the flesh, yet now henceforth know we Him no more" (II Cor. 5:16). We no longer know Christ as the lowly Jesus who suffered at the hands of evildoers. Nor do we know Him as the King of Israel who will one day overthrow the kingdoms of this world and establish His kingdom of righteousness on the *earth*.

Today, Christ is in royal exile. Dispensationally, this will continue to be the case throughout the present age of Grace. Therefore, we know Christ as the Lord of glory who is currently conducting a *heavenly ministry*. The heavenly character of this dispensation is seen throughout the Pauline revelation. The members of the Body of Christ are said to have a heavenly hope and calling, blessed with all spiritual blessings in the heavenlies, seated with Christ in heavenly places, etc.

Moreover, Christ is seated at the right hand of the Father in a position of *exaltation*, "far above all principality, and power, and might, and dominion, and every name that is named, not only in this world, but also in that which is to come. And hath put all things under His feet" (Eph. 1:21,22). These passages plainly state Christ has been given absolute power and authority over His entire creation because He humbled Himself unto death, even the death of the Cross. If the Father has "put all things under His feet," how do we explain the ongoing rebellion of men and angels who continue in their evil ways? Simple, this is the administration of Grace—sin is not being judged today. While Christ has the authority to do so, He has chosen not to exercise His power in accordance with the riches of His grace.

The apostle adds these words of clarification: "But when He saith all things are put under Him, it is manifest that He is excepted, which did put all things under Him. And when all things shall be subdued unto Him" (I Cor. 15:27,28). Notice carefully the phrase "all things *shall* be subdued unto Him." In short, the day is fast approaching when the Lord will exercise His rightful authority to judge the affairs of men. The Book of Revelation bears record that God will ultimately triumph over sin in His universe. He will have the *final* word. In that day, every knee shall bow and every tongue shall confess that Jesus Christ is Lord, to the glory of God the Father!

The exaltation of Christ also includes His Headship over the Church, which is His Body. The true Church is not an organization that's made up of noisy denominational machinery. Rather it is a living organism that derives its life from Christ who "filleth all in all" (Eph. 1:22,23). We learn from I Corinthians chapter 12 that the head is said to be a member of the Body. Therefore, headship has to do with the *mind of Christ*, which is accessed through the Pauline revelation (Phil. 2:1-5).

Since the spirit of Christ dwells within us God could have supernaturally given us the mind of Christ, but He has chosen to reveal it to us in written form. Thus, we are instructed as individual members of His Body to be filled with a knowledge of His will. May the Lord burden each of us to set our affections on things above and not upon the things of this earth.

5

Bitter Waters Made Sweet

"And you hath He quickened, who were dead in trespasses and sins: wherein in time past ye walked according to the course of this world, according to the prince of the power of the air, the spirit that now worketh in the children of disobedience: among whom also we all had our conversation in times past in the lusts of our flesh, fulfilling the desires of the flesh and of the mind; and were by nature the children of wrath, even as others."

—Ephesians 2:1-3

I have never read this portion without thinking about the relevance of the Word of God. It's timeless! And this is certainly true with the theme before us. Since the entrance of sin into the world, the way of man has been anything but easy. Job seemed to have his finger on the pulse of the matter when he wrote, *"man is born unto trouble, as the sparks fly upward."* It is interesting though, that when adversity arises men are quick to blame God, or inquire why He allows such things. But shall we blame God for what man has brought upon himself? God forbid! Man is a product of his own folly. *"Wherefore, as by one man sin entered into the world, and death by sin; and so death passed upon all men, for that all have sinned"* (Rom. 5:12).

Some claim that if they had been in the garden everything would have been different. I certainly have no reason to doubt them. In all probability, they would have pushed

Adam aside to reach for the forbidden fruit before he did! You see God saw the entire human race *in Adam,* as only He could. So when Adam stretched forth his hand to partake of the forbidden fruit, each of us were reaching for it as well—we are his posterity, thus we share in his *guilt.* God could have condemned the whole human race to the lake of fire and have been perfectly justified in doing so. Thankfully, we did not receive what we justly deserved, for *"The Lord is merciful and gracious, slow to anger, and plenteous in mercy"* (Psa. 103:8).

A faithful parishioner surprised his pastor by asking: "Doesn't it make you nervous preaching on sin with all those experts sitting out there in the congregation?" Humorous as this may seem, the parishioner's statement conveys a very significant truth: sin is *universal* and knows no boundaries. Every soul, with the exception of Christ, has been born in sin, which means that all are in danger of eternal condemnation were it not for the grace of God.

THE ANATOMY OF SIN

"Their throat is an open sepulchre; with their tongues they have used deceit; the poison of asps is under their lips: whose mouth is full of cursing and bitterness. Their feet are swift to shed blood: destruction and misery are in their ways" (Rom. 3:13-16).

The scene here becomes increasingly bleak as Paul describes the general state of the natural man, which has been rightfully called the *anatomy of sin.* His throat is said to be "an open sepulcher" (vs. 13). When we visit our family doctor complaining of flu symptoms, one of the first things he does is to examine our *throat.* Often his comments during the examination range from: "Oh my!!" to "Well, that doesn't look good!!" Of course, this doesn't do much for one's frame of mind. But while we're gagging on the tongue depressor, he's making an observation about our general state of health. Spiritually, the same is true of the natural man, only his throat is an open *grave*, which reeks of deceit, cursing, bitterness, murder, destruction and misery!

Little wonder, the apostle says, we were once "dead in trespasses and sins" (Eph. 2:1). Throughout the Word of God "death" denotes *separation,* whether physically, spiritually or eternally. According to Ephesians 2:1, man is spiritually separated from God. If the taproot of the family tree was Adam and he's dead due to sin, obviously we the branches are spiritually separated as well. We've overstepped the boundary of God's righteousness and fallen short of the glory of God.

> "In time past ye walked according to the course of this world, according to the prince of the power of the air, the spirit that now worketh in the children of disobedience" (vs. 2).

As Gentiles we followed the *course* of this world system. Like a river, we meandered through life aimlessly fulfilling the desires of the flesh. We were unaware that the prince of the power of the air was manipulating us through the world of money, the world of fashion, the world of entertainment, the world of sports, the world of politics, etc. Satan controls the world system through things that appeal to the flesh. This "spirit" or *influence* still holds sway over the children of disobedience to this very hour. If this course is not altered it will lead men to perdition.

> "Among whom also we all had our conversation in times past in the lusts of our flesh, fulfilling the desires of the flesh and of the mind; and were by nature the children of wrath, even as others."

Notice the apostle levels an indictment against Jews as well. As a former blasphemer, Paul, like his countrymen, walked in the lust of the flesh. In Paul's case he was driven by ambition, ascending above many of his equals in the religious world (Gal. 1:14 cf. I Tim. 1:13). Thus, the Jews like the Gentiles are by nature the children of wrath. Webster defines the term *nature* as "the inherent character or basic constitution of a person or thing." The nature of a boa constrictor is to squeeze its prey to death; therefore, it can never be trusted no matter how docile the reptile may seem. Although outwardly man may appear good, essentially he is morally corrupt. The nature of man is *depraved*.

TOTAL DEPRAVITY

This doctrine has suffered severely at the hands of well-meaning Bible teachers. Consequently, their desire to establish a theological system of interpretation has caused them to lose sight of what the Scriptures actually teach. Let's begin by clearing up some misunderstandings. One eminent Bible teacher has this to say:

"This doctrine has suffered from many misconceptions, for the average person would define total depravity by saying that it means that man is as bad as he can be. However, if we adopt that as an acceptable definition, immediately our theology is brought into question because we know men who are not as bad as they can be. We know many men who are good men, kind men, generous men, moral men, men who contribute much in the home and in the community.

"Rather, the doctrine of depravity says that man is as bad *off* as he can be. There is a vast difference between being as bad as he can be and being as bad *off* as he can be. The doctrine of depravity has to do, not with man's estimation of man, but rather with God's estimation of man....When we measure men by man, we can always find someone who is lower than we are on the moral or ethical scale, and the comparison gives us a feeling of self-satisfaction. But the Scriptures do not measure men by man; they measure men by God who has created them. The creature is measured by the Creator and is found to be wanting."[1]

I think we all agree that the natural man is "totally depraved." However, we must not confuse "total depravity" with "total inability." According to Romans 3:12, man is *rotten* to the core, as far as God is concerned. Contrary to what Arminius taught, there is no spark of good in him.[2] Left to himself, the natural man will *not* seek God and would inevitably end up in the lake of fire. The *operative* phrase here is "left to himself."

> "But God, who is rich in mercy, for His great love wherewith He loved us, even when we were dead in sins, hath quickened us together with Christ, (by grace ye are saved)" (Eph. 2:4,5).

The bitter waters of man's depravity are made *sweet* by the revelation, "But God, who is rich in mercy." Thankfully, God has taken the *initiative* to make a provision of salvation and bring mankind in contact with the gospel, which is the means through which the Spirit *convicts* the unsaved sinner (John 16:7-11; Eph. 6:17 cf. Heb. 4:12). We believe that the *sovereignty of God* and *human responsibility* are both essential in the salvation of any soul. So then, when the gospel of salvation is preached to an unregenerate soul, the Holy Spirit supernaturally pierces through the enmity of his heart, allowing the light of the glorious gospel to shine in (II Cor. 4:3-6). Once the sinner is under conviction, he is *responsible* to God to believe the terms of the gospel—that Christ died for his sins, was buried, and rose again the third day.

But can the natural man who is dead in trespasses and sins believe the gospel? Some ask, "How can a dead person believe?" To which we would respond, "How can a dead person be *disobedient?*" (Eph. 2:2). Both answers *necessitate* the utilization of man's intellect and will. We reject the notion that God imparts faith to the natural man thus, enabling him to believe. If this were true, it would completely eliminate human responsibility, especially in regard to the unbeliever who would be condemned to the lake of fire for rejecting a gospel he could have never believed. The Scriptures declare: "faith cometh by hearing, and hearing by the Word of God." Notice that faith comes by *hearing* the Word of God, not implantation.

Let's go a step farther: Did Adam in a *fallen* state understand what God said to him in the garden? The record is clear that he most certainly did—the Word of God pierced straight through his stony heart of flesh. God created man as an intelligent, rational being who has the capacity to make decisions. Even though this image has been marred by sin, when the Spirit convicts a soul through the gospel, man has the *ability* and the responsibility to believe. Can he resist if he so chooses and reject the good news? He often does (see Acts 7:51).

"But God, who is rich in mercy, for His great love wherewith He loved us, even when we were dead in sins, hath quickened us together with Christ, (by grace ye are saved)" (Eph. 2:4,5). If *all* are dead in trespasses and sins, then it can also be said that the love of God and His righteousness extends to *all*. This is a recurring theme throughout the Pauline epistles:

"Even the righteousness of God which is by faith of Jesus Christ unto all and upon all them that believe: for there is no difference" (Rom. 3:22). God's gracious provision is unto "all" which clearly indicates that redemption is *unlimited*. Christ died for the sins of the world. However, the Word of God declares that salvation, and subsequently the righteousness of God, is only conveyed *"upon all them that believe."*

The moment we believe the gospel we are quickened—that is, regenerated by the Spirit, baptized into the Body of Christ and identified with His death, burial, and resurrection.

THE AGES TO COME

"And hath raised us up together, and made us sit together in heavenly places in Christ Jesus: that in the ages to come He might show the exceeding riches of His grace in His kindness toward us through Christ Jesus" (Eph. 2:6,7).

What a grand statement! God has "made us sit together in heavenly places in Christ Jesus." We should note that the verbs in this passage are in the present tense. As far as God is concerned we are *righteous* in Christ; therefore, He sees us already seated with Him in the heavenlies, as we will be in eternity. We are going to rule and reign with Christ over cities of angels. What we need to do is make a practical application of this positional truth in our everyday lives. Amazingly, believers find it difficult to judge in the smallest of matters in the local church. Most seem to have forgotten that our conduct and willingness to suffer for Christ will determine our reigning position with Him (II Tim. 2:11-15).

"That in the ages to come He might show the exceeding riches of His grace in His kindness toward us through Christ Jesus" (Eph. 2:7). The grace of God has been defined as "God's Riches At Christ's Expense." He paid it all that we might enjoy eternity with Him. In the ages to come, beyond time as we know it, God is going to show us the exceeding riches of His grace in His kindness. What more could He do for us that He hasn't already done?

We are going to be displayed as the *trophies of His grace*. Thus, the host of heaven will glorify God through us on the basis that He has brought so many sons to glory. The phrase "exceeding riches of His grace" may also imply that God will make known *new* riches yet untold. As the ages roll on He will personally show the members of the Body of Christ every detail of His handiwork that He prepared for us before the foundation of the world. John Newton had it right when he wrote: "Amazing grace, how sweet the sound."

Just how does a sinner *receive* the riches of His grace? *"For by grace are ye saved through faith; and that not of yourselves: it is the gift of God: not of works, lest any man should boast"* (Eph. 2:8,9). Here again we have the sovereignty of God and human responsibility, running side by side like two trains traveling in the same direction. God always strikes a *balance* between these two lines of truth, which is something we would do well to emulate. Salvation is by God's grace. It has been said, *grace* is receiving from God that which we do not deserve. If we received what we justly deserve every last soul would be condemned to the horrors of hell.

But Christ, who knew no sin, stepped across the stars into this world of sin and woe to be made "sin for us...that we might be made the righteousness of God in Him" (II Cor. 5:21). Calvary covers it all—it's a finished work. With redemption secured through the blood of Christ, God calls upon the sinner to place his *faith* in what Christ has accomplished on his behalf. Faith is simply our *response* to God's gracious provision of salvation.

Since it is contrary to God's creative purpose to ever impose His will upon man's will, we are given the *choice* either to believe or to reject the gospel. The sinner is responsible to place his faith in Christ, and should he fail to do so, he will suffer the eternal consequences of his unbelief. Those found in their sins will be left *without excuse* before a holy and righteous God, who has appointed a day to judge the world in righteousness (Acts. 17:31 cf. Rev. 20:11-15).

Down through the centuries there has been an interesting debate between theologians regarding the phrase, "and that not of yourselves: it is the gift of God." Some believe the gift of God is "faith." That is, God must give the sinner "faith" to believe the gospel since he's dead in trespasses and sins. In short, a corpse doesn't have the capacity to believe.

This interpretation, however, has a number of shortcomings, the least of which is cause for concern. To begin with, the grammatical construction of Ephesians 2:8 does not support this position. "For by grace are ye saved through **faith** [Gr. *Pistis*]; **and that** [Gr. *kai touto*] not of yourselves: it is the gift of God." Notice the pronoun "that" in the original language is *neuter* while "faith" is in the *feminine* gender. Seeing that these genders aren't in agreement with one another, the pronoun "that" could not possibly refer to "faith." Consequently, faith cannot be the gift of God.

Furthermore, if God must impart faith for the sinner to believe the gospel, then regeneration precedes belief. If this were true, as we said earlier, it would completely eliminate human responsibility, especially in regard to the unbeliever who would be condemned to the lake of fire for rejecting a gospel he could have *never* believed.

Although John Calvin is normally credited with teaching that faith is the gift of God, the Dutch Reformers have unfairly misrepresented him. Charles Hodge, who might be considered the archbishop of Calvinism, plainly acknowledged that Calvin believed *salvation*, not faith, is the gift of God. "What is said to be the gift of God? Is it salvation, or faith?...These words *kai touto* only serve to render more prominent the matter referred to. They may relate to faith....or to the salvation spoken of....Beza, following the fathers [Church fathers], prefers the former reference; Calvin, with most of the modern commentators, the latter."[3]

We, too, believe that *salvation* is the gift of God. Not only does this fit the context in which the passage is set, and the grammatical construction, it also harmonizes with the over-all theme of Paul's epistles. In fact, the apostle follows the same order in Romans 6:23 as he did in Ephesians 2:1,8: "For the wages of sin is death; but *the gift of God is eternal life* through Jesus Christ our Lord."

"Not of works, lest any man should boast" (Eph. 2:9). This passage, which is a part of the former sentence, also attests that Paul had salvation in mind. Surely we would never say faith is "not of works." *Faith* and *works* are mutually exclusive of one another. However, it is common to hear someone say that they are working for their salvation. Beloved, if good works could save you, then Christ died in vain! You see, we must come God's way. Please read these words very, very carefully. Read them as if your eternal destiny depended upon it—because it does!! "But to him that worketh not, but believeth on Him that justifieth the ungodly, his faith is counted for righteousness" (Rom. 4:5). Not one soul will be able to boast in heaven that they earned their way to glory. Salvation is of the Lord. We are merely unworthy sinners saved by *grace* alone.

"For we are His workmanship, created in Christ Jesus unto good works, which God hath before ordained that we should walk in them" (Eph. 2:10). The idea of *workmanship* has to do with that which is made. It is the work of God to *fashion* us into the image of His dear Son. This brings to mind the story of a rowdy, disruptive little boy in a Sunday school class who continually frustrated his teacher. One morning the teacher asked him, "Why do you act like that? Don't you know who made you?" To which the little guy replied, "God did! But He isn't through with me yet."

We might say that we, too, are a work in progress. When Michaelangelo completed the painting of *The Last Judgment* at the Sistine Chapel in 1541 it was breathtaking. But this pales by comparison to the work of God foreordained before the foundation of the world. The Church, the Body of Christ is His *masterpiece* that will be exhibited in glory for all to see throughout eternity.

To prepare us for that day, we were "created in Christ Jesus unto good works, which God hath before ordained that we should walk in them." These works have nothing to do with earning our way to heaven. While works do not save us, we are called to "good works" after we're saved. God has a plan and purpose for each of our lives. Thus, we are to present our bodies a living sacrifice, which is our reasonable service. The areas of the Lord's work that we might become involved are too many to name: evangelism, missions, teaching, music, counseling, youth work, sweeping the church basement, etc.

Please note that, today, believers "should" walk in good works. This strongly implies that they *may*, then again they *may not*. According to the kingdom gospel God required fruits as an evidence of their salvation. "Every tree that bringeth not forth good fruit is hewn down, and cast into the fire. Wherefore by their fruits ye shall know them" (Matt. 7:19,20). While today it is God's desire that every believer *should* live a godly life in Christ Jesus, we are not under the law but under grace. Thus there may be times when we have difficulty ascertaining who knows the Lord. That's the *nature* of grace!

ONE NEW MAN

"Wherefore remember, that ye being in time past Gentiles in the flesh, who are called Uncircumcision by that which is called the Circumcision in the flesh made by hands; that at that time ye were without Christ, being aliens from the commonwealth of Israel, and strangers from the covenants of promise, having no hope, and without God in the world" (Eph. 2:11,12).

Every year on June 14th, our country celebrates Flag Day! On this date, we proudly display the "Stars and Stripes" to commemorate that America is the "land of the free and the home of the brave." Although the flag is not esteemed very highly these days, we have a rich heritage. The flag represents *liberty*, and were it not for the ultimate sacrifice of those who gave their lives on the battlefield, a banner of oppression might well be flying over our heads.

The origin of "Old Glory" was conceived by the Second Continental Congress in 1777. It was a fitting symbol of our nation's struggle against tyranny. The thirteen stripes which grace the flag represent the thirteen original colonies. The colors red, white and blue are significant as well—"red" depicts the *courage* and *sacrifices* of the nation's defenders; "white" characterizes the desire for *liberty*, and "blue" portrays *loyalty* and *unity* of our citizens. Delaware had the distinct honor of being the first to have their star placed on "Old Glory" in 1787, and Hawaii was the recipient of the *last* star in 1959. Fifty united states proclaiming "liberty and justice for all."

As the *Stars and Stripes* wave in the wind, it is a solemn testimonial that "freedom's light" was purchased at a great price. We must never, never forget our roots. "Those who cannot remember the past are condemned to repeat it."[4] As it has been said, "We tend to write our benefits in dust and our injuries in marble." The sense of these thoughts might also be applied to the spiritual realm. God wants us to remember our past that we might be more *appreciative* of our present spiritual blessings. And, indeed, we have much to be thankful for!

A Dark Past

There is an old saying that applies to the Gentiles in time past: "You have no one to blame but yourself." When "they knew God, they glorified Him not as God, neither were thankful; but became vain in their imaginations, and their foolish heart was darkened....For this cause God gave *them up* unto vile affections" (Rom. 1:21,26). Once this took place, God channeled His blessing through Abraham's seed. Consequently, the nations came to be known as the Uncircumcision—Gentiles in the flesh. "In the flesh" does not speak of lineage, rather it points to the fact that they were *uncircumcised.* Insofar as the Gentiles were *outside* of the Abrahamic covenant, there was little hope of them ever being saved. Although religious circumcision did not guarantee salvation to a child of Abraham, it did show *favor* and *opportunity.*

The promise of the Messiah, who would deliver His people from their sins, was given to *Israel.* Christ sprang out of the tribe of Judah; He was a Jew who came unto His *own* (John 1:11). We did not have a redeemer; we were "without Christ, aliens from the commonwealth of Israel." Since the covenants of promise find their fulfillment in Christ, we were *homeless,* strangers to the Theocracy. The Gentiles, *as* Gentiles, were not citizens of the kingdom, therefore we had no rights or privileges. For example, an alien living in the United States is destitute of any rights under our Constitution. He cannot vote, own his own business, or take advantage of entitlement programs such as Social Security. These rights are only reserved for U. S. citizens.

The Gentiles were "without hope" and "without God in the world." In time past, we lived a *hopeless* existence. Death was the great unknown as seen in the ancient Egyptians' understanding of things. They erected funeral edifices known as pyramids to bury their kings. It was their belief that the body had to be preserved through mummification so the soul could exist forever. The Egyptians were so skillful in this scientific process that morticians today are mystified by how they accomplished such an astonishing feat. Egyptologists believe that the sloping sides of the pyramids followed the slanting rays of the sun, by which the soul of a departed Pharaoh could ascend to the gods. Of course, when the apostle states the Gentiles were "without God," he meant *without a knowledge* of the true and living God. The Egyptians believed that their kings were gods. In fact, they worshipped a pantheon of gods—Oris the god of vegetation, Re the sun god, Amon the god of the air and fertility, etc.

As we can see, our past history was not a pretty picture. Quite literally millions upon millions of Gentiles were swept into *perdition* because when "they knew God, they glorified Him not as God." But let's look at a practical illustration of Ephesians 2:11-12 in action.

A Snapshot of Ourselves in Goliath

"And there went out a champion out of the camp of the Philistines, named Goliath, of Gath, whose height was six cubits and a span" (I Sam. 17:4).

Goliath *personifies* the Gentile world in time past. It was common in those days for armies to send a *representative* into battle. Each side would select the best among them to determine the outcome of the engagement (I Sam. 17:8-10). In this instance, the Philistines chose Goliath. He was their "champion," that is, one who stood between two camps. Undoubtedly, he had successfully exercised this task before to the chagrin of his enemies.

When the armies of Israel saw Goliath step out onto the plain, I'm sure they nearly had a cardiac arrest! And for good reason: Goliath was a giant who stood 9 feet 7 inches tall. He was a seasoned fighting machine whose coat of armor probably weighed more than most men. The record also informs us that the staff of his spear was "like a weaver's beam," with the spear's head weighing nearly twenty pounds (I Sam. 17:4-7). Picture that coming at you with the velocity of a torpedo! Little wonder, when word spread throughout the camp of Israel that a volunteer was needed to do battle against this *uncircumcised* heathen, everyone suddenly came down with a serious case of FEAR!!! (I Sam. 17:24).

Only a young man named David had the courage to face this formidable foe. Of course, his family and King Saul thought he had taken leave of his senses. Sometimes, we receive more opposition from our family and friends when going about the Lord's work than we do from our enemies. "And Saul said to David, Thou art not able to go against this Philistine to fight with him: for thou art but a youth, and he a man of war from his youth" (I Sam. 17:33).

But David was not deterred by the King's argument. Rather, David showed Saul how the Lord was with him as he tended his father's sheep. When a lion and a bear sought to plunder the flock, David killed them both with his bare hands. "Thy servant slew both the lion and the bear: and this uncircumcised Philistine shall be as one of them, seeing he hath defied the armies of the living God" (I Sam. 17:36). David looked upon Goliath as nothing more than a *wild animal*—a brute being who deserved to die for defying the living God! If there were dictionaries in David's day, his picture would have appeared by the word "courage." Memories of past blessings often embolden us, and it surely did in David's case.

As David and Goliath stepped into the arena, to the human eye this was an obvious mismatch. Probably David barely came up to his opponent's belt buckle. Be that as it may, there was one thing both the armies of Israel and Goliath failed to comprehend: *God was with David!* Goliath, of course, thought this was merely a fool's joke; "this scrawny, little kid is going to do battle with me?" "Am I a dog, that thou comest to me with staves? And the Philistine cursed David by his gods" (I Sam. 17:43). While the giant was humoring himself, David took a smooth stone (more aerodynamic) from his pouch, placed it in his sling, and whipped it at Goliath. That missile came out of David's hand with such force, it "sunk" into Goliath's forehead, crushing his skull—and great was his fall! (I Sam. 17:49).

The following comparison summarizes the above:

Position By Covenant	Position By Nature
1. David was *circumcised* as a child of the covenant.	1. Goliath was *uncircumcised*, a mere dog.
2. David was a *citizen* of the commonwealth of Israel.	2. Goliath was an *alien* and a *stranger*.
3. David received the *favor* of God.	3. Goliath was under the sentence of *death*.
4. David enjoyed the *hope* and blessing of the Kingdom.	4. Goliath lived a *hopeless* existence.
5. David personally *knew* the true and living God.	5. Goliath worshipped idols of stone and wood.

A CHANGE IN VENUE

A Dispensational View of Peace

"But now in Christ Jesus ye who sometimes were far off are made nigh by the blood of Christ. For He is our peace, who hath made both one, and hath broken down the middle wall of partition between us" (Eph. 2:13,14).

The phrase "but now" indicates that a very important dispensational *change* has taken place in God's dealings with mankind. In time past, the Gentiles were clearly "without Christ," BUT NOW, we who were once afar off may draw near to God by the blood of Christ. This is God's secret purpose which He saw fit to reveal *only* to Paul. Today, there is a new creation—Jews and Gentiles in *one* Body! "For He is our peace, who hath made both one."

Those who grew up in the 1960's came to be known as the "peace" generation, even though they had little regard for the establishment. But did you know that when this term appears in Holy Scripture it is used in a very general sense, and must always be qualified by the context? For example, there is a vast difference between the phrase "peace on earth" and the phrase "peace with God." To this Paul adds "Christ is our peace." It is important to consider each of these phrases in their dispensational settings.

While the subject of *peace* always seems to be approached in a devotional sense, we believe this is a great injustice to the Word of God and withholds valuable truth from the saints.

a. Peace on Earth

"For unto you is born this day in the city of David a Savior, which is Christ the Lord. And this shall be a sign unto you; ye shall find the babe wrapped in swaddling clothes, lying in a manger. And suddenly there was with the angel a multitude of the heavenly host praising God, and saying, glory to God in the highest, and on earth peace, good will toward men" (Luke 2:11-14).

This passage raises an interesting question: When will peace be brought to the earth, and by whom? First of all, when we turn in our Bibles to the gospel according to Luke, we must bear in mind that Luke's gospel is an integral part of the prophetic Scriptures. The theme of prophecy, as we know, is Christ's reign upon the earth for a period of one thousand years. Thus, when we study Luke's chronicle of the birth of Christ, the nation Israel is in view. The promise to reign with Christ in the kingdom to come was given exclusively to her.

A proper understanding of verse 14 is based on verse 11, where we read *"For unto you is born this day in the city of David a Savior, which is Christ the Lord."* We need to thoughtfully observe here the phrase "for unto you." We must ask to whom does the "you" refer in this passage? Unquestionably it is a direct reference to the *saved* Hebrew shepherds who were keeping watch over their flock by night. They were representatives of Israel: "Unto you," that is, Israel, a Savior is born. A Savior who would confront the sins of His people and redeem them back to Himself. But we also note that the Savior is the *Christ*, the long-promised Messiah who will confront the chaos of this world. Indeed, He will be the King of kings and Lord of lords. It is in this context that our phrase, "peace on earth" comes into view. When the Messiah returns in His second coming to set up His kingdom, He will bring peace for the first time to this world of sin. He will overthrow the kingdoms of this world and establish His own kingdom of peace and righteousness (Rev. 11:15). This wonderful truth is confirmed for us in Isaiah 9:6 where we read these words:

> *"For unto us a child is born, unto us a Son is given; and the government shall be upon His shoulder: and His name shall be called Wonderful, Counselor, The mighty God, The everlasting Father, THE PRINCE of PEACE."*

Isaiah uses a phrase similar to Luke's, "For unto us." He was one of Israel's major prophets. Insofar as Isaiah was a Hebrew, when he states "Unto us," he means unto us Israelites. Next we note, "A child is born....a Son is given." My friends, here we have something of great significance. The birth of this child is a reference to Christ taking on a human form that He might be born in Bethlehem's manger. But as to the Son, He was not merely born, He was *given*. You see, the one who took on human form is also the eternal Son of God. From everlasting to everlasting, He is God.

As we read on, the Scriptures reveal that a government will be upon His shoulder. Not human government, but rather a divine government—a theocracy over which He will rule. Isaiah also states that this Holy One of God will be the *Prince of Peace* and of His government and *peace* there shall be no end. But when should the world expect this to come to pass? When the Lord Jesus Christ returns *after* the Tribulation period to set up the throne of His glory. We oftentimes refer to this period as the millennial reign of Christ. Now someone may be thinking, "But here in America we are enjoying a time of peace." This may be true, but this cannot be said in other parts of the world. Furthermore, the peace we presently enjoy could end at any time. It is very important, as believers in Christ, to always live in light of this truth.

b. Peace with God

"Therefore being justified by faith, we have peace with God through our Lord Jesus Christ" (Rom. 5:1).

The Apostle Paul introduces us to our second phrase when he declares that believers have "peace with God." While we may live in light of the fact that world peace continues to elude us, we can have peace with God through our Lord Jesus Christ. If we have this peace, everything can collapse around us but we have the assurance that nothing will ever separate us from the love of God in Christ Jesus. I am sure most of us have heard it said at one time or another: "It's high time they made their peace with God." Those who try to make their peace with God are to be pitied. There are literally millions at this very hour who are striving for this peace, but they will not find it because they are searching in all the wrong places. They are seeking it in their own strength and wisdom and the end result will be disillusionment.

How is this peace obtained? Allow me to begin by showing how it is *not* obtained.

> *"Now to him that worketh is the reward not reckoned of grace, but of debt.* But to him that worketh not, but believeth on Him that justifieth the ungodly, his faith is counted for righteousness"* (Rom. 4:4,5).

First we learn that you cannot receive *peace with God* on your own merit. It is not possible to obtain this peace through good works, repetitious prayers, fasting, or confirmation. As a matter of fact, you can go to church services every day of your life and not experience this peace.

> "Cometh this blessedness then upon the circumcision only, or upon the uncircumcision also?" (Rom. 4:9).

Secondly, you cannot acquire this peace by keeping ordinances such as circumcision or water baptism. You can have all the oceans of the water poured over you but it will never grant you the forgiveness of your sins or peace with God.

> "For the promise, that he should be heir of the world, was not to Abraham, or his seed, through the law, but through the righteousness of faith" (Rom. 4:13).

Beloved, you can try your very best to keep all 613 commandments and ordinances contained in the Law of Moses, and for all your efforts you will still not enjoy this peace.

How do we receive peace with God? By *faith*—if we simply believe that Christ died for our sins and rose again, not only are we justified freely by His grace, we also receive assurance that we are right with God. This means that God has nothing against us, having judged our sins at Calvary. The believer can never again be brought into the danger of the hellfire judgment to come. God is at *rest* with us forever.

c. Christ is Our Peace

"For He is our peace, who hath made both one, and hath broken down the middle wall of partition between us; having abolished in His flesh the enmity, even the law of commandments contained in ordinances; for to make in Himself of twain one new man, so making peace" (Eph. 2:14,15).

Who could have possibly known that at Calvary, "God was in Christ, reconciling the world unto Himself"? (II Cor. 5:19). Thus, for those who have believed, Christ is our *peace*. As we have seen, the apostle makes numerous references to peace in his epistles, each of which have various shades of meaning: Grace and peace from God, the Father, peace with God, peace of God, the gospel of peace, etc. The "peace" that Paul speaks of here in Ephesians is Christ *Himself*. He has destroyed the enmity or the hatred between Jews and Gentiles, and has made both one.

Christ has broken down the middle wall of partition, that is, the *law* with its animal sacrifices, feasts, baptisms, Sabbaths, etc. This wall stood tall and strong for over fifteen hundred years. It barred the Gentiles access to the true and living God. There was no place this was more acutely evident than the temple. The following inscription was recently unearthed from Herod's temple in Jerusalem by archeologists:

"No Gentile may enter the barricade which surrounds the Sanctuary and enclosure. Anyone who is caught doing so will have himself to blame for his ensuing death."[5]

But now, we are *free* from the law. Christ has "abolished in His flesh the enmity, even the law of commandments contained in ordinances" (Eph. 2:15). Charles Hodge makes this insightful statement: "Christ delivered us from the obligation of fulfilling the demands of the law as a condition of justification." He accomplished this by redeeming us from the curse of the law. The curse of the law was the pronouncement of "death" due to sin. But Christ who knew no sin was made a curse for us (Gal. 3:13). In other words, He died *our* death, freeing us from the bondage of the law.

This paved the way for the creation of a "new man" (Eph. 2:15). The term "new" used here by the apostle is the Greek word *kainos*. This particular term does not mean something recently completed. Rather, it has the idea of new "in kind and quality—unlike anything existing before." When the automobile made its debut at the turn of the 20th century, it replaced the horse and buggy. It was an entirely *new* form of transportation that never existed before. The same is true of the entity Paul calls the "new man," not to be confused with the new nature. Jews and Gentiles make up the one "new man." This was unheard of prior to the revelation that was committed to Paul.

Today, Christ has reconciled *both* in one Body. You see, God has concluded both Jews and Gentiles in unbelief that He might have mercy upon *all* (Rom. 11:32). Consequently, He has declared a truce today, giving His enemies an opportunity to be *reconciled*. But to be the beneficiary of this amnesty, we must believe the gospel to make the reconciliation complete. For example, people who work in the city of Chicago tend to rack up a lot of parking tickets, sometimes amounting to thousands of dollars. Once every five years or so, the city will extend a brief "grace period" to clear their books. Notices are sent to each violator informing them that if they appear in traffic court, plead guilty, and pay a nominal fine (usually a fraction of what is owed), they will avoid having their driver's license suspended. However, this offer only benefits those who take *advantage* of it. Those who reject the offer incur the wrath of the state.

> "And came and preached peace to you which were
> afar off, and to them that were nigh. For through Him
> we both have access by one Spirit unto the Father" (Eph.
> 2:17,18).

This passage has troubled some of the brethren, insofar as it seems to imply that Christ preached this message during His earthly ministry. Of course, we know this could not have been the case since this truth was hidden. The answer lies in the fact that the revelation of the joint Body was to be manifested in *due time* through Paul's gospel (I Tim. 2:3-7 cf. Titus 1:1-3). So, it is through Paul's message that Christ is making known that Jews and Gentiles are reconciled in one Body by the Cross. Interestingly, each member of the Trinity plays a consequential role to make this a reality. Hence, through Christ's finished work, both Jews and Gentiles now have full access to the Father by the Spirit.

As "Old Glory" is the emblem of our countrymen's sacrifice, the Cross of Christ, for the Gentiles, is our emblem signifying a new and living way.

THE DWELLING PLACE OF GOD
Laying the Foundation

> "Now therefore ye are no more strangers and foreign-
> ers, but fellowcitizens with the saints, and of the house-
> hold of God; and are built upon the foundation of the
> apostles and prophets, Jesus Christ Himself being the
> chief corner stone" (Eph. 2:19,20).

Some years ago during a trip to Colorado our family visited Pike's Peak which, needless to say, was one of those unforgettable experiences. As we clattered up the side of the mountain on the old Cog Railway, our conductor, a young college student, pointed out various points of interest. He also had a great sense of humor which made the trip even

more enjoyable. At an elevation of over 14,000 feet everything begins to move in slow motion, including the Cog en-
gine that was pulling us up the final 30 percent grade to the
summit. The scenery was absolutely breathtaking. How anyone could look out over those "purple mountain majesties"
and fail to see the creative hand of God is beyond me.

In similar fashion, Paul's letter to the Ephesians brings
us to the very summit of the Pauline revelation. From this
vantage point we are able to see various points of interest
as we look out over the riches of God's grace. Like the splendor of the Rockies, the grace of God never ceases to amaze
us! Here in Ephesians 2:19,20 we learn that those who are
saved in this dispensation make up a *holy temple* where
God dwells through the Spirit. The first question one is
inclined to ask is: "Does this in any way conflict with the
Mystery Program?" Quite the contrary, it serves to demonstrate the fact that there are *connections* between the two
programs of God.

The term "now" used here by Paul signals that a significant dispensational change has taken place. With the fall
of Israel God turned to the Gentiles; therefore we who were
once far off are NOW made nigh by the blood of Christ. In
time past we were the offscouring of the earth. Back then
the Gentiles were called the Uncircumcision, a term that
was used in a derogatory sense by those who were of the
Circumcision. We were *dogs*, "without Christ...strangers
from the covenants of promise, having no hope, and without
God in the world" (Eph. 2:11,12).

But now we are no more strangers but *fellowcitizens* with
the saints. In essence the apostle is saying that the Ephesians were fellowcitizens with the other members of the
Body of Christ, which is true of all those who have trusted
Christ down to this very day. Our citizenship here in America

signifies that we reside in the *same* country and that each of us has certain inalienable rights. Likewise, as members of the Body of Christ, we are fellowcitizens of a heavenly country, blessed with all spiritual blessings, having been granted rights and privileges as the sons of God (Phil. 3:20).

Paul broadens the scope when he reveals that we are also numbered with the *household of God*. In this context the phrase "household of God" is a collective reference to all of the blood-washed saints from every age. As sinners saved by grace, we are a part of that great company of people called the *redeemed*, in contrast to those who are *lost*. Thanks be unto God that we are saved and included in the plans and purposes of God as individual members of Christ's Body.

The apostle goes on to add that we are "built upon the foundation of the apostles and prophets." Exactly who were these apostles and prophets? Some insist that this refers to the 12 apostles and the Old Testament prophets. But they laid the foundation, which is Christ, according to *prophecy*. The apostles taught, based on the teachings of the law and prophets, that Christ was the Messiah, that He was the rightful heir to the throne of David—hence, the King of Israel. Is this what we proclaim to our hearers today? Surely the members of the Body of Christ are *not* built on this foundation. If these were the apostles and prophets of the kingdom the order would be reversed, for in God's Prophetic Program the prophets preceded the apostles, as seen in the gospel according to Luke:

> "Therefore also said the wisdom of God, I will send them *prophets* and *apostles*, and some of them they shall slay and persecute" (Luke 11:49).

Who, then, were these mighty defenders of the faith that held these prominent positions in the early part of this present dispensation? We believe that these were the apostles and prophets of *grace* who preached Christ according to the revelation of the Mystery. Of course, Paul is the *primary* apostle of this dispensation, but there were those who also held this office in a *secondary* sense. When Paul wrote to those at Thessalonica about his ministry among them he states: "Nor of men sought we glory, neither of you, nor yet of others, when we might have been burdensome, as the APOSTLES of Christ" (I Thes. 2:6). These apostles of Christ are identified for us by the Holy Spirit as being Paul, Silas, and Timothy (I Thes. 1:1). As far as the prophets are concerned, Agabus comes to mind as one of the foretellers of this administration. You will remember that it was Agabus who warned Paul not to go to Jerusalem, lest he suffer the consequences (Acts 21:10-13). In Paul's epistles the order is always the same, apostles first, followed by the prophets, for this is the order in which they were given.

> "And God hath set some in the Church, first apostles, secondarily prophets, thirdly teachers" (I Cor. 12:28).
>
> "Which in other ages was not made known unto the sons of men, as it is now revealed unto His holy apostles and prophets by the Spirit" (Eph. 3:5).
>
> "And He gave some, apostles; and some, prophets; and some, evangelists; and some, pastors and teachers" (Eph. 4:11).

So then, as members of the Body of Christ, we are built upon the foundation of the apostles and prophets of grace who proclaimed the Lord of glory in His exaltation. Christ is the chief cornerstone which is synonymous with the foundation. It is the point of reference from which all measurements are taken. Thus, if we want to measure up to God's standard today, we, too, must acknowledge Paul's apostleship and message.

THE BUILDING OF A TEMPLE

We place a high premium on rightly dividing the Word of truth, and rightfully so. But it is equally important to recognize the *connections* between the two programs of God. For example, the Savior who shed His blood for Israel is the same Savior who died for our sins. The Spirit who indwelt the saints at Pentecost is the same Spirit who indwells believers in the age of Grace. As we have seen, the members of the Body of Christ are also numbered with the household of God and therefore joined to the *living temple* which God planned and purposed before the foundation of the world. This helps to explain why Paul uses the metaphor of a "temple" when speaking of us collectively.

> "In whom all the building fitly framed together groweth unto an holy temple in the Lord" (Eph. 2:21).

Using the diagram of the Old Testament temple as an illustration, the living temple of God basically follows the same pattern.

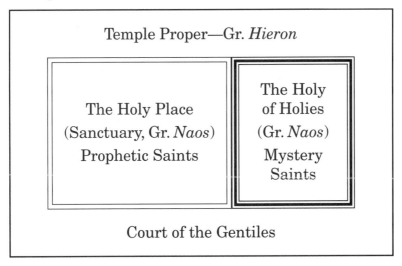

Temple Proper—Gr. *Hieron*

The Holy Place (Sanctuary, Gr. *Naos*) Prophetic Saints

The Holy of Holies (Gr. *Naos*) Mystery Saints

Court of the Gentiles

On the left side of our diagram we have the Holy Place, which represents all of those who have been saved under the Prophetic Program. The living stones that have been placed into this side of the structure rest on the sure foundation, which is Christ relative to His *earthly ministry*. This explains why Peter says to his readers: "Ye also, as lively stones, are built up a spiritual house, an holy priesthood, to offer up spiritual sacrifices, acceptable to God by Jesus Christ" (I Pet. 2:5). With the setting aside of the nation Israel in unbelief, God has temporarily discontinued the construction on this part of the building. He has, however, revealed another set of plans for a *new* addition to the structure.

A new masterbuilder, Paul, is summoned, through whom God reveals His *secret* purpose, which was hidden from ages and generations past. Consequently, Paul was very careful NOT to "build upon another man's [Peter's] foundation" (Rom. 15:20). Instead he pours out a new section of foundation in his epistles, which is Jesus Christ according to His heavenly ministry.

> "According to the grace of God which is given unto me, as a wise masterbuilder, I have laid the foundation, and another buildeth thereon...For other foundation can no man lay than that is laid, which is Jesus Christ" (I Cor. 3:10,11).

Today then, God is cutting out stones from the quarry of sinful humanity, saving them by the riches of His grace and placing them into the temple. It is interesting that the term "temple" used here by the apostle in Ephesians 2 is the Greek word *Naos*, which refers to the sanctuary, and in this context to a specific section of it called the *Holy of Holies*. In this holy sanctum dwelt the very presence of God Almighty. Only the High Priest was permitted to enter this area once a year on the Day of Atonement. Anyone else was under the sure sentence of death if they even dared to draw near. *But now*, through the blood of Christ, God *dwells* in our midst, thus, we can "come boldly unto the throne of grace, that we may obtain mercy, and find grace to help in time of need" (Heb. 4:16). It is a solemn thought indeed that every believer in Christ dwells in the very presence of God. Surely this should cause us to order our steps accordingly.

> "In whom ye also are builded together for an habitation [dwelling place] of God through the Spirit" (Eph. 2:22).

When Solomon constructed the temple in Jerusalem he commanded, "and they brought great stones, costly stones, and hewed stones, to lay the foundation of the house." Solomon paid a king's ransom to purchase the stones for his temple, but it is nothing to be compared with what it cost our Savior to purchase us from the quarry of sin. Every stone that was placed in Solomon's temple was made ready *before* it was brought to the structure so that, "there was neither hammer nor axe nor any tool of iron heard in the house, while it was in building" (I Kings 6:7). The stones were cut to such precision at the quarry that when they were brought to the site each fit perfectly into its place without a sound. In like manner, the sound of the hammer was only heard on a hill called Calvary, as they drove nails into the hands and feet of our Lord. The living stones that were chiseled from His finished work are still being slipped quietly into the temple of God. We are perfect and complete in Him.

Paul further teaches us that the temple is "fitly framed together" and that we are "builded together." This indicates that our placement in the building is a sovereign act of God. Furthermore, just as one stone rests upon another, so we too rely upon each other as believers in Christ. We are to bear one another's *burdens*.

Many years ago I received a phone call in the middle of the night saying that one of the expectant mothers of our assembly had been rushed to the hospital. By the time I arrived at the medical facility the infant was stillborn and already with the Lord. There is no greater burden to bear than to lose a child. The grief is overwhelming at first, but these dear saints weathered the storm well. Words seem inadequate at such times, so I pulled up a chair and spent the rest of the day with the family. There were long periods of silence followed by a need to talk about the things of the Lord. For the most part I only spoke when they felt like talking. Sometimes the best way to help bear another's burden is to simply be there.

Another way in which we rely upon each other is for *encouragement*. God often encourages us through other saints. There are some believers that you can't help but feel uplifted by when you are in their presence. I remember the story of the godly Grandmother who always had a kind word for the pastor's message. One Sunday the pastor had to be out of town so a young, inexperienced guest speaker was called to fill the pulpit. His message was an absolute disaster. All eyes were on the seasoned veteran of the Cross as she made her way to the vestibule. Everyone wondered what she could possibly say to the young man by way of encouragement. Grandma patted him on the hand and said: "I want to thank you for that wonderful Scripture passage you read this morning, it lifted my heart into the heavenlies. Isn't God's Word wonderful—thank you again!!"

Just as one stone in Solomon's temple held up the other stones, in like fashion we need to uphold one another in prayer. May the Lord help us not only to keep others before the throne of grace, but also to be thankful that we are partakers of His *eternal purpose*.

6

The Treasures of Grace

"For this cause I Paul, the prisoner of Jesus Christ
for you Gentiles, if ye have heard of the dispensation of
the grace of God which is given me to youward."

—Ephesians 3:1,2

The old hymns of the faith are often melodies of dispensational truth. Prior to the American Revolution, Philip Doddridge set these words to song: "Grace 'tis a charming song, harmonious to the ear; heaven with the echo shall resound, and all the earth shall hear. Grace taught my wandering feet to tread the heavenly road; and new supplies each hour I meet, while pressing on to God. Saved by grace alone! this is all my plea: Jesus died for all mankind, and Jesus died for me."

Across the grandeur of God's past dealings with mankind, there were occasional displays of "grace." For example, "Noah found grace in the eyes of the Lord." Here we must differentiate between *grace* within a dispensation and the present *dispensation of Grace*. Today God has opened the floodgates, allowing His matchless grace to inundate a lost and dying world. Matchless grace, yes; please note again the word "Gentiles" in the above passage of Scripture. This is a truly wonderful thing, that Paul is sent to the *Gentiles*. Who can deny that this was unheard of in the Old Testament? Gentiles saved by grace alone! "O the depth of the riches both of the wisdom and knowledge of God! how unsearchable are His judgments, and His ways past finding out!" (Rom. 11:33).

A WALK DOWN MEMORY LANE

Although God had made a provision for the Gentiles to be saved through Israel in prophecy, a cursory reading of the Old Testament will produce this conclusion: No one was *sent* to the Gentiles. They were "strangers from the covenants of promise, having no hope, and without God in the world" (Eph. 2:12). Consequently, the past history of the Gentiles is one of *ruin*. They were merely pagans who perished under the sentence of God's judgment time and time again. When a nation stood in the path of Israel returning to the Promised Land, God destroyed them.

With a mighty hand the Lord delivered Israel from the fleshpots of Egypt. But shortly after their departure, Pharaoh hardened his heart. Thus he summoned all the chariots of Egypt and amassed an army that struck fear into the hearts of the Israelites who were camped by the Red Sea. They probably heard the thunder of approaching chariots first, then looked up to see a cloud of terror staring them in the face. It appeared they were trapped between the jaws of death—a watery grave before them or a sword awaiting behind. But the Lord was with His people that day. As we know, God miraculously parted the Red Sea and Israel crossed safely to the other side on *dry ground.*

The Egyptians (Gentiles) on the other hand tasted the wrath of God. "And the Lord said unto Moses, stretch out thine hand over the sea...and the waters returned, and covered the chariots, and the horsemen, and all the host of Pharaoh that came into the sea after them; *there remained not so much as one of them....*And Israel saw the Egyptians dead upon the sea shore" (Ex. 14:26,28,30). This was only the beginning of sorrows for these godless heathen who were instantaneously swept into the pit along with their weapons of warfare (Ezek. 32:27,28).

Shortly after Israel crossed the Jordan River on her return to the Promised Land, she learned that there were enemies in the land. Thus she was to rid the land of the uncircumcised Gentiles that obstructed her way. Under the command of Joshua, God instructed His people to show *no* mercy on those who were lower than the dust of the earth. As the walls of Jericho came crashing down, the record states: "And they utterly destroyed all that was in the city, both man and woman, young and old, and sheep, and ass, with the edge of the sword" (Josh. 6:21).

This conquest was followed by another victory at Ai. "And so it was, that all that fell that *day*, both of men and women, were *twelve thousand*, even all the men of Ai. For Joshua drew not his hand back, wherewith he stretched out the spear, until he had utterly destroyed all the inhabitants of Ai" (Josh. 8:25,26).

For those who may be wondering why God dealt so harshly with the nations, it must be remembered that these heathen had given themselves over to *unspeakable atrocities*. They were guilty of idolatry (sacrificing their little ones to pagan gods), gross immorality, homosexuality, and various other perversions. In addition, each of these nations was riddled with *disease*. This helps us understand why Israel burned everything in their wake (Josh. 6:24 cf. 8:28). God was merely purging the land of sin and its devastating effects.

Historically, the Assyrians were perhaps the most brutal people of their day. They had earned a reputation among the nations for developing some of the most inhuman forms of torture known to man. This ranged from flaying the skin of their enemies to running poles through their victims and lining them along the entrance of the cities they had conquered. Thus, when Hezekiah learned that Sennacherib, the king of Assyria, had Israel in his sights, he was visibly shaken. He prayed: "Now therefore, O Lord our God, I beseech Thee, save Thou us out of his hand" (II Kings 19:19).

"And it came to pass that night, that the angel of the Lord went out, and smote in the camp of the Assyrians an hundred fourscore and five thousand [185,000]: and when they arose early the next morning, behold, they were all *dead* corpses" (II Kings 19:35). Amazing! One angel in about an eight hour period obliterated the entire Assyrian army encamped before Jerusalem.

The biography of the Gentiles in time past is a long *funeral* procession. Their blood ran like a river through the Old Testament. Surely, this should give us a deeper appreciation of the grace of God, for Paul says: "*But now* in Christ Jesus ye [Gentiles] who sometimes were afar off are made nigh by the blood of Christ" (Eph. 2:13). And who had God sent to the Gentiles to tell them about this good news? *Paul.* He is the apostle of the Gentiles. Paul was the first to tell us how God is saving Gentiles, as Gentiles, by His grace.

THE DISPENSATION OF GRACE

"If ye have heard of the dispensation of the grace of God which is given me to youward" (Eph. 3:2).

Perhaps one of the most notable characteristics of this dispensation is, the heavens are *silent*. In prophecy, this meant that God was *displeased* with His people. However, today, God is declaring grace and peace. He has reconciled the world to Himself, not imputing their sins unto them. God is giving all men everywhere an opportunity to be saved.

Sadly, some have wrongly concluded that this silence of the heavens is due to an apathy on God's part. Probably you have even heard it said, "Evil is running rampant in our streets. Why, doesn't God do something?" "Look at Hitler, he murdered six million innocent Jews in the Holocaust.

120

Why, didn't God rain fire down from heaven on this ungodly dictator?" But what Hitler did pales by comparison to the evil deeds of Stalin who murdered twenty million under his regime. Yet, they say, he died peacefully in his sleep.

Even though it may appear that evil men sometimes prosper, mark these words and mark them well, a day of *reckoning* is coming. While the sins of those who commit such wickedness are not being imputed at this time, they are reserved for the day of vengeance (Rom. 2:5,6). Wicked men may think that they have gotten away with murder, so to speak, but God will *remember* at the judgment to come. Then shall they be consumed in terror as they are cast into the lake of fire which burneth forever and ever (Rev. 21:8).

For the time present, however, God is manifesting the riches of His grace. In His longsuffering He is not willing that any should perish, but that all would receive His gracious offer of reconciliation. The following true story is taken from a page of Charles Finney's life which illustrates this point.[1]

"Mr. Finney had a man come up to him one night, a rough looking fellow, and said, 'Will you come and visit me? I'd like to see you. First, I want to know whether you believe what you preached tonight.' Finney said, 'Yes I believe what I preached.' The man replied, 'I want you to come and see me.' He gave him the address, and went on his way. He had barely disappeared from sight when four men hurriedly came to Mr. Finney and asked: 'What did that man say to you?' 'He asked me to come visit him.' They replied, 'Don't go, he's the worst man in this community. He has a saloon and a gambling den, and you may be placing yourself in harm's way.' Mr. Finney said, 'I promised to go and I must go.'

"The next day the man met him at the front door of his office. Mr. Finney went in, the man shut the door and took a revolver out of his pocket and held it in his right hand.

Mr. Finney looked at it, and the man said, 'Don't be afraid, I'm not going to hurt you. This revolver has killed four people. I killed two of them and my bartender killed the others. You said last night that the blood of Jesus washed away all sins. Is there any hope for me?' Mr. Finney said, 'That's what I preach and that's what I believe. The blood of Jesus Christ, God's Son, cleanses us from all sin.'

"The man said, 'This is my office. This side here is my saloon. I sell everything there. I have men come there who bring their week's wages and spend every cent. Their wives come to me carrying their little babies in their arms, pleading with me to send the men home. But I curse at them and put the women out with their children. Mr. Finney, is there any hope for me?' Mr. Finney said, 'The blood of Jesus Christ, God's Son, cleanses us from all sin.'

"The man said, 'On the other side is the gambling den. If a man gets out of the saloon with any money, we get it there. Men come who have worked in the bank, they bring the bank money, they gamble it and lose, and then shoot themselves right in my gambling place. We have that often, but that's how I make my money. Mr. Finney, is there any hope for me?' Mr. Finney said, 'The blood of Jesus Christ, God's Son, cleanses us from all sin.'

"The man said, 'Across the street is my beautiful home. I have a wife and a little girl. I married this young woman in New York and told her I was in a thriving business, that I had plenty of money—I didn't tell her what it was, when she came here and saw that I had a saloon and gambling den it nearly broke her heart. She didn't die, but she's never been happy. My little girl is about 12. I go home and I beat them. I pushed my little girl against the stove and she has a burn from her shoulder to the elbow. She'll never be the same again. Mr. Finney, do you think there is any hope for me?' Mr. Finney said, 'The blood of Jesus Christ, God's Son, cleanses us of all sins.' [The evangelist went on to share with this man how God loved him and that Christ died for his sins, was buried, and rose again]. The man said, 'All right, Mr. Finney, you may go,' and he let him out the front door."

It is said word came to Mr. Finney the following day that the man was wonderfully saved from his sins. From that day forward he became a faithful husband, a loving father, and served the Lord until the end of his life. That's grace! It has been said that "the grace of God is often most cherished by those who have walked the farthest from its light." Only the *matchless grace* of God could so transform a life from the depths of despair into a vessel that is fit for the Master's use.

> "For this cause I Paul, the prisoner of Jesus Christ for you Gentiles, if ye have heard of the dispensation of the grace of God which is given me to youward" (Eph. 3:1,2).

Before we leave this portion, it should also be noted here that Paul refers to himself as the *prisoner* of Jesus Christ to whom was committed the dispensation of Grace. Interestingly, Paul never considered himself a prisoner of Rome. Rather, he had been apprehended of Christ on the road to Damascus. The chains that bound him that fateful day were chains of love. Paul was a firm believer in the providence of God—he saw the things that had happened to him as the hand of God. This is clearly exhibited in his words to the saints at Philippi:

> "But I would ye should understand, brethren, that the things which happened unto me have fallen out rather unto the furtherance of the gospel. So that my bonds in Christ are manifest in all the palace, and in all other places" (Phil. 1:12,13).

In other words, had the apostle not been wrongly accused at the hands of his countrymen in Jerusalem, he probably would have never been incarcerated in Rome. Paul viewed this as the permissive will of God which enabled him to carry the gospel to a place it may have never reached otherwise. As a result, the infamous Praetorian guard was introduced to Christ, and some of Caesar's own house became members of the *household of God* (Phil. 4:22).

Needless to say, the apostle's confinement at Rome temporarily suspended his travels. But even in this the Lord had a purpose. With the saints now grounded in the rudimentary things of grace, the time had come to bring them into a fuller knowledge of the revelation of the Mystery. This could easily be accomplished through the written page. Thus Paul began an extensive writing ministry during the years of his imprisonment which is still producing fruits to this day. These writings include: *Ephesians, Philippians, Colossians, Philemon, Hebrews* and *I & II Timothy*. As we know, these particular epistles bring us to the very pinnacle of grace truth.

Another benefit of Paul's imprisonment is that God effectively uses it to teach us that the apostle could not have been teaching the law, otherwise the Jews would not have been seeking his life. Their intense persecution of the apostle was due to his ministry among the *Gentiles*. When Paul recounted how the Lord had instructed him to go "far hence unto the Gentiles," his countrymen were infuriated.

"And they gave him audience unto this **word**, and then lifted up their voices, and said, Away with such a fellow from the earth: for it is not fit that he should live" (Acts 22:22). Notice they gave him an audience "unto this **word**," that is, the word *Gentiles*. This was the straw that broke the camel's back, as it were. It was unthinkable that someone would be sent to the Gentiles. This only confirmed their worst fear that Paul had sought to bring Trophimus, an uncircumcised Gentile, into the temple (Acts 21:27-31). Of course, this was totally untrue, but it gave them sufficient reason to call for his life. Although the Jews were thwarted in this attempt, it did land Paul in a Roman prison.

Some things in life are a given, as they say. Take your eyes off the road for a moment and the driver in front of you is sure to have applied his brakes when you glance back. If you're dining out, you no sooner fill your mouth with food and the waitress is standing there to ask you a question. However, due to the fact that we live in a sin-cursed world, sometimes we are called upon to face the *unexpected*. Consequently, the next time the wheels come off your Christian life, remember Paul's personal experiences. Instead of going to pieces, consider what the Lord may be teaching you. Perhaps He has placed you in a particular set of circumstances to *comfort* someone or tell them about the Savior. Whatever the case may be, learn to be content in whatever state you may find yourself.

THE REVELATION OF THE MYSTERY

"If ye have heard of the dispensation of the grace of God which is given me to youward: how that by revelation He made known unto me the mystery; (as I wrote afore in few words, whereby, when ye read, ye may understand my knowledge in the mystery of Christ)" (Eph. 3:2-4).

They say the darkest hour of the night is just before dawn. Such is often the case with those who are searching for the truth. The eyes of their understanding are blinded by Satan to keep them from the glorious light of Paul's gospel. But those who are more interested in pleasing God than men are customarily rewarded with the key which unlocks the sacred secret. In the course of time, it becomes apparent that God has *two programs* in His Word—Prophecy and the Mystery.

What does the Mystery mean to you? The Mystery to some is just that, a mystery. Simply put, they couldn't defend it if their life depended upon it. Perhaps the most common explanation is that it has something to do with the "mysteries" of the kingdom found in Matthew chapter thirteen. But this interpretation fails to take into consideration the two programs of God. Those who are better acquainted with dispensationalism teach that the Mystery is Jews and Gentiles in one Body. We applaud their attempt to rightly divide the Word, but in fact this conclusion falls somewhat short of the whole truth.

While the joint Body is an essential part of our message, it is only one in a series of doctrines which make up the Mystery. The *Mystery*, then, is a divine program which introduces us to the heavenly ministry of Christ (Eph. 1:19-23). But why is a knowledge of it so important?

First and foremost, the Mystery unfolds God's plans and purposes for the Church, the Body of Christ—it is His *will*, and every child of God should desire to have a knowledge of His will (Col. 1:9,10 cf. 1:25,26). In addition, it completely eliminates confusion within the camp.

A short time ago, I was invited to hold some special meetings down south. The first evening I went to the platform early to gather my thoughts for my message. A few minutes before the service I realized that I had forgotten to pick up a bulletin. But since we were about to begin I was reluctant to leave the front. As I turned to my left I noticed a hymnal lying beside me that had a bulletin sticking out from under the front cover.

A sense of relief came over me as I glanced at it to see where to turn in the hymnal. When we stood, the congregation began to sing "How Great Thou Art." I was confused for a moment because my program had "Great Is Thy Faithfulness" as the first hymn. Something was terribly wrong! Although there were similarities in the order of service, a closer look at my bulletin revealed that the hymns were different, the Scripture reading was incorrect, and the message had nothing to do with my subject. I was following the wrong program!!!

Sadly, many in Christendom are committing the same mistake. They are seeking to carry out the Prophetic Program only to find themselves in an awkward position. We have all had the experience of trying to force something into a place where it doesn't belong. In short, the old proverbial "square peg in a round hole." Of course, if you use a large enough sledgehammer it will eventually fit, but not according to design.

The same is true of those who unwittingly place themselves under the Prophetic Program. They must go to great lengths to wrest the Scriptures from their natural setting to make them say something God never intended them to say. May we remind the reader again, *all Scripture is for our benefit, but it is not all written to us, nor is it all about us.* We must rightly divide the Word of truth, otherwise we are guilty of forcing the "square" doctrines of prophecy into the "round hole" of the Mystery.

The Unique Character of the Mystery

"How that by revelation He made known unto me the Mystery; as I wrote afore in few words" (Eph. 3:3).

Notice that the Mystery or the gospel of the grace of God was committed to Paul. Insofar as this message was "hid in God" from the beginning of the world, it necessitated a *direct*

127

revelation from Him. Thus, the Lord appeared face to face with Paul on the road to Damascus. This was merely the beginning of over thirty years of revelations the apostle would receive regarding the doctrines of grace.

Brethren, the Mystery is found *exclusively* in Paul's epistles. And until the Church submits itself to this indisputable fact, it will be forever "tossed to and fro, and carried about with every wind of doctrine, by the sleight [trickery] of men, and cunning craftiness, whereby they lie in wait to deceive" (Eph. 4:14). Every teacher who claims to have had a vision, heal the sick, or says that Old Testament prophecy is being fulfilled today, is a case in point.

The two great revelators of Holy Scripture are *Moses* and *Paul*. God dispensed the law to Moses; therefore, he was the Lord's spokesman under the *old economy*. For example, he says to a new generation preparing to enter the Promised Land:

> "Now therefore hearken, O Israel, unto the statutes and unto the judgments, which *I teach you*, for to do them, that ye may live, and go in and possess the land which the Lord God of your fathers giveth you. Ye shall not add unto the word which *I command you*, neither shall ye diminish ought from it, that ye may keep the commandments of the Lord your God which *I command you*" (Deut. 4:1,2).

Notice the frequent usage of personal pronouns in the phrases "*I* teach you," "*I* command you," and again, "*I* command you." To some it may sound like Moses was an egomaniac. On more than one occasion he was charged with taking too much upon himself. In other words, who did he think he was to tell the children of Israel what to do! Be that as it may, Moses was God's divinely *appointed* Deliverer. To disobey the commands of Moses was to disobey the Word of the Lord.

You will recall when Miriam and Aaron spoke against Moses, the anger of the Lord was kindled against them: "With him [Moses] will I speak mouth to mouth, even apparently, and not in dark speeches; and the similitude of the Lord shall he behold: wherefore then were ye not afraid to speak against my servant Moses?" (Num. 12:8). The judgment of God was swift and sure—Miriam was afflicted with *leprosy* for seven days that she might be ashamed.

Although we are living under a *new economy*, things haven't changed much. Today, many of the Lord's people foolishly exclaim: *Paul, Paul, Paul,* all you people talk about is *Paul*! He was nothing more than a boaster! One lady even went so far as to inform me that "Paul was a male chauvinist pig!" Apparently, she did not agree with what the apostle taught regarding the role of women in the home and the church. In consideration of the above, I immediately took two steps backward, in the event the earth opened up and swallowed her whole!!

I graciously said to this lady: "Those were strong words that you spoke against our Lord." Boy, am I a glutton for punishment! She snapped back, "I said nothing of the kind!!!" Oh, but you did, the Scriptures plainly say: "If any man think himself to be...spiritual, let him acknowledge that the things that I write unto you are the *commandments of the Lord*" (I Cor. 14:37). You see, Paul is God's divinely *ordained* apostle, through whom He has made known the riches of His grace. To reject Paul's apostleship and message is tantamount to rejecting the heavenly ministry of Christ. Little wonder Paul says, "Be ye followers of me, even as I also am of Christ" (I Cor. 11:1).

In Ephesians chapter one, the apostle briefly surmises that God has "made known unto us the *Mystery of His will,* according to His good pleasure which He hath purposed in Himself." The *Mystery of His will* simply means that we are included in God's eternal plans and purposes. While the prophetic saints will inherit the new earth which includes the New Jerusalem, the inheritance of the Body of Christ is to spend eternity with Christ in the heavenlies (Eph. 1:9-12). Thus, here in Ephesians chapter three, the phrase "as I wrote afore in few words" is referring back to Paul's comments in chapter one. As the apostle continues his train of thought, he gives us a fuller picture of the various aspects of the revelation of the Mystery.

"Whereby, when ye read, ye may understand my knowledge in the Mystery of Christ" (Eph. 3:4).

By this point in time Paul was well-grounded in the message of Grace, as the above passage confirms. However, the Ephesians were still being established in the faith. Consequently, the apostle wanted them to more fully understand the significance of the "Mystery of [Greek, *the*] Christ," that is, *the Body of Christ*. Interestingly, the Body of Christ was a secret that was withheld from ages and generations past.

Therefore, one will search in vain to find any reference to the Church, the Body of Christ in the Prophetic Scriptures. One nation was preeminent throughout the pages of prophecy—*Israel*! As they say, the proof is in the pudding!

The days of Abraham:	"And I will make of thee a great *nation* [Israel]" (Gen. 12:2).
The days of Moses:	"And ye shall be unto me a kingdom of priests, and an holy *nation*. These are the words which thou shalt speak unto the children of *Israel*" (Ex. 19:6).

The days of the Kings:	"And what one *nation* in the earth is like Thy people *Israel*, whom God went to redeem to be His own people?" (I Chron. 17:21).
The days of the Prophets:	"but *Israel* doth not know, My people doth not consider. Ah sinful *nation*, a people laden with iniquity" (Isa. 1:3,4).
The time of Christ:	"but being high priest that year, he prophesied that Jesus should die for that *nation*" (John 11:51).
The day of Pentecost:	"Therefore let all the *house of Israel* know assuredly" (Acts 2:36).

Not until the Apostle Paul did God see fit to reveal the secret of the *Body of Christ*. Think of it! "That the Gentiles should be fellowheirs [Gr. joint-heirs], and of the same Body [Gr. joint-Body], and partakers [Gr. joint-partakers], of His promise in Christ by the gospel" (Eph. 3:6). This was unheard of in time past.

Today, then, God is saving *individual* Jews and Gentiles out of the nations, thus forming a new entity called the *joint-Body*. Just as the members of our physical body are joined together, the members of Christ's Body also bear a relationship with one another. If you fall and crack a rib, the pain greatly limits your ability to move—there's life in those bones! In like fashion, if a child of God falls from grace, it sends shock waves through the other members who are in proximity of the fallen member. Upon being baptized by the Holy Spirit into the Body, we also become joint-heirs and shall be seated *together* with Christ in heavenly places.

131

A CONTROVERSIAL PASSAGE

"Whereby, when ye read, ye may understand my knowledge in the mystery of Christ) which in other ages was not made known unto the sons of men, as it is now revealed unto his holy apostles and prophets by the Spirit" (Eph. 3:4,5).

Those of the Acts 2 persuasion argue that the Mystery was made known to ages and generations past, but not as fully as it is now revealed to his apostles and prophets. In other words, Paul was not the first to receive it. They base this conclusion on Ephesians 3:5.

The proper exegesis of this passage hinges on the phrase *"as it is now revealed."* Therefore, we must determine whether the term "as" is used in the *comparative* or the *contrastive* sense. Perhaps an illustration will prove to be helpful: I might say: My golf game is *as* good *as* yours. Here the "as" is used in the comparative sense—I am comparing your game with mine. Turning to the contrastive side of our term we might say: The ancient Egyptians did not have computers *as* we do today. Applying our illustration to the passage in question we have two possibilities:

1. The Mystery was revealed prior to Paul, but not *as* (comparative) fully as it is today.

2. The Mystery was not revealed to ages and generations past *as* (contrastive) it is today through Paul's gospel.

The Acts 2 dispensationalists opt for number one. Those of us who have come to see Paul's distinctive ministry defend number two; thus, we have two opinions—but who is to say which one is correct? We are reminded at such times of the thought-provoking words of Elijah: "How long halt ye between two opinions?" The solution lies in the answer to the question, "What saith the Lord?" The following passages prove beyond a shadow of a doubt that the "as" is used in the *contrastive* sense in Ephesians 3:5, which can only mean the revelation of the Mystery was initially committed to Paul.[2]

> "Now to Him that is of power to establish you according to my [Paul's] gospel, and the preaching of Jesus Christ according to the revelation of the Mystery, which has been KEPT SECRET since the world began" (Rom. 16:25).

> "If you have heard of the dispensation of the grace of God which is given me [Paul] to youward: how that by revelation He made known unto me the Mystery....And to make all men see what is the fellowship of the Mystery, which from the beginning of the world hath been HID in God, who created all things by Jesus Christ" (Eph. 3:2,9).

So then, while Paul received the Mystery by direct revelation from the Lord of glory, the apostles and prophets, and those since, have received it through the *illumination* of the Spirit (Gal. 1:11,12 cf. Eph. 3:5). A knowledge of this glorious message is only obtainable through the enlightenment of the Holy Spirit. And it has been our experience that those who are in search of the key that unlocks the sacred secret are never denied access.

THE PROMISE

> "That the Gentiles should be fellowheirs, and of the same Body, and partakers of His promise in Christ by the gospel" (Eph. 3:6).

The apostle adds that we are joint-partakers of "His promise in Christ by the gospel." We believe that this too is another unique characteristic of the Mystery that was committed to Paul. Namely, that the Gentiles would be given the free gift of *eternal life*, in spite of the nation Israel. Paul says to Titus: "In hope of eternal life, which God, that cannot lie, promised before the world began" (Titus 1:2). But to whom did the Father make this promise? Undoubtedly, He made it to *Himself*. Probably everyone has made a promise to themselves at one time or another in their life.

I remember my grandfather telling the story of the time he was riding his Harley-Davidson (against his mother's wishes) and someone ran him off the road. When the motorcycle hit the curb it threw him over the handlebars. He landed on the side of an embankment only to look up to see his motorcycle flying through the air. It missed his head by two inches before tumbling into a ravine below. As a result, he made a promise to himself that day to never ride a motorcycle again, and he didn't (nor have I). Although men, for one reason or another, sometimes fail to fulfill their promises, God *cannot* lie (Num. 23:19). If He has promised to give us eternal life, we have the full assurance that He will honor His Word.

How well I remember the day that I received an unexpected call from the family that my father had taken a turn for the worse. He had been battling heart disease for two years but was slowly losing ground. When I walked into his hospital room, the shadow of death was upon his face. Thankfully, his mind was still clear, enabling us to reminisce a bit and talk about the things of the Lord. As I boarded the plane to fly home from Pittsburgh, I wondered if I would ever see my father again on this side of glory. As it turned out, that was the last time I ever saw him alive. He passed away about a week later.

Death is an *enemy*. It robs us of our loved ones. Even though medical science has cheated the Grim Reaper at times, the words of Pastor J. C. O'Hair ring in my ears: "The death rate is still one apiece."

"The story is told of an Arabian merchant who sent his servant to the city of Baghdad to buy provisions. While in the marketplace, the servant saw the figure of Death who appeared to threaten him. In panic, the servant fled to tell his master of the encounter. He begged for the use of a horse so that he could escape to the distant town of Samara.

"Later that day, the merchant also visited the Baghdad marketplace. Seeing 'Death,' he asked, 'Why did you make a threatening gesture at my servant this morning?' Death answered, 'That was not a threatening gesture, but rather a start of surprise. I was astonished to see him here in Baghdad because tonight I have an appointment with him in the far-off town of Samara.'"[3]

Boy, talk about having a bad day! Death is *inescapable*. In fact, he may be looking over your shoulder as you are reading these words. Sorry, I didn't mean to scare the wits out of you! But, I would like you to understand that through Christ's finished work at Calvary, He has *destroyed* "him that had the power of death, that is, the devil; and deliver[ed] them [us] who through fear of death were all their lifetime subject to bondage" (Heb. 2:14,15). "O death, where is thy sting? O grave, where is thy victory?"

If my memory serves me correctly, I believe it was Franklin Roosevelt who said: "We have nothing to fear, but fear itself." How true! The victory has been secured for us at Calvary. Death for the believer is merely a door into *eternal life*. Thanks be unto God for the promise of life everlasting. However, if you have rejected Christ, He will soon be standing at the door as your *judge* (Rev. 3:20).

THE WISDOM OF GOD

"Mr. Watson, come here; I want you." These were the first words ever spoken over an invention called the telephone.

Of course, the inventor who uttered this famous phrase was Alexander Graham Bell. Bell had devoted his entire life to helping the deaf to speak. Both his mother and wife were deaf, which inspired him in his lifelong work. Perhaps his most celebrated student was Helen Keller.

A well-known lecturer, Bell became a professor of vocal physiology at Boston University in 1873. It was during this period he began work on his renowned invention. Since Bell was not proficient with his hands, he recruited the services of Thomas Watson, who enthusiastically designed the apparatus for transmitting sound electrically. One failure after another plagued the project, but finally their long nightly vigils began producing tangible results. On a cool windswept Boston evening in March 1876, the first sentence was successfully transmitted by telephone. Alexander Graham Bell's historic words were spoken to his assistant, Thomas Watson.

Little did Mr. Bell realize that his *discovery* was to revolutionize the field of communications. The endless hours of toil were instantly forgotten when his voice echoed over the receiver. Although this event was a major turning point in history, it pales in comparison to the discovery of the *manifold wisdom of God.* Today, God is speaking to us through Paul's epistles to communicate the riches of His grace. The manifold wisdom of God has to do with His *secret purpose* for the Church, the Body of Christ. As we shall see, this is the greatest discovery of all!

a. The Hidden Wisdom of God and Paul's Apostleship

"Whereof I was made a minister, according to the gift of the grace of God given unto me by the effectual working of His power" (Eph. 3:7).

Why Paul? God already had called the twelve apostles of the kingdom. Although Judas had fallen in transgression, the seat of his apostolic office was filled by Matthias preceding the day of Pentecost. Insofar as Paul was *unconverted* at the time, he could not have possibly fulfilled the qualifications set down by the Holy Spirit to be numbered with the twelve (Acts 1:21-26).

Of course, there are many dispensationalists who would agree with this interpretation, but teach that God ordained Paul to be the thirteenth apostle of the kingdom. Perhaps you have heard the saying, "They jumped out of the frying pan into the fire." In other words, we have gone from bad to worse, which is certainly the case with this view. The number *twelve* is stamped throughout the pages of prophecy, thus eliminating the possibility of a thirteenth apostolic office (Matt. 19:28 cf. Rev. 21:12-21).

What logical explanation then can we give for Paul's apostleship? Before the foundation of the world, God foreordained that He would raise up a *new* apostle to reveal His eternal purpose for the parenthetical age of Grace in which we now live. Hence, Paul says: "But when it pleased God, who separated me from my mother's womb, and called me by His grace, to reveal His Son in me, that I might preach Him among the heathen [Gentiles]" (Gal. 1:15,16).

When God rolled up the building plans of prophecy and temporarily placed them aside, He made known a secret set of plans. With this program came a completely *new* set of blueprints. According to the counsel of His will, He had *predetermined* to call Paul as the masterbuilder of the project. So then, the instructions for our building program are found in Paul's epistles. Little wonder the apostle says: "I have laid the foundation, and another buildeth thereon. But let every man take heed how he buildeth thereupon" (I Cor. 3:10). It is essential to use *Pauline* construction materials (grace doctrines), simply because someday soon the Building Inspector will examine our workmanship to determine if we followed His codes.

This helps us understand the apostle's statement here in Ephesians, that he was *"made* a minister, according to the gift of the grace of God given unto me." Those who question Paul's apostleship claim he was merely self-ordained. However, this passage clearly states otherwise. God *called* Paul to be the apostle of the Gentiles and commissioned him to dispense the ministry of reconciliation (Acts 26:16 cf. Rom. 11:13). He was given the *gift* of grace according to the effectual working of His power to carry out this divine commission.

Although seminaries do their best to turn out preachers, unless they are truly called of God their ministries will avail little. The gift of God's grace enables those who are charged with this calling to effectively expound the gospel. It brings insight, discernment, truth, and leadership capabilities. Sadly, the concept of a great preacher today is a "commanding presence" and "eloquence." But does this coincide with the biblical record? Surely, Paul was the greatest preacher ever to proclaim the gospel of the grace of God. Yet, he had this to say about the Corinthians' perception of him:

> "For his letters, say they, are weighty and powerful; but his bodily presence is weak, and his speech contemptible" (II Cor. 10:10).

Well, so much for a "commanding presence" and "eloquence." Beloved, the means through which God accomplishes His will isn't human ability or strength; rather, it is the effectual working of *His power*. God is the one who convicts, forgives, enlightens, blesses, strengthens, comforts, and restores the brokenhearted. Paul says, "We have this treasure in earthen vessels, that the excellency of the power may be of God, and not of us." Why? "That your faith should not stand in the wisdom of men, but in the power of God" (I Cor. 2:5).

Although Charles Spurgeon did not fully understand the Word, rightly divided, he was nevertheless faithful to the light God had given him. Mr. Spurgeon is a good example of how those who preach the gospel are merely *instruments* in the hand of God. D. L. Moody related the following story regarding one of his visits to London:

"We had an early meal and Mr. Spurgeon suggested that we go into a quiet room to pray. As Mr. Spurgeon got down to pray, a great burden came upon him and he sank down almost to the floor. The burden of his prayer was, 'Lord, I am not worthy; not worthy to preach in Thy name!' And he was like that for two hours. Then the burden was lifted, but he was so wet with perspiration that they had to change all of his clothing. He was put into a cab, for it was late, and hurried to the auditorium to preach where thousands were waiting.

"They had to help him to the platform because of his physical weakness from that burden, and that burden was, 'Lord, I am not worthy to preach!' Mr. Spurgeon preached for one hour. Marvelous strength of body was given to him. Everyone seemed to move back and forth with the swaying of his body. The entire congregation broke down in tears as he preached on, 'He was delivered for our offences and raised again for our justification.' How many were saved that night no one will know until eternity."

Of course, there is always the danger of some abusing the authority structure that God has ordained for the Church (II Tim. 2:16-19 cf. Heb. 13:17). Those who are *called* to preach the gospel must take great care not to think too highly of themselves. Godly leadership never lords itself over God's heritage; instead it sets a godly *example* for all to follow (I Pet. 5:3). It has been correctly said: "When a minister of the gospel exalts himself and begins to work in his own human strength, and according to his own plans, he competes with God and forfeits his spiritual power."[4]

There are none who have done more for the cause of Christ than Paul. Yet he was the first to *humbly* acknowledge:

> "Unto me, who am less than the least of all saints, is this grace given" (Eph. 3:8).

> "For I am the least of the apostles, that am not meet to be called an apostle, because I persecuted the church of God. But by the grace of God I am what I am: and His grace which was bestowed upon me was not in vain; but I labored more abundantly than they all: yet not I, but the grace of God which was with me" (I Cor. 15:10).

Did you catch all those key phrases? "Unto me...is this *grace given.*" "*By the grace of God* I am what I am." "*His grace which was bestowed* upon me.*" "The *grace of God which was with me.*" Those who falsely accuse Paul of being a boaster should read these passages. Paul clearly understood that everything he had accomplished for Christ was not due to his own ability, but to the *grace of God.* Therefore, it is unwise to compare ourselves among ourselves: "For it is God which worketh in you both to will and to do of His good pleasure" (Phil. 2:13). We would do well to remember the poignant words of the hymn writer: "To God be the glory, great things He hath done!"

b. The Hidden Wisdom of God and the Dispensation of the Mystery

> "that I should preach among the Gentiles the unsearchable riches of Christ;

> "And to make all men see what is the fellowship of the Mystery, which from the beginning of the world hath been hid in God, who created all things by Jesus Christ" (Eph. 3:8,9).

If you were to search the archives of ancient history (B.C.), would you expect to find a reference to the telephone as a form of communication? You are probably thinking, that's absurd! The telephone wasn't invented until 1876 (A.D.). This is precisely the point Paul is making in regard to the revelation he received from the Lord of glory. The apostle calls the message he preached among the Gentiles the *unsearchable* or *untraceable* riches of Christ. In other words, the doctrines of Grace taught by Paul are *untraceable* in the Prophetic Scriptures (Genesis—Acts 9 and James—Book of Revelation).[5]

Now, if you are from Missouri, the "show me state," we challenge you, or anyone for that matter, to find these Pauline teachings in the above Prophetic writings: Israel set aside in unbelief; the Church, the Body of Christ made up of Jews and Gentiles without distinction; commission of reconciliation; salvation by grace through faith alone; terms of salvation— Christ's death, burial, and resurrection presented as good news; our spiritual baptism into Christ by the Holy Spirit; blessed with all spiritual blessings in the heavenlies; seated with Christ in the heavenlies; a heavenly hope and calling; the Pretribulational Rapture; etc. Inasmuch as you are searching for the *unsearchable*, you may want to keep an eye out for references to telephones as well!

This brings us to our *responsibility* as members of the Body of Christ. We are to "make all men see what is the fellowship [*oikonomia*—dispensation] of the Mystery." For some unknown reason, the King James translators *departed* from the *Majority Text* here.[6] Apparently, they drew the Greek word *koinonia* translated "fellowship" from a smaller family of manuscripts. Since the rendering *koinonia* is only supported by scant manuscript evidence, we prefer to follow the rendering of the *Majority Text*, as do the vast majority of Greek authorities. More importantly, we believe this translation best fits the *context*.

141

We must also keep before us that the KJV translators did not have a knowledge of Paul's gospel, which undoubtedly influenced their decision-making process in some cases. Here we are reminded of the counsel of the KJV translators themselves. In their letter *To The Reader*, they state:

"Some, peradventure, would have no variety of senses to be set in the margin, lest the authority of the Scriptures for deciding of controversies, by that show of uncertainty should somewhat be shaken. But we hold their judgment not to be so sound in this point....Doth not a margin do well to admonish the reader to seek further, and not conclude or dogmatize upon this or that peremptorily [i.e. "leaving no opportunity to question or debate]?...They that are wise had rather have their judgments at liberty in differences of readings, than to be captivated by one, when it may be the other."

While the *King James Version* of the Bible can be classified as "Old Faithful," there is a need at times to consult the original languages in order to arrive at the *proper sense*. Furthermore, we are in the enviable position of having additional manuscript evidence, which corroborates the *Majority Text* that was unavailable to the KJV translators. Thankfully, God has placed numerous "reference works" at our disposal to assist us in this effort, since most students of the Word are not Hebrew and Greek scholars.

Having said this, it is our *responsibility* then to "make known the dispensation [Gr. *oikonomia*] of the Mystery." Consequently, we are to proclaim the whole counsel of God in light of the Pauline revelation. We are to open our mouth boldly to preach Christ according to the Mystery, placing special emphasis on His heavenly ministry. Great care must be taken to distinguish between the *old economy* and the *new economy*. That is, between law and grace, Israel and the Body, Christ's earthly kingdom and His heavenly kingdom, etc.

Bryan Leech has made this insightful observation: "Our lives should be a living illustration of the truth, but they are frequently hard to read and even some times misleading." Unfortunately, many who have been graced with a knowledge of the Mystery are living undercover. They fear the retaliation of the Christian community if they defend Paul's gospel. But are we serving God or men? Whether or not we stand for this message, God has given us a knowledge of His will; therefore, we are ultimately responsible to make it known, and we will be judged accordingly.

Yes, it is a sacrifice! You will likely be criticized! You may even be ostracized! And probably you will be misrepresented! Pastor J. C. O'Hair used to say, "When you stand for the truth, you have to have the hide of a rhinoceros and the heart of a dove." But these things will pass like a morning mist when you hear the sweet voice of our Savior say, *"Well done, thou good and faithful servant!!!"*

Most Christian leaders seem to think that their responsibility is to provide programs and entertainment for the congregation. They reason that this will draw larger crowds, which is an indication of God's blessing. But the same result could be produced by inviting a Christian sports celebrity to a large church auditorium here in Milwaukee. We could literally pack the house. Numbers do not necessarily indicate God's blessing. In fact, God often passed by the multitudes and did His greatest work among small groups of saints who were obedient (Matt. 13:2,10-17; Acts 1:15; Col. 4:15).

> "which from the beginning of the world hath been hid in God, who created all things by Jesus Christ" (Eph. 3:9).

As we have seen, the Mystery is *untraceable* in the Old Testament. It was not hidden in prophecy nor foreshadowed in the types. Rather, it was hid in the mind of God.

When God revealed His secret purposes, the angels of heaven were astonished, Satan and his host were dumbfounded, and the inhabitants of the earth mused at the wonderful workings of God among the *Gentiles*. "O the depth of the riches both of the wisdom and knowledge of God! how unsearchable are His judgments, and His ways past finding out!" (Rom. 11:33).

Interestingly, Paul reminds us that the Mystery was hid in God, who created all things by Jesus Christ. This is significant for this reason: We are taken back to *creation* to refresh our memory that, "In the beginning God created the heaven and the earth." He has a program for the earth and Christ's reign upon it. And He also has a plan and purpose for the heavens where the Body of Christ will reign with Him in glory. Of course, the latter is the theme of the Pauline epistles.

7

The Manifold Wisdom of God

"To the intent that now unto the principalities and powers in heavenly places might be known by the Church the manifold wisdom of God."

—*Ephesians 3:10*

It is nearly impossible to walk into a store these days without seeing *angels*. These heavenly creatures are *everywhere*. Go ahead, admit it, you've seen them too, haven't you? Of course, we are referring to all the paraphernalia that bears the image of these unseen beings.

Without any rhyme or reason, it seems to be common knowledge that there are both male and female angels who have large wings and exhibit halos most of the time. Some appear to be childlike, while others are depicted as adults watching over little ones. Moreover, they are always pictured in *serene* settings, never lifting their hand to judge mankind. Sadly, they are often revered more than God Himself. The current interest in angels has correctly been called "angelmania." However, any time the world seeks to understand or describe the things of God, we can be sure it will be *distorted*.

Tradition plays a large role in the contemporary portrayal of the angelic host. For the most part, it is based upon Greek mythology and medieval art. But here again the Word of God must serve as our final authority—all else is merely speculation. Before we can fully appreciate the significance of Paul's reference to the angelic realm in the above text, we must first understand more about these heavenly emissaries. Actually, the Scriptures have a great deal to say about them.

As we have seen, *confusion* is predominant when it comes to the subject of angels. Surprisingly, this is even true within the household of faith. So, with God's help, we shall search the Scriptures to determine their origin, number, appearance, nature, and purpose. More importantly, what is their *role* today, if any, during the dispensation of Grace. This fascinating tour will take us through both programs of God.

IN THE PRESENCE OF ANGELS

a. Everything You Wanted to Know About Angels but were Afraid to Ask

Origin: The angelic host is a product of God's creative genius. Paul states: "For by Him [Christ] were all things created, that are in heaven, and that are in earth, visible and invisible, whether they be thrones, or dominions, or principalities, or powers: all things were created by Him, and for Him" (Col. 1:16). Bearing in mind that Christ created all things, angels are *invisible* (to humanity) supernatural *spirits* who reside in heaven. Inasmuch as God relishes diversity, we can safely conclude that angels are individuals who are as different as snowflakes. Like man, they are *finite* beings in wisdom, knowledge, authority and power. Although enormously *inferior* to God, the angels of heaven are superior to mankind at this point in time (Heb. 2:5-8).

We believe the angelic host was very high on the list of God's creation agenda. When the Lord spoke to Job out of a whirlwind, He inquired of the patriarch: "Where wast thou when I laid the foundations of the earth?...When the morning stars sang together, and all the sons of God shouted for joy?" (Job 38:4,7). The phrases "morning stars" and "sons

146

of God" are unequivocally references to angels. This is substantiated by their very presence at the dawn of creation as God spoke and worlds came into existence. In other words, they were *eyewitnesses* of all His creative acts. Interestingly, since the *fall*, they are not said to sing again until the redemption of all things (Rev. 5:8,9).

Number: We do not have a number in our numerical system which would allow us to count the angelic host. The writer of Hebrews says: "But ye are come unto Mount Zion, and unto the city of the living God, the heavenly Jerusalem, and to an *innumerable company* of angels" (Heb. 12:22). According to W. E. Vine, the Greek word the apostle uses here denotes "indefinitely, a myriad, a numberless host." One-third of this multitude rebelled against God and defected with Satan shortly after creation (Rev. 12:3-9). Probably even this number is beyond our numerical system. Thus, the angelic host now falls into two major classifications—*elect* and *fallen*. Contrary to popular opinion, your Uncle Clarence did not become an angel when he died. This is merely the fabrication of Hollywood. The number of elect angels is *fixed*, and therefore never increases or decreases.

Appearance: Angels were created ministering spirits and are always referred to in the *masculine* gender (Heb. 1:7). As far as we can ascertain, there are only two orders of angelic beings who are said to have wings—the Cherubims and Seraphims (Ezek. 10:18-21 cf. Isa. 6:1-4). This means that the vast majority of angels *do not* have wings, which is confirmed by the numerous appearances they made to the patriarchs, prophets and apostles.

Although spirits, angels have the uncanny ability to *transform* themselves into human form. If one were to appear at your door selling Bibles, you would be totally unaware that an angel was in your midst. In fact, Paul says: "Be not forgetful to entertain strangers: for thereby some have entertained angels unawares" (Heb. 13:2).

In the days of Sodom and Gomorrah, Lot had no idea that the two *men* who met him at the gate of Sodom were angels. He carried on a normal conversation with them and begged his visitors to enter his house so he could wash their *feet* and prepare them a meal. That evening Lot made a *feast* for his guests and they had an enjoyable time of fellowship together. As they were preparing to *retire* for the evening, the men of Sodom called to Lot, and said unto him, "Where are the *men* which came in to thee this night? bring them out unto us, that we may know them." The record states that the angels pulled Lot into the house and struck the men of the city with blindness. These weren't ordinary visitors; they were on a search and destroy mission. The next morning, they rained fire and brimstone upon the cities of the plain, forever wiping them from the face of the earth (Gen. 19:1-26).

Nature: While angels are normally invisible, they frequently appeared in spirit form during biblical times to discharge God's will. Consequently, we are to understand that, like man, they possess a *personality*—intellect, emotions, and will.

The intellect gives them the ability to know and reason. On resurrection morning, the angel that appeared at the tomb freely conversed with Mary. Thus, he instructed the women to go tell the disciples the Lord had risen. Furthermore, he imparted a *revelation* to them that the Lord would await their arrival at Galilee (Matt. 28:7).

It has been said that music is the language of the soul; it's an expression of our feelings. Angels, then, also have *emotions*. As they beheld the handiwork of God on creation morning, they sang together and shouted for joy. Like us (or at least as we should be), they are caring, sensitive, compassionate beings who are deeply moved at times. Our Lord said of them: "There is joy in the presence of the angels of God over one sinner that repenteth" (Luke 15:10). Moreover, these heavenly beings seem to have a *curious* side (I Pet. 1:12).

The fact that angels worship God and execute His commands clearly shows a consensus of *will*. Surely the words of Lucifer are a chilling reminder of the time there was a rebellion in the ranks of the angelic host. "For thou hast said in thine heart, I *will* ascend into heaven, I *will* exalt my throne above the stars of God [elect angelic host]: I *will* sit *also* upon the mount of the congregation, in the sides of the north [Satan's desire to reign in the millennial kingdom on earth—see Psa. 48:1-3]: I *will* ascend above the heights of the clouds [he desires all the glory]; I *will* be like the most High" (Isa. 14:13,14).

Purpose: In addition to worshipping God day and night, angels are "all ministering spirits, sent forth to minister for them who shall be heirs of salvation" (Heb. 1:14). They held a high profile in past prophetic events and will play an even more prominent role in the coming day of the Lord. For example: An angel of God led Israel out of the land of Egypt (Ex. 14:19). Angels were present at the giving of the law at Mt. Sinai and ordained it in the hand of a mediator (Psa. 68:17 cf. Gal. 3:19). They assisted Israel in the conquest of the Land (Ex. 23:20). When Daniel the prophet stood face to face with a group of man-eating lions, God sent His angel to protect him (Dan. 6:22).

An angel appeared to Zacharias at the altar to inform him that his wife Elisabeth would bear a child in her old age. Of course, this was none other than John the Baptist who would one day be the forerunner of Christ (Luke 1:11-14). In regard to the young, our Lord instructed His disciples: "Take heed that ye despise not one of these little ones; for I say unto you, That in heaven their angels do always behold the face of my Father which is in heaven" (Matt. 18:10).

Although angels are often viewed as serene caretakers, they are also the mighty warriors of God who administer His judgments. As God unleashes His wrath in the coming Tribulation period, the record states that an angel will take a "censer [canister], and fill it with fire of the altar, and cast it into the earth: and there were voices, and thunderings, and lightnings, and an earthquake." This is followed by seven angels blowing seven trumpets. As the scene closes these agents of *wrath* will have *destroyed* one-third of the natural resources of the earth, one-third of the heavenly bodies (sun, moon, and stars), and killed one-third of the earth's population (Rev. 8,9). Well, so much for serenity!

b. Angels Who Attend Church

"To the intent that now unto the principalities and powers in heavenly places might be known by the Church the manifold wisdom of God, according to the eternal purpose which He purposed in Christ Jesus our Lord: in whom we have boldness and access with confidence by the faith of Him" (Eph. 3:10-12).

The Apostle Paul makes approximately *fifty* references to the angelic host in his epistles. Here we must pause to say, however, that the ministry of angels during the administration of Grace is in accordance with the Mystery Program. Today, there are few, if any, manifestations of angels. Insofar as the heavens are silent, the angelic host is silent for the most part as well. Any variation from this would be an *exception* of God, as those living at the Rapture will be an exception to Hebrews 9:27.

We would not be too quick to say though that they are inactive in this dispensation. In fact, there seems to be a strong case that both the elect and fallen angels are extremely *active* behind the scenes. Remember, we are engaged in a spiritual warfare. "For we wrestle not against flesh and blood, but against principalities, against powers, against the rulers of the darkness of this world, against spiritual wickedness in high places" (Eph. 6:12). When armies fight, there is a flurry of activity on both sides of the battlefield.

As God's *secret service* agents, there are at least three areas where angels play an essential role in the Church, the Body of Christ.

Witnesses: Although the angelic host was well aware of the wisdom of God as it related to creation and the Prophetic Program they assisted in revealing, Paul writes to the saints at Ephesus: "To the intent that *now* unto the principalities and powers in heavenly places might be known by the Church the manifold wisdom of God" (Eph. 3:10). The term *manifold* here means, "varied," that is, multifaceted or multicolored. Hence, the wisdom of God is many-sided; it is like looking through a kaleidoscope with its various shapes, sizes, and colors. In this context, we believe the apostle limits the phrase *manifold wisdom of God* to the revelation of the Mystery. In other words, Paul's revelation unveils the *hidden wisdom* of God for the Church that was kept *secret* from past generations. Not even the elect angels knew anything about God's eternal purpose for the Body of Christ.

The apostle uses the term "now" dispensationally to show that a change has taken place. Today, then, the principalities and powers in the heavenly realm are *learning* about the Mystery *through us.* If angels shed tears, they probably wept when Paul wrote to Timothy that "all they which are in Asia be turned away from me." To turn from Paul was to *abandon* his apostleship and message! Consequently, the Church wandered aimlessly through the Dark Ages until the light finally dawned again in the Reformation.

Undoubtedly with the recovery of Grace truth today, the angels are again rejoicing as they gather up every morsel of the manifold wisdom of God. If you have tasted of the riches of His grace you understand there is a simplistic side to Paul's gospel, yet it can also be very *complex*. Like us, the angels are adding word upon word, and line upon line to their knowledge of His eternal purpose. It is astonishing to ponder though that we are their *examples*.

Conduct: The apostle seems to liken the spiritual realm to an arena where we are fighting the good fight of the faith in the presence of angels. There is good reason to believe that our *conduct* is constantly being observed by unseen eyes. Therefore, we should walk worthy of our calling "with all lowliness and meekness, with longsuffering, forbearing one another in love." Paul was always mindful that he was being watched and lived accordingly:

> "For I think that God hath set forth us the apostles last, as it were appointed to death: for we are made a *spectacle* unto the world, and to *angels*, and to men" (I Cor. 4:9).

Although the custom of head covering among women is no longer observed in the western hemisphere, in Paul's day it was an integral part of their culture and worship. Since it was a symbol of *subordination* the apostle instructed the women at Corinth that they should worship with their heads *covered* "because of the angels" (I Cor. 11:10). This could well be because of the insubordination of their counterparts in the days of Noah.

Well stricken in years, the apostle admonishes young Timothy: "I charge thee before God [or in the sight of God], and the Lord Jesus Christ, and the elect angels, that thou observe these things without preferring one before another, doing nothing by partiality" (I Tim. 5:21). May we remind the reader, it is very possible that the angelic host could be summoned as an eyewitness of our conduct, at the Judgment Seat of Christ—a humbling thought indeed! While God is omniscient, He often works *through* His creation to accomplish His purposes.

Deliverance: Those who are numbered with the household of faith agree that we are engaged in a spiritual warfare with the forces of evil. We wrestle not against flesh and blood, but with the rulers of darkness. With this type of activity going on behind the scenes, surely the angels of God *assist* us in the battle at times, especially since they were created for us (Heb. 1:14). Only the Lord knows how many times these celestial beings have come to our aid.

Some suppose that with the coming of the Holy Spirit the ministry of angels is unnecessary and would be incompatible. We know, however, that Philip was *filled* with the Spirit, yet an angel of the Lord instructed him where to meet the Ethiopian eunuch. Upon leading the eunuch to the Lord, the Spirit caught Philip away to Azotus. Here the angel of the Lord and the Holy Spirit worked in tandem without a conflict of interest (Acts 6:3-5 cf. 8:26-40).

You will recall that after Herod killed James he planned to execute Peter. But the night preceding Peter's execution, an angel appeared to him in prison and struck him on the side. Before Peter knew fully what was happening, the angel led him past two guards, through an iron gate that opened unattended before them, and the angel vanished into the night. Surely Peter was under the *control* of the Holy Spirit, yet an angel of the Lord delivered him from harm's way (Acts 12:5-11).

I doubt that there is anyone reading these lines who would question for a moment that Paul was *indwelt* by the Holy Spirit, but here again an angel of God is said to have appeared to

153

him. In the midst of a storm at sea, when all hope seemed to be lost, an angel consoled the apostle, saying, "Fear not, Paul; thou must be brought before Caesar: and, lo, God hath given thee all them that sail with thee" (Acts 27:21-26). While the Holy Spirit, as God, holds a position of supremacy over the angelic host, we believe their ministries to be *compatible*.

Perhaps a word of caution should be added here. As we have seen, angels are intelligent, powerful, supernatural agents who render the highest service to God. But we must never lose sight of the fact that the angels of heaven were created by Christ, and for Him. Therefore, they are *never* to be worshiped, nor should we esteem them too highly. The Apostle John was so overwhelmed by the apocalyptic visions he had seen that he fell at the feet of the angel who showed him these events. The angel's response is unforgettable: "See thou do it not: for I am thy fellowservant" (Rev. 22:8,9).

THE VICTORIOUS CHRISTIAN LIFE

Man will never come to know God through human wisdom. He must first drink freely of Christ, the "water of life," before he will be able to comprehend the spiritual things of God.

The mind of the believer should be a fertile field where the seeds of God's Word are sown, whereby he might grow in the grace and knowledge of our Lord Jesus Christ. Thus, the Christian life is a growth process which begins the day we are saved and continues throughout eternity. Furthermore, to live the victorious Christian life we must learn how to apply God's power in every given circumstance. It is sad many times to see believers respond to problems in their own strength, simply because they do not know how to draw from God's vast reservoir of power. But how can we have the victory over adversity on a day-by-day basis?

a. Victory Over Adversity

"Wherefore I desire that ye faint not at my tribulations for you, which is your glory" (Eph. 3:13).

The Apostle Paul was well-qualified to address this subject, since he lived a life of adversity. Therefore, his counsel will prove invaluable as he instructs us how to triumph in Christ. In II Corinthians 11:24-26 the apostle sets forth a list of things he endured in his service for Christ:

"Of the Jews five times received I forty stripes save one. Thrice was I beaten with rods, once I was stoned, thrice I suffered shipwreck, a night and a day I have been in the deep. In journeyings often, in perils of waters, in perils of robbers, in perils of mine own countrymen, in perils by the heathen, in perils in the city, in perils in the wilderness, in perils in the sea, in perils among false brethren."

Most of us have not even come close to suffering for the cause of Christ as Paul did. Little wonder that the apostle says here in Ephesians: *"Wherefore I desire that ye faint not at my tribulations for you, which is your glory."* It is inevitable that personal tribulations will overtake us. They may take the form of spiritual conflicts, the death of a loved one or possibly severe illness. You see, it is not a question of, if problems *will* come, but *when* they will come. Mark these words well: We need to learn how to have the victory over adversity *before* it looms as a giant before us. It's too late to begin preparing once we are in the middle of a crisis, simply because in our weakness our emotions often take control— thus we are less likely to be as objective.

"For this cause I bow my knees unto the Father of our Lord Jesus Christ, of whom the whole family in heaven and earth is named, that He would grant you, according to the riches of His glory, to be strengthened

> with might by His Spirit in the inner man; that Christ
> may dwell in your hearts by faith; that ye, being rooted
> and grounded in love" (Eph. 3:14-17).

Here are some things we need to incorporate into our lives to prepare ourselves for the day of calamity: First, in the order of enumeration, we must cultivate a daily *prayer* life, not just in time of need, but praying without ceasing. If we get into the *habit* of regularly going to the throne of grace to speak to our heavenly Father, when trouble raises its ugly head we will naturally want to turn to Him for assistance. I am sure all of us have had the experience of bearing heavy burdens, and the relief we experienced when we shared them with others. How much more so with God, for the Scriptures teach us to *"cast all your care upon Him: for He careth for you."* We can take great comfort in the fact that God is sovereign and in *control* of all things. No matter what the outcome, we can be sure that God has worked all things out according to His will and ultimately for our good! His will is always best for us!

The next step in preparing for the day of adversity is to strengthen our inner man. Paul says, *"That He would grant you, according to the riches of His glory, to be strengthened with might by His Spirit in the inner man."* Every child of God has an old nature and a new nature. Since we do not want to have the old nature control us, it is important to yield to the new man, which is created in holiness and righteousness.

The story is told of an Eskimo in Alaska who used to travel to town every weekend with two of his huskies. One was black and the other was white. One day he was standing talking with some of the townspeople when he pointed to his dogs, stating that he was going to give the command for the two dogs to fight and he predicted that the black dog would win. Sure enough the black dog won. A week passed and the Eskimo returned to town. This time he predicted the white dog would win the fight. Sure enough he was right again.

This went on for about six weeks with the Eskimo always correctly picking which dog would win. On the way back home one day a friend asked the Eskimo how he always knew which dog was going to win. The Eskimo responded that it was really quite simple. If I want the black dog to win I simply starve the white dog all week. On the other hand, if I want the white dog to win I starve the black dog.[1]

This is exactly what we need to do in our Christian lives: *starve the old nature and feed the new!* But how is this accomplished? We must discipline ourselves to *deny* our fleshly appetites and fill our minds with the wonderful Word of God. I do not mean merely to read the Bible devotionally; rather, we must study this blessed Book. We need to acquire a knowledge of God's will, or we'll be left to our own human reasoning in times of trial. Suppose you were to lose a close loved one unexpectedly. Where would you turn in the Scriptures for comfort or to comfort other family members? You should be familiar *beforehand* with passages such as: II Corinthians 1:3,4; I Thessalonians 4:13-17 and Romans 8.

The inner man is also strengthened by the Holy Spirit. Ephesians 5:18 bears witness to this great truth:

> "And be not drunk with wine, wherein is excess; but be filled with the Spirit."

It is obvious that strong drink controls the drunkard; this is why he often stumbles about. Sometimes we even say that "he is under the influence." Following this thought, the apostle instructs the Ephesians, and us, that we should be under the control or *influence* of the Holy Spirit. Beloved, the filling of the Spirit is the *key* to having power in the

Christian life. You cannot have more of the Spirit, but He can have more of you! If you yield to Him, He will cause you to be more spiritually minded. I am sure each of us has had the occasion of being in the presence of someone who is spiritual. They had a well-rounded knowledge of the Word of God, and were so gracious that it was humbling to be in their presence. You were so impressed by them that it made you wonder how they managed to become so spiritually minded. The answer is really quite simple—they allowed the Spirit to take control of every aspect their life. Being "filled" with the Spirit is always the *goal,* though none of us has ever fully attained it.

Next, we must make Christ the *center* of our lives if we ever expect to have the victory over sin. This is what the apostle sets forth in Ephesians 3:17 when he says, *"That Christ may dwell in your hearts by faith."* The term "dwell" in this passage means to "settle down." Have you ever visited someone and felt unwelcome? When believers are disobedient or harbor sin in their hearts the Lord is made to feel unwelcome. Many times when a child of God plans his or her week the Lord is conspicuously left out. Regrettably, only a few stolen minutes of time are given to the Savior, but just the opposite should be true. We should begin our week by putting Christ *first.* Start by setting time aside for Bible study and prayer. You may also want to consider how you might become more involved in the Lord's work.

Also remember, that while we have liberty in Christ we are never to use our liberty for an occasion to the flesh. Therefore, never indulge in anything that might dishonor the name of Christ. It is true that there are some areas in the Christian life which we might call *gray* areas. Sometimes we do not have a specific Scripture verse that addresses the situation. Then simply ask yourself this question, "If I partake of this, will it honor and glorify God?"

b. A Guiding Light

"that ye, being rooted and grounded in love, may be able to comprehend with all saints what is the breadth, and length, and depth, and height" (Eph. 3:17,18).

Here Paul sets down the *dimensions* of the Mystery. Thus, it is of the utmost importance for us to understand that God is doing something new and different among men today. Since a change has taken place, we need to know specifically where to turn in God's Word to understand the *breadth*, the *length*, the *depth*, and the *height* of His grand theme (Rom. 16:25). As we have noted, during the age of Grace we must turn to Paul's epistles for our doctrine, walk, position, and destiny. When we rightly divide the Word of truth we learn that God is carrying out His Mystery Program today. Thus, Paul desires that we "comprehend with all saints" the dimensions of the Mystery.

He begins with the *breadth,* which is a reference to the fact that *all* believers are included, that is, both Jews and Gentiles. In other words, we are not to stop with the nation Israel, but go on to perfection, by acknowledging that in the administration of Grace, God is forming the Body of Christ in which all believers are members (Eph. 4:4; I Cor. 12:27).

Next, we have the *length,* which refers to the *longsuffering* of God. When God set Israel aside in unbelief He would have been perfectly justified in judging the world for the rejection of His dear Son. Instead, He unveiled a new program, lavishing the world with the riches of His grace, thus giving all men everywhere an opportunity to be saved (I Tim. 1:15,16).

The length is followed by the *depth.* The depth speaks of the finished work of Christ. While the prophet of old predicted the death of Christ, it was not until the raising up of the Apostle Paul that we learn the *significance* of the once-for-all-sacrifice. Paul presents the good news of the Cross: how our Savior gave Himself a ransom for the sins of the world (I Tim. 2:3-6).

The fourth dimension is the *height,* which is undoubtedly a reference to our exaltation with Christ in the heavenlies. While Israel had an earthly hope, we have the hope of heaven. We should familiarize ourselves with this dimension, for when trials beset us it is comforting to know that some day soon we shall be with Christ, which is far better.

LOVE WHICH PASSETH KNOWLEDGE

"And to know the love of Christ, which passeth knowledge, that ye might be filled with all the fulness of God" (Eph. 3:19).

In this passage, the apostle contrasts the *spiritual knowledge* of the believer (to know), with *human knowledge* (passeth knowledge). We are living in a time when a high premium has been placed on human intelligence. Technology is advancing so rapidly that a product is barely to the marketplace before it's obsolete. Human knowledge has progressed to the point where man has created small microchips, the size of a pencil eraser, that can store volumes of information. While man glories in his accomplishments in the area of high tech, God is still the *infinite* One in knowledge. Consequently, as believers in Christ we should never be intimidated by the intelligentsia of this world's system because we hold a superior position in Christ. Moreover, the wisdom of this world is foolishness with God. Someone may have a Ph.D. with a vast amount of knowledge in various fields, but when we share the Word of God with him, suddenly he finds himself in a very awkward position. Why? Simple, these things are *spiritually* discerned. The natural man will never know God through human knowledge.

Those who are saved, however, have available to them a *knowledge* of spiritual things that far surpasses human knowledge. Having the eyes of our spiritual understanding opened, we are now able to comprehend the Word of God. It is God's Word where we first learned about the love of Christ. It was Christ's love for us that sent Him to Calvary to die for our sins, to redeem us back to God (Rom. 5:8). His love also keeps us secure for, as the apostle says, "Who shall separate us from the love of Christ?" (Rom. 8:35). In addition, the love of Christ constrains us or motivates us to serve Him. Of course, we can never repay what He has accomplished for us, but out of gratitude for what He has done for us we should *desire* to live for Him (II Cor. 5:14,15). With this knowledge of the love of Christ we can enjoy the fullness of God.

These are the keys which enable us to live the victorious Christian life. By God's grace we can live above the circumstances. This may be difficult, but when the believer handles a trial with composure, God is glorified. Always remember, the only Bible some people will ever read is *your life.* We are "epistles, known and read of all men." If you make an application of these passages in your life you will experience the fullness of God. True joy and true fulfillment are only found in Christ Jesus our Lord!

8

Time and Eternity

"I therefore, the prisoner of the Lord, beseech you that ye walk worthy of the vocation wherewith ye are called."

—Ephesians 4:1

During the past one hundred years God has raised up many navigators in the faith who have charted new courses to long lost truths in the Blessed Book. Their untiring labors were like the lighthouse by the seashore guiding lost voyagers safely home. When they stood in the pulpits of America, they made the Scriptures come alive as dispensational truth after dispensational truth was unfolded.

In the course of time, *doctrine* became a rallying point as many donned the gospel armor to fight the good fight of the faith. With a full head of steam the Christian faith forged ahead into new territory. However, one of the problems that gradually developed during that era was a serious neglect of emphasis on Christian conduct. Many leaders, given to intellectualism, were zealous to make known the doctrine but became cold and indifferent to practical matters. They thundered home the truth, but failed to speak the truth in love.

Unfortunately, some assemblies started taking on the mannerisms of their leaders, and in an unloving way began to shun the newcomers to the faith. Strapped with the perception that Christians are not very gracious and are often inconsiderate, a new generation of leaders arrived on the scene. They concluded that most believers were suffering from what was known as a cold shoulder complex, which was caused by an over-emphasis on doctrine with little or no attention given to practical Christian living.

These new torchbearers (some of whom are the prominent New Evangelical leaders today) sought to swing the pendulum 180 degrees in the opposite way. They overreacted to the problem and sought to move the Church away from a conservative position on the Scriptures to a more liberal view. Their battle cry was "Let's forget our doctrinal differences and simply love one another!" They began telling their hearers to "Act like the world, look like the world and talk like the world to win the world." *Compromise* became a way of life as they invited the masses to come to church, promising them a good time.

This, of course, created a new problem. What do you do with an assembly of people to whom you refuse to proclaim doctrine? Their answer to the problem was to *entertain* them with contemporary Christian music and humorous skits. This was coupled with testimonies from well-known celebrities, topped off with *short* devotionals on "How to get along." To keep the people coming back they supplemented numerous social programs with well-orchestrated activities for the young and old alike.

While this may be an acceptable solution to the New Evangelical, it should not be acceptable to us. Surely such a scheme is destined to failure. Those who devise such plans will soon fall victim to their own folly. Always remember, if it is not the Word of God that is holding your attention then you are attending church for all the wrong reasons.

Sadly, many of these same problems have filtered down to some of our Grace churches, thus putting us in the same spiritual dilemna. While we acknowledge the above problems to be painfully true, the solution to both is to simply create a BALANCE between doctrine and walk. If we fail to do this, as we have already seen, the results can be catastrophic. Doctrine and walk are like two children in the same family. If you spend all of your time with one child you are naturally going to neglect the other child. As parents, we must discipline ourselves to distribute our time evenly between both children, taking great care to never show favoritism towards one over the other. Similarly, doctrine and walk go together. Sound doctrine demands a godly walk, and a godly walk results from sound doctrine!

Continuing our analogy, normally in the family circle, a younger brother will look up to his older brother for encouragement and guidance. This is also true in the Christian life. Our walk finds direction from the doctrine we hold. In a nutshell, your doctrine (based on right division) is going to affect your walk. Allow me to show you exactly what I mean.

LIVING UNDER THE LAW

"Ye shall keep the Sabbath thereof; for it is holy unto you: everyone that defileth it shall surely be put to death: for whosoever doeth any work therein, that soul shall be cut off from among His people" (Ex. 31:14).

If you had lived back at the time that God imparted the Law to Moses, you would have found yourself face-to-face with the doctrine of the Sabbath. The Sabbath was always to be observed on the seventh day (Saturday), at which time the people of God were to rest and worship. It was not enough to merely confess that the Sabbath was given by Jehovah and merrily go on your way. The dispensing of this commandment directly touched the lives of those who were subservient to it.

The Israelite's walk was dramatically affected by this doctrine, making it necessary for them to prepare for the Sabbath days in advance. Those under this Law were *not permitted* to do any type of manual labor, thus all food preparation had to be done in advance (Ex. 31:14). No fires were to be kindled (Ex. 35:3). Even the gathering of sticks was prohibited, carrying with it the sentence of death if disobeyed (Num. 15:32-36). They were also forbidden to buy or sell on the Sabbath, and could journey no more than one mile on this holy day.

Those under the Law were diligent to keep their conduct in accordance with the commandments under which God had placed them. In their case God didn't suggest that it was a good idea; He *demanded* obedience or the consequences would be death!

LIVING UNDER GRACE

"For sin shall not have dominion over you: for ye are not under the Law, but under grace" (Rom. 6:14).

With the abolition of the Law by Christ's death at Calvary, and the subsequent setting aside of Israel, God raised up a new apostle, committing to him the dispensation of Grace (Eph. 3:1-3). Today, the Gentiles have the privilege of living under God's administration of Grace committed to Paul, which means we are to follow the instructions of Christ found in Paul's epistles (I Cor. 11:1; 14:37). When God implemented this new program of Grace, which He calls the "Mystery", He instituted many changes. For example, today we no longer observe the Sabbath, but rather worship on the first day of the week. Also, we have *liberty* on this day to do as we please, within the boundaries of the Scriptures, of course. We can work if necessary, travel as far as we wish, and prepare and eat all the food we may enjoy. Personally, I believe the day is best set aside for worship combined with rest, although every man may do as he sees fit.

The precedent for worshipping on the first day of the week (Sunday) is delivered to us by the Apostle Paul. Paul was the first to teach that God had made a change in the believer's day of worship.

> "and came unto them to Troas in five days; where we abode seven days. And upon the first day of the week, when the disciples came together to break bread, Paul preached unto them" (Acts 20:6,7).

You will note here that the apostle stayed in Troas for a period of seven days. The Spirit of God does not mention this by chance, but rather by *design*. Of the seven days Paul visited this city it is interesting that he did not preach on the Sabbath. Rather he chose *Sunday*, the first day of the week, to proclaim the gospel. The apostle gathered the saints together on the first day to break bread with them in a time of fellowship followed by a season of worship.

The first mention of Sunday worship in Paul's epistles is found in I Corinthians 16:2:

> "Upon the first day of the week let every one of you lay by him in store, as God hath prospered him."

Since we are to follow Paul as he followed Christ, we also set Sunday aside as our special day of worship. It is a celebration of our Lord's resurrection. In so doing we are acknowledging the fact that a change has taken place in dispensations, which has resulted in a new set of instructions for the Church, the Body of Christ today. Hopefully, this comparison will help us understand that the doctrine God has placed us under will determine how we should walk to honor and glorify Him. A change in doctrine also means a change in walk.

WALKING WORTHY OF THE DOCTRINE

"I therefore, the prisoner of the Lord, beseech you that ye walk worthy of the vocation [calling] wherewith ye are called" (Eph. 4:1).

Frail creatures of dust identified with the sin of Adam can never, in their own strength, walk worthy of this high and holy calling. In our own strength we will fail miserably to fulfill these words. It is only *in Christ* that we can accomplish this, "to the praise of His glory." But how do we walk worthy in Christ? First, we must understand what we have in Him. We have been chosen in Christ, adopted, accepted in the Beloved, redeemed through His Blood, forgiven and sealed by the Holy Spirit (Eph. 1:1-14). But there is more, much more. Because of Christ's finished work, we have been given a heavenly position with the promise of being with Christ for eternity (Eph. 2:6; I Thes. 4:16,17). When we acknowledge and fully appreciate these doctrines of grace, they should motivate us to live a godly life in Christ Jesus.

Also, to walk worthy in the doctrine we must learn to *prove* all things.

"Proving what is acceptable unto the Lord. And have no fellowship with the unfruitful works of darkness, but rather reprove them" (Eph. 5:10,11).

Proving here has the idea of testing something to make sure it measures up. If you were boarding a plane bound for Chicago and the stewardess said, "I think you should know that this pilot has never flown before," I am sure your response to that would be "I think I'll take the next bus!" I would say that was a wise decision in light of the fact that the pilot hasn't yet proven himself.

Spiritually, we must discipline ourselves to *test* everything according to God's Word to make sure, "what is acceptable unto the Lord." For instance, when we consider the matter of separation as taught in the Pauline Epistles, is it right or wrong to establish partnerships with the unsaved? Is it right or wrong as believers, to date and marry the unsaved? When we put these things to the test in accordance with the Word of God, the believer is instructed to "have *no* fellowship with the unfruitful works of darkness." In other words, we are not to be "unequally yoked together with unbelievers" (II Cor. 6:14).

Note, the apostle does not say, "don't have too much fellowship," he clearly says NO fellowship. Believers are not to be unequally yoked together with the unsaved for any reason. A yoke is what holds two animals together, so they can pull a heavy load. Two horses evenly yoked together can accomplish a great deal for their master. However, if we were to yoke a horse and an ox together it would be impossible for them to work together. The horse and the ox are going to be unevenly yoked because the horse stands taller than the ox at the shoulder. Also, the stride of the horse is much longer than that of his counterpart. Accordingly, when the horse lurches forward, the ox having a shorter stride, is going to pull the horse both in a downward and backward direction.

This is also true of the saved and the unsaved. If you fellowship with the unfruitful works of darkness, it won't be very long before the unsaved begin to draw you back into the things of this world system. They will pull you down into the depths of sin, thus causing you to disgrace the name of Christ. You see, the unbeliever does not share your joy of salvation, your love of the truth, and your desire to live according to God's Word. To be accepted in the sight of the unbeliever, it will become more and more necessary for you to say less and less about the things of the Lord.

Gradually you will find yourself slipping back into the ways of the world.

But possibly someone is thinking, "How can you be so sure, maybe I'll have the opportunity to win them to Christ." It has been my experience that just the opposite is true. The unbeliever normally draws the believer back into the evils of the world. God tells us to "come out from among them and *touch not the unclean thing.*" Believers are in the world, but not of the world. In short, we must separate ourselves from the unsaved, lest we be overcome by temptation. But I can hear someone saying, "There God goes again interfering in my life, destroying all my fun!" Well, beloved, what we call fun is many times what God calls sin. When God instructs us to separate ourselves we must always remember it is for our own good. A separated life will draw us *closer* to Him.

We cannot put enough emphasis on the importance of maintaining a BALANCE between our doctrine and walk. They should be inseparable, like a bride and groom who have just exchanged their vows at the wedding ceremony. Whatsoever God has joined together let no man put asunder!

WALKING WORTHY OF OUR CALLING

In the Old Testament, God required His people to observe certain dietary laws. Only *clean* animals were permitted to be eaten. They were clearly identified as those beasts that "parteth the hoof...and cheweth the cud" (Deut. 14:6). Although the issue of *health* was the basis for these laws, the spiritual significance of these regulations was paramount. Types and laws in the Old Testament were often pictures of great spiritual truths.

Now, I'm not a farmer by any stretch of the imagination, but I do know that after a cow grazes it will regurgitate its stomach contents and begin chewing the cud. This mulling over of its food a second time symbolized the importance of *meditation*. Israel was to feast on the law of God and then meditate upon it day and night. The divided hoof symbolized the need for God's people to live *separated* lives. So through His Word, the Potter molded a nation that the other nations of the world soon came to fear.

Inasmuch as the things that "were written aforetime were written for our learning," the above illustration can easily be applied to ourselves. According to His determinate counsel, the Potter is presently molding a *new* vessel from the mire of humanity: the Church, the Body of Christ. Today we have been given a new revelation upon which to meditate; but God still requires us to live *separated* lives unto Him. Consequently, those of us who have feasted upon the riches of His grace have a much greater responsibility to walk worthy of our calling.

a. Our First Steps

"I therefore, the prisoner of the Lord, beseech you that ye walk worthy of the vocation wherewith ye are called" (Eph. 4:1).

The term "walk" is a figure of speech that is used by the apostle to describe our *manner of life*. How we conduct ourselves, in Christ, speaks volumes to those around us. Perhaps an illustration here will be helpful. Suppose for a moment that we sit down together in Central Park to observe those who are visiting the park. Without exchanging a word, we would probably be able to tell a great deal about those passing by. For example, the first to stroll in front of us is a young mother with a toddler trailing behind. This little guy can't take two or three steps without stumbling and falling. Obviously, he is learning to walk. Approaching from the other direction is a man weaving all over the sidewalk. As he staggers along his demeanor indicates that strong drink is controlling his actions. Next, a well-dressed man wearing an expensive suit passes by us rather briskly. There is little doubt that he is a businessman who is apparently late for an appointment.

So then, if a man walks according to the course of this world and practices the deeds of the flesh, we conclude that he is a son of Adam. But if this same man responds to the gospel, a dramatic change takes place, and he begins to desire the things of God. In fact, his chief end is to glorify God. Before long his attitude, actions, desires, manner of speech, and dress all become subject to the Word of God, or at least they should be.

Those who are babes in Christ tend to have an insatiable hunger for the sincere milk of the Word. Parents who have a newborn can relate to this, especially when the 2:00 a.m. feeding rolls around. That sweet, little, screaming bundle of joy wants to be fed NOW!!! I read somewhere where one husband thought he had found an acceptable solution to these early morning theatrics. Struggling to pull his head up from the pillow, he said to his wife, "Honey! You get up with the baby, and I'll stay here in bed and pray for you." As it turned out, he was probably the one who ended up needing prayer! Spiritually, babes in Christ also require frequent feedings, encouragement and a lot of tender loving care. As they begin to walk in grace, it is inevitable they are going to stumble and fall flat on their face. Like the eagle that flutters over her young, we should step forward to help them up, dust them off and give them a word of reassurance.

Every believer is either a *babe* in Christ, *spiritually minded*, or a *carnal* Christian. Interestingly, our manner of life identifies us with one of these three categories. This is why it is so important to *walk worthy* of our calling. But how is this accomplished? And, is it possible for the fallen sons of Adam to walk well-pleasing unto the Lord?

b. The Key Ingredient

Paul's opening statement in Ephesians 4:1, "I therefore, the prisoner of the Lord, beseech you that ye walk worthy", forms a natural transition between the doctrinal portion of the writing in the first three chapters and the *practical* application taught in the latter three chapters. The very order here strongly suggests that whatever doctrines are committed to God's people, they always govern their conduct. This is true in every dispensation.

Perhaps we should consider another example to further substantiate our point. Under the law Israel was obligated to observe seven yearly festivals known as the "feasts of Jehovah." According to Leviticus 23, they were: Passover, Unleavened Bread, Firstfruits, Pentecost, Trumpets, Day of Atonement, and Tabernacles. Each of these feasts had specific *regulations* attached to them, ranging from the sacred rites of offering blood sacrifices, to every household offering two wave loaves. Since these festivals were "holy gatherings of the Lord," all of them fell under the classification of Sabbaths and should be distinguished from the weekly Sabbath. Thus every Jewish habitation ordered their steps according to the law. In short, the doctrine of these feasts affected their *conduct*.

A case in point is found surrounding our Lord's crucifixion and resurrection. "The Jews therefore, because it was the preparation, that the bodies should not remain upon the Cross on the Sabbath day, (for that Sabbath day was an *high day*)" (John 19:31). Of course, the preparation day was the day preceding the Passover when the Israelites prepared for the upcoming festival. Notice that John is careful to point out that the Savior's body could not remain on the Cross because the approaching Sabbath (Passover) was a high day in which no strenuous work was permitted. The two days following this "high day" were also Sabbaths—Unleavened Bread and the regular weekly Sabbath (Lev. 23:6,7 cf. Matt. 28:1). Furthermore, it should be noted that the phrase in Matthew 28:1 in the original is *plural*, literally "In the end of the Sabbaths."

These *three Sabbaths* in a row disrupted all activity. Of course, this allows for the literal fulfillment of the Master's prediction that He would remain in the tomb for three days and three nights (Matt. 12:40). This also helps explain why the graves that were opened the day Christ died were unable to be closed until *after* His resurrection (Matt. 27:45-54). And, it sheds light on why the women were hindered from coming to the sepulcher sooner to anoint the body of our Lord (Mark 16:1-4).

With the introduction of the present administration, God has dispensed a *new* doctrinal handbook for the Church, the Body of Christ. Thus, our walk is governed by the doctrines of grace. Hence, "let no man therefore judge you in meat, or in drink, or in respect of an holy day, or of the new moon, or of the Sabbath days: which are a shadow of things to come; but the body [substance] is of Christ" (Col. 2:16,17). According to this passage, the observance of feast days and Sabbaths were merely shadows of the *reality* that we now have in Christ.

We frequently hear members of the "Christian community" say, "Oh, let's forget about all those complicated doctrines and simply live the Christian life." Such statements show an acute disregard for the basic principle that *doctrine is the foundation upon which our walk rests*.

c. The Journey

"I therefore, the prisoner of the Lord, beseech you
that ye walk worthy of the vocation wherewith ye are
called, with all lowliness and meekness, with longsuffering, forbearing one another in love" (Eph. 4:1,2).

True *fulfillment* in the Christian life is only possible when
we live in accordance with the spiritual blessings that have
been bestowed upon us. When Paul instructed the Ephesians
to "walk worthy of their calling," he used the Greek word *axios*
(worthily) which Kenneth Wuest says is "...an adverb, meaning 'in a manner worthy of.'" Mr. Wuest adds this interesting
observation: "The adjective form means, 'having the weight of
(weighing as much as) another thing.' Thus, Paul exhorts the
Ephesian saints to see to it that their Christian experience,
the Christian life they live, should weigh as much as the
profession of Christianity which they make. In other words,
they are to see to it that they practice what they preach, that
their experience measures up to their standing in grace."[1]

We concur that this is the primary sense of the apostle's
words. But insofar as Paul uses a term that is so closely
associated with weights and measures, it could well be that
there is an underlying thought here. Namely, on the scales
of the Christian life there ought to be a *balance* between
doctrine and walk.

Some are so doctrinally minded that they become insensitive to the spiritual needs of others. But, do not the Scriptures warn us "And though I...understand all mysteries, and
[have] all knowledge...and have not love, I am nothing" (I Cor.
13:2). Seeking to remedy this condition, some have swerved
so far in the opposite direction that their motto is "Away
with doctrine; let us make love the sole theme of our lives!"
However, this is a blatant rejection of such passages as: "let
him acknowledge that the things that I write unto you are

175

the *commandments of the Lord*" (I Cor. 14:37); "But thou hast fully known my *doctrine*" (II Tim. 3:10); and "All Scripture is given by inspiration of God, and is profitable for *doctrine*" (II Tim. 3:16). The Word of God always strikes a *balance* between our standing and state. Therefore, we would do well to heed the apostle's example to "Speak the truth in love."

> "With all lowliness and meekness, with long-suffering, forbearing one another in love" (Eph. 4:2).

The beginning of our journey to walk worthy is found here in Ephesians 4:2. *Lowliness:* We are not to think too highly of ourselves. This first step in our walk deals a deathblow to the present day self-esteem movement. Those who are walking in lowliness aspire to live a Christ-centered life. But someone is sure to ask: "Isn't my primary responsibility to love my wife?" Beloved, if we place Christ *first*, then we will voluntarily obey His Word, which says: "Husbands, love your wives, even as Christ also loved the Church, and gave Himself for it" (Eph. 5:25). When a believer feels neglected for one reason or another, if he is living for Christ, he gladly submits himself to the biblical injunction: "let each esteem other better than themselves."

Meekness means to be mild-mannered, gentle, under control at all times. It is said this word was used of wild horses who were tamed. "They still had their strength and spirit, but their will was under the control of a master." The same should be said of every believer in Christ. Insofar as God never causes us to do anything contrary to our will, it is of the utmost importance that we remain in the center of His *will*. Meekness must never be confused with weakness. The Scriptures state: "Moses was very *meek*, above all the men which were on the face of the earth" (Num. 12:3). Yet, he courageously confronted the rebels in Israel who challenged his God-given leadership, the outcome of which sent many of them to their death!

Longsuffering is being patient with the circumstances that one may find himself in. You will recall when God revealed to Abraham that He would multiply his seed as the stars of heaven, he waited *patiently* for the fulfillment of the promise (Heb. 6:13-15). Sometimes, we are like a horse chomping at the bit, impatient for *immediate* results. But God's ways are not our ways. Thus, we must learn to be longsuffering and to accept that God is working all things out according to the counsel of His will. If we will simply rest in His sovereignty, "the peace of God, which passeth all understanding, shall keep your hearts and minds through Christ Jesus."

Forbearing one another in love is one attribute that is sorely lacking in the lives of most saints. As soon as a little rain falls into an otherwise peaceful setting, most believers are all too willing to absolve themselves of any responsibility in the Lord's work. In short, they *quit*! But, for the sake of the One who loved us and gave Himself for us, should we not endure a little hardness as a good soldier of Jesus Christ? Did not our Savior endure cruel mocking, a crown of thorns, scourging and, yes, even death itself to redeem us? How shall we ever look into His eyes and say, "I didn't care enough to fight the good fight of the faith." Shame on us! These insightful words of an aged preacher who was brokenhearted over the actions of some in his congregation are poignant indeed: "Longsuffering is learning to bear with other Christians who are not just what we think they ought to be." After all, God forbears with them, so should we!

A GRAND STATEMENT OF FAITH

"Endeavoring to keep the unity of the Spirit in the bond of peace. There is one Body, and one Spirit, even as ye are called in one hope of your calling; one Lord, one faith, one baptism, one God and Father of all, who is above all, and through all, and in you all" (Eph. 4:3-6).

177

Notice that the Spirit of God, not the local assembly, has established this sevenfold unity. These seven planks form the doctrinal foundation upon which the super-structure of the Mystery rests. It is indeed a grand statement of faith. Due to the fact that the Spirit has established it, adherence to the sevenfold unity isn't negotiable, it is *required*. A complete exegesis of this subject is found in the author's book, *Exploring the Unsearchable Riches of Christ*. In fact, one entire chapter is devoted to each plank of the statement.[2] Therefore, we will only be giving a brief presentation here to ensure that the reader is pointed in the right direction.

It is imperative to remember that each part of the sevenfold unity of the Spirit is *unique* to Paul's gospel. Moreover, each is *spiritual* in nature, not physical. We have before us the unsearchable riches of Christ:

1. *One Body:* This is the *new creation* that God foreordained that we should be holy and without blame before Him in love. The Body of Christ is a living organism made up of Jews and Gentiles without distinction. We are members one of another—*one* in Christ, who is our Head (I Cor. 12:12,13; II Cor. 5:17; Eph. 1:22,23).

2. *One Spirit:* The person of the Spirit is the same yesterday, today, and forever. However, His *role* during the dispensation of Grace has changed dramatically. Today it is the Spirit who baptizes us into the Church, the Body of Christ. He also illuminates those who are seeking a fuller knowledge of God's will, which is accomplished by enlightening them to the Mystery (I Cor. 12:13; Eph. 3:1-5; Col. 1:8-10 cf. 1:25-27).

3. *Even as ye are called in one hope of your calling:* We certainly have no objections to those who limit the apostle's words here to the *Rapture*. We, too, believe that this glorious event is indeed included in the phrase. But Paul is

addressing the *one hope of our calling*, wherein we find that believers have been *called* into His grace in Christ. Christ is our hope according to I Timothy 1:1: "Paul, an apostle of Jesus Christ by the commandment of God our Savior, and Lord Jesus Christ, which is *our hope.*" Thus, the hope of salvation (Rapture—deliverance from the wrath to come), the hope of the resurrection, the hope of heaven, and the hope of eternal life, are all *vested* in Him (Gal. 1:4; I Thes. 5:8; I Cor. 15:19; Col. 1:5; Titus 1:2).

4. *One Lord:* The person of Christ is *immutable*. Like the Spirit, He is the same yesterday, today, and forever. With the King in royal exile due to His rejection, Christ is conducting a heavenly ministry today with the Church, which is His Body. As the *Head* of the Body, He is seated at the right hand of the Father as the God of all grace, not willing that any should perish but that all would receive deliverance from the judgment to come (Eph. 1:19-23; 2:13-16; Col. 1:15-19).

5. *One faith:* While this might well be a reference to the entirety of Paul's revelation, which he calls *the faith*, we feel this would be somewhat redundant when the same could be said of the sevenfold unity under consideration. It seems to us that the apostle has the *faith of Christ* in mind, as it relates to the terms of salvation. With the change in dispensations, Paul was given the *secret* of the gospel which is *Calvary*. God was in Christ reconciling the world unto Himself. Thus, when we believe the gospel of salvation; that Christ died for our sins, was buried, and rose again, we are justified by *His faithfulness* (I Cor. 15:1-4; Gal. 2:16; Eph. 6:19).

6. *One baptism:* This is the baptism that *saves*. Even most of our Baptist friends would agree with this conclusion. The moment we trust Christ as Savior, the Holy Spirit *spiritually* baptizes us into Christ. According to Paul's revelation, this baptism simultaneously places us into the Body of Christ

and identifies us with His death, burial, and resurrection (Rom. 6:3,4; I Cor. 12:13; Gal. 3:27; Col. 2:12).

7. *One God and Father of all, who is above all, and through all, and in you all:* We serve one God who eternally exists in three persons; Father, Son, and Holy Spirit. The Godhead is co-equal and co-eternal. As we have seen, God the Father is making known His *eternal purpose* for the Church during the age of Grace. He is working in and through us to the praise of His glory (Eph. 1:3-6; 3:11; Phil. 2:12-15).

CHRIST'S ASCENSION
ACCORDING TO PAUL'S GOSPEL

The context of Ephesians 4:8-16 can perhaps best be summarized by a humorous event in history which we recently came across:

"During the reign of Oliver Cromwell, the British government began to run low on silver for coins. Lord Cromwell sent his men on an investigation of the local cathedral to see if they could find any precious metal there. After investigating, they reported: 'The only silver we could find is the statues of the saints standing in the corners.' To which Cromwell replied: 'Good! We'll melt down the saints and put them into circulation.'"[3]

This doesn't sound like a bad idea! Sadly, far too many times the saints of God grow cold and indifferent in the Lord's service—like those statues standing in the corners. The enemy sends a few hardships their way and most are more than ready to throw in the towel. Oh! that God might melt our hearts and put us back into *circulation* for Him. Thankfully, He has gone before us to prepare the way. Thus, a proper understanding of the ascension of Christ according to Paul's gospel provides the means through which a believer might grow in grace.

a. The Ascensions of Christ

"Wherefore He saith, When He ascended up on high, He led captivity captive, and gave gifts unto men. (Now that He ascended, what is it but that He also descended first into the lower parts of the earth? He that descended is the same also that ascended up far above all heavens, that He might fill all things)" (Eph. 4:8-10).

The biblical record clearly supports that Christ ascended *twice* to His Father's throne near the close of His earthly ministry. Our Lord's ascension from the Mount of Olives, following His post-resurrection ministry, is perhaps the most universally acknowledged. Of course, here Christ is portrayed as being seated at His Father's right hand until His enemies are made His footstool, at which time He will visibly return in glory to execute judgment upon all those who obey not the gospel of the kingdom (Acts 1:9-11; 2:32-36 cf. II Thes. 1:7,8). But forty days prior to this glorious event He had ascended to the Father for an entirely *different* purpose. This ascension took place at the time of His resurrection—*the first day of the week!*

After the initial flurry of activity that fateful day, our Lord appeared to Mary Magdalene, who was yet troubled by His disappearance. "Jesus saith unto her, Mary. She turned herself, and saith unto Him, Rabboni; which is to say, Master. Jesus saith unto her, Touch me not; [or, do not detain me] for I am not yet ascended to my Father: but go to my brethren, and say unto them, I ascend unto my Father, and your Father; and to my God, and your God" (John 20:16,17). We believe this ascension is in harmony with the activities of the High Priest on the day of atonement.

Every year on the day of atonement, the High Priest would shed the blood of a goat to atone for the sins of the chosen nation. He alone was permitted to pass through the holy place and enter into the holy of holies. The High Priest always entered the holiest of all on the right side of the veil—God's position of favor. Once in the presence of the Almighty, he sprinkled the goat's blood seven times upon the mercy seat *before the Lord*. Then he was instructed to return to the congregation, but not before sprinkling the blood upon the brazen altar, thus cleansing it for the ensuing year (Lev. 16:15-19).

If we put all these pieces of the puzzle together, the following image begins to gradually emerge. The day Christ died, He descended into the lower parts of the earth to the unseen world known as *Hades*. He remained there for three days and three nights in a disembodied state. According to Luke's gospel, Hades was divided into two compartments, paradise and torment, with a great gulf fixed between.[4]

Peter informs us that during this period He "preached unto the spirits in prison [torment]; which sometime were disobedient, when once the longsuffering of God waited in the days of Noah" (I Pet. 3:19,20). Wuest makes the interesting observation that the verb "preach" here "is not *euaggelizomai*, 'to preach the gospel', but *kerusso*, 'to make a proclamation.'" Undoubtedly, the Lord declared unto them the *hopelessness* of their plight. Thus, these words or ones akin to it have echoed down through the succeeding generations, "Your *unbelief* has sentenced you to a life of torment forever and ever."

The Master's words to the thief on the cross substantiates that He also spent time in *paradise* during His three day absence from the earth. "And Jesus saith unto him, Verily I say unto thee, Today shalt thou be with me in paradise." Imagine the jubilation of these righteous dead who for the first time were introduced to their *Redeemer*.

After His resurrection and brief appearance to Mary, Christ led *captivity captive*. But what is the significance of this phrase? "When He ascended up on high, He led captivity captive." In the Old Testament this terminology is closely associated with *liberation*. For example, according to Judges chapter 5, Israel had again been delivered from "the noise of the archers," this time under the faithful leadership of Barak. Upon freeing the host of Israel from the evils of the Canaanites, Deborah and Barak sang: "Awake, Awake, Deborah: awake, awake, utter a song: arise, Barak, and lead thy captivity captive, thou son of Abinoam." This was a song of victory as they marched through the camp displaying those of their own kindred who had been *recovered* from bondage.

Although the sins of those in paradise had been atoned for, the blood of bulls and goats could never remove those sins. Consequently, these sins past, though covered, hindered them from residing in the presence of a holy and righteous God. Therefore, it was needful for these righteous dead to remain in the lower parts of the earth until the shadow became a reality through Christ's shed blood. Upon the completion of His finished work, He ascended on High to *present* Himself to the Father as proof of the fact He had offered the once-for-all sacrifice. This was in fulfillment of the above type (Heb. 9:11-14,23-28).

What a sight that must have been on resurrection morning when He ascended to the Father. With the finished work now a reality, and the sins of those past generations removed as far as the east is from the west, Christ led captivity captive, thus *liberating* those confined to the center of the earth. They, too, were presented to the Father as the first trophies redeemed by the blood. Little wonder He didn't want to be detained by Mary; there were more pressing matters that required His attention. God always does everything decently and in order.

Of course, the hope of these prophetic saints is *earthly*. They are merely *temporary* residents of heaven where they anxiously await the millennial kingdom. This helps explain Enoch's prophecy that when the Lord returns in His Second Coming to the earth to execute judgment, He will come "with ten thousands [myriads] of His saints" (Jude 1:14,15). Today, then, *paradise* is located in the third heaven (II Cor. 12:1-4).

b. The Ascension and the Mystery

As Paul develops the theme of the ascension, he does so in accordance with the *Mystery*. Here we learn that God had a secret purpose in mind for the Church, the Body of Christ. Paul's knowledge of the Old Testament would put most believers to shame today. The Spirit of God made good use of his understanding of those things written aforetime. In fact, He often guided the inspired apostle to borrow a selection that was in harmony with his message, but added a *new* morsel of truth making it unique to Paul's revelation.

For example, the apostle begins by quoting from Psalm 68 in Ephesians 4:8: "Wherefore He saith, When He ascended up on high, He led captivity captive," but adds: "and gave gifts unto men." Interestingly, Paul normally uses the Greek word *charisma* when he speaks of the spiritual gifts that are given to believers for His service. In this context, however, he uses the Greek word *doma* referring to the character of the gifts that are given. What or who are these gifts? The extended context clearly gives us the answer: "He gave some, apostles; and some, prophets; and some, evangelists; and some, pastors and teachers" (vs. 11).[5] So then, apostles, prophets, evangelists, pastors and teachers are *gifts* Christ has given to the Church, which is His Body that it might edify itself in love.

"And he gave some, apostles; and some, prophets; and some, evangelists; and some, pastors and teachers" (Eph. 4:11).

Inasmuch as the gifts of apostles and prophets had to do with the original imparting of the Word of God, when the Holy Scriptures were completed these gifts were *withdrawn*. We now have the written revelation of God which is the final authority in all matters of faith and practice. Here we must be careful not to throw the baby out with the bath water. Simply because God has withdrawn the apostles and prophets does not necessitate an action on His part to withdraw all His gifts from His Church, as some have concluded. We believe the late J. Oswald Sanders hit the nail on the head when he wrote: "The supernatural nature of the Church demands a leadership that rises above the human. The overriding need of the Church, if it is to discharge its obligation to the rising generation, is for leadership that is authoritative, spiritual and sacrificial."[6]

It must be remembered that as the inspired apostle penned the words of this letter, Ephesians brings us into the very pinnacle of Body truth. Without diminishing from the apostle's early writings to the Gentiles, his later writings establish the *norm* for the present dispensation. And it is here in Ephesians that we learn that the Lord gave some *evangelists*, and some *pastors* and some *teachers*. Those who have been *called* to these positions will meet the qualifications of I Timothy 3 and should be adequately trained for the Lord's work. According to the riches of His grace, God bestows insight, discernment, wisdom, and leadership capabilities upon those who receive these callings. In times of intense persecution and discouragement the call of God is the only thing that has kept many servants of the Lord from leaving the ministry.

We believe that the position of *evangelist* is a very special calling of God. He is given a special measure of grace to leave his family and homeland, and travel halfway around the world to a foreign country to preach the gospel. The evangelist has a burning *desire* to win lost souls to Christ. They seem to be oblivious to danger as they go from village to village, planting churches. A true missionary understands the importance of training *nationals* to carry on the work in his absence. If a government closes its borders to missionaries, as many have done, the gospel will continue through the fruits of his labors. Although we may not be called to be an evangelist, we are *all* "to do the work of an evangelist" (II Tim. 4:5).

While every *pastor* is a teacher, not every teacher is a pastor. The word "pastor" in Ephesians 4:11 is the Greek word *poimen* which denotes a *shepherd*. Paul effectively employs the analogy of the sheepfold in a *secondary* sense to show that it is the shepherd who feeds, protects and leads the flock. For the sake of order, God has ordained various authority structures to govern the home, government, and His Church. Paul says to Timothy: "Let the elders that rule well be counted worthy of double honor, especially they who labor in the Word and doctrine" (I Tim. 5:17). Here the apostle distinguishes between the *ruling elders* and the *teaching elder*, who would be the pastor of the local assembly.

The ruling elders provide spiritual leadership for the local church in cooperation with the pastor. They should all strive to work *together* to resolve problems that arise, and provide a spiritual atmosphere where the saints can gather to worship in harmony. Moreover, we must never lose sight of the fact that the head of Christ is God, the head of man is Christ, the head of woman is the man. In like manner, the pastor standing in the pulpit is the head of the assembly, otherwise confusion reigns. Pastors are *never* to lord their authority over the flock of God. They are to set a godly example through their leadership that every saint would be more than willing to follow. Furthermore, a pastor or teacher should not be unfaithful to his calling. As we know, many have departed from the faith, seeking their own personal gain. One who truly has a pastor's heart will be more interested in the spiritual well-being of those entrusted to him than seeking his own glory.

In addition, the apostle gives us the job description of the gifts Christ has given to the Church.

EMPLOYED IN HIS SERVICE

"For the work of the ministry, for the edifying of the Body of Christ: till we all come in the unity of the faith, and of the knowledge of the Son of God, unto a perfect man, unto the measure of the stature of the fulness of Christ. That we henceforth be no more children, tossed to and fro, and carried about with every wind of doctrine, by the sleight of men, and cunning craftiness, whereby they lie in wait to deceive. But speaking the truth in love, may grow up into Him in all things, which is the head, even Christ" (Eph. 4:12-15).

The evangelists, pastors and teachers are responsible before God to faithfully proclaim the whole counsel of God in view of Paul's revelation. They should always encourage their hearers to rightly divide the Word of truth. The best teacher always serves as a guide. Of course, the saint's responsibility is to be a Berean and study to see if these things are so.

I know I'll probably be shot at high noon for this, but pastors are not called to paint the fellowship hall, evangelize the neighborhood, print the church bulletin or provide taxi service for the congregation. The pastor should be at his study preparing stimulating messages that have some life to them. Messages that will challenge, encourage, and build up the saints of God. As those under his ministry mature in the faith, *they* are to do the work of the ministry.

If this divine order is adhered to closely, those under our spiritual care will "henceforth be no more children, tossed to and fro, and carried about with every wind of doctrine, by the sleight [trickery] of men, and cunning craftiness, whereby they lie in wait to deceive" (Eph. 4:14). Pastors and teachers who are willing to stand faithfully and uncompromisingly for *sound* doctrine are God's *answer* to false doctrine and those who lie in wait to deceive. If we speak the truth in *love*, it will expose error. A child of God rooted and grounded in the faith is not easily deceived.

Question: Would you say that the warning of the foregoing passage is valid today? If you answered yes, then the gifts of evangelist, pastors and teachers are still being given simply because the above problems persist. God's gifts to the Church are His early *warning* system against error. Ask your pastor what he feels are the three greatest threats to the message of Grace and you will probably receive three mini sermons. This serves to confirm that he is the one standing on the front lines, or should be, in the defense and confirmation of the gospel.

How long will God continue to give these gifts to the Body of Christ? Paul insists: "Till we ALL come in the unity of the faith, and of the knowledge [Gr. *epignosis*—full knowledge] of the Son of God, unto a perfect man, unto the measure of the stature of the fullness of Christ" (Eph. 4:13). Paul warns us about those who, whether wittingly or unwittingly, would spread unsound doctrine among us. We are living in a time when some of the brethren seem to deem it important to find something new.

Surely, it could not be said there has ever been a period in Church history, past or present, that the "unity of the faith" has been attained, much less a "full knowledge" of the Son of God. But this is exactly what some would have us believe; that is, that the *unity of the faith* has been attained. Perhaps we should put this to the Berean test.

Creation: Some believe God created all things in six literal twenty-four hour days. Others teach the "ruin and reconstruction theory," that God created, destroyed, and re-created. This is commonly called the "gap theory" which places millions or billions of years between the original creation and the re-creation.

Redemption: The battle has raged for centuries over whether Christ died for the sins of all mankind or merely for the sins of the elect. Which do you believe?

Things to Come: It is well known there are those who believe the events covered in the Book of Revelation are entirely futuristic. Many would challenge this assertion as absurd. They teach that the early chapters of the Apocalypse describe the various stages of Church history up to the present "Laodicean" age. If we agree that there are two camps of interpretation on any biblical subject, then we have yet to come into the unity of the faith.

There is not one scintilla of evidence that the "unity of the faith" has ever been attained by *all*. Even in Paul's day, the saints were wielding the sword of the Spirit *against* one another (II Tim. 1:15 cf. 2:17-19). In addition, we must inquire: Has the Church come to a full knowledge of the Son of God? That is, of His person, work and present heavenly ministry. We shall answer this question with a question: Has the Church, which is His Body, acknowledged the preaching of Jesus Christ according to the revelation of the Mystery?

Thus, the responsibility of God's *gifts* to His Church is to proclaim the whole counsel of God in light of the Pauline epistles. Why? That the saints might be established in the faith! There is also an *experiential* side to this truth as well. When God *called* me into the ministry nearly three decades ago, it was *definitive*. Other pastors have testified of similar experiences, which confirms that the "gifts and callings of God are without repentance" (Rom. 11:29). *Beware* of those who would rob you of this precious truth!

While we are all to be striving toward the unity of the faith, the Church is far, far from attaining this lofty goal. When believers come to the unity of the faith we will all be of *one mind* concerning Paul's apostleship and message. Merely inquire if the dispensationalists see eye to eye with the covenant theologians, or if those who preach the kingdom gospel agree with those who preach Paul's gospel, and you will probably be tarred and feathered.

Consequently, we do not believe the Body of Christ shall attain to the unity of the faith or a full knowledge of Christ according to the revelation of the Mystery until the Rapture. In the meantime, may God give us the grace to follow the divine order He has set down to put the saints back into circulation to the praise of His glory.

VITAL SIGNS

> "But speaking the truth in love, may grow up into Him in all things, which is the Head, even Christ: from whom the whole Body fitly joined together and compacted by that which every joint supplieth, according to the effectual working in the measure of every part, maketh increase of the Body unto the edifying of itself in love" (Eph. 4:15,16).

Vital signs are essential. As the apostle checked the *pulse* of the Body of Christ he found it to be alive and well. Since the Body was still in the infancy stage at the time of this writing Paul was anxious for it to *grow*. Growth is a miracle of God. The why and how we grow physically, and why we stop growing at a particular point, is a great mystery. But we do know that there are certain required elements to sustain the growth process such as nourishment, exercise, and time.

In regard to the Body of Christ, the apostle says that we are to "grow up into Him in all things, which is the Head, even Christ." Notice we are to *mature* "into Him in all things." The goal is Christlikeness. Let's begin with that which is obvious. The Body matures as its members ingest the Word of God, exercise themselves unto godliness, and look forward to the time of Christ's imminent return. What's often overlooked is that maturing in Christ also includes acknowledgement of our union and relationship with one another.

Hence Paul states that the Body is, "fitly joined together and compacted by that which every joint supplieth." The statement "fitly joined together" (Gr. *sunarmologeo*) is also found in Ephesians 2:21 where it's referred to as a building "fitly framed together" (Gr. *sunarmologeo*). In both cases it has the idea of that which is *connected*. For example, as we consider the wonder of the human body, the femur (thighbone) is connected to the tibia (shinbone) by the kneecap. Each is essentially dependent upon the other in order for the leg to function properly. The same can be said of the Body of Christ; every member is bound together in a vital union. Thus, when a member falls from grace, those who are in close proximity *feel* the pain of the one who has fallen.

This union produces a *relationship* between each member that's unlike any other. The apostle describes it as being *knit* or "compacted by that which every joint supplieth, according to the effectual working in the measure of every part." In other words, every joint or member has a *purpose* through which the influence of Christ passes to the other members, similar to the human body's circulatory system. Furthermore, every member has been endowed with *spiritual gifts* according to the sovereignty of God, which enables us to minister to the other members of the Body (see Romans 12). God not only calls us, He also gives us the capacity to perform that area of *service* He has called us to. Our part is to be willing vessels through whom His grace and gifts may be manifested. Thus, whenever the "roll is called up yonder," God will receive all the honor and glory.

The above is clearly witnessed in the local assembly—one preaches the Word, one teaches Sunday school, one plays the organ, one sings, one prays, one has a burden for lost souls, another a desire that all men come to see what is the fellowship of the Mystery, etc. On a grander scale this is how the Body increases with the increase of God, thus edifying itself in love (Col. 2:19).

9

God's Recipe for a New Heart

"This I say therefore, and testify in the Lord, that ye henceforth walk not as other Gentiles walk, in the vanity of their mind."

—Ephesians 4:17

We have clearly seen how doctrine governs our manner of life, but it should be noted that there are also other dispensational aspects to our *walk*. For example, under the kingdom gospel the Lord taught His disciples: "Beware of false prophets, which come to you in sheep's clothing, but inwardly they are ravening wolves. Ye shall know them by their fruits....Every tree that bringeth not forth good fruit is hewn down, and cast into the fire" (Matt. 7:15,16,19). These *fruits* manifested themselves in the following ways: generosity, honesty, nonviolence, truthfulness, contentment, etc. (Luke 3:8-14). In the former administration, the fruitless were pruned from believing Israel and in the future day of judgment they will be cast into the lake of fire. So then, bearing fruit in one's life was not an option, but a *necessity*.

When the present dispensation was committed to Paul, the very nature of "grace" gave birth to a new revelation in regard to our Christian walk. Sadly, many have failed to acknowledge this change, which has caused some to be judgmental of those who have never blossomed. Based on the foregoing kingdom teaching, they conclude that these so-called believers were never saved to begin with.[1] However, this assumption is incorrect as the following passages indicate:

"even so we also *should* walk in newness of life" (Rom. 6:4).

"For we are His workmanship, created in Christ Jesus unto good works, which God hath before ordained that we *should* walk in them" (Eph. 2:10).

"I...*beseech* you that ye walk worthy of the vocation wherewith ye are called" (Eph. 4:1).

Each of the above statements imply that while the believer *should* live a godly life in Christ Jesus, this is *not* always the case. In fact, a large percentage in Christendom fall into this very classification. If I say to a friend that he should see a physician about a chronic heart problem, the very nature of my statement does not guarantee he will heed my advice. Although "grace" *beseeches* us to conduct ourselves in a Christ-like manner, believers are often prone to wander. Surely, the Corinthians did not persevere in the faith, nevertheless Paul called them saints (I Cor. 1:2). They were guilty of envy, strife, contention, divisions, fornication, heresy, greed and numerous other indiscretions. Nonetheless, they were saved by the grace of God even though there was *little* evidence of fruit in their lives. There is, however, grave consequences for living such a careless life—*loss* at the Judgment Seat of Christ!

A DIVINE WARNING

"This I say therefore, and testify in the Lord, that ye henceforth walk not as other Gentiles walk, in the vanity of their mind" (Eph. 4:17).

Here the apostle warns us to "walk not as other Gentiles." In other words, the possibility of slipping back into our former manner of life is ever before us. Paul began the chapter with a positive statement, "walk worthy," but here he turns to the negative, "walk not." Life is full of important decisions! After all, the average day begins by deciding whether to have *Frosted Mini-Wheats* or *Wheaties, Breakfast of Champions!* As we journey down the road of life, we naturally *avoid* those things that would bring us into harm's way. If you happen upon a bridge that has been washed out, do you proceed or turn around? The same application must be made in our spiritual lives. Hence, when we are instructed not to act like the Gentiles, the apostle is encouraging us to exercise *discernment*.

The unbelieving Gentiles walk in the vanity of their minds, that is, they ascertain things on the basis of mere human reasoning. In short, they *think* differently. This futile thought process manifests itself in various ways. Take, for example, the research that is being done on alcoholism. Medical science surmises that perhaps a defective gene causes some to be more susceptible to strong drink than others. Thus, based on this unsound premise, they conclude that alcoholism is a *disease*, and therefore the alcoholic is not responsible for his actions—he can't help himself! To say that this is a figment of their imagination would be an understatement.

Some years ago, I was driving through Apollo, Pennsylvania where I saw a piece of twisted wreckage alongside the road. Upon slowing down, I discovered that it was an automobile, or at least what was left of it. Apparently someone survived the crash because there were beer cans strategically placed beside the car along with a sign at the rear bumper which read, "And they told us we were going to have fun." Someone lied.

The Word of God emphatically declares that drunkenness is one of the *sins* of the flesh (I Cor. 6:9,10 cf. Gal. 5:17-21). It is an *addictive habit* that is acquired from unscrupulous friends or family members. "Woe unto him that *giveth* his neighbor drink, that puttest thy bottle to him, and makest him drunken also" (Hab. 2:15). "Wine is a mocker, strong drink is raging: and whosoever is deceived thereby is not wise" (Prov. 20:1).

Not long ago, a large group gathered from around the world to supposedly get in touch with the earth's energy force. They were convinced that through meditations, chants, and mind exercises they could bring lasting peace to the earth. Apparently, the group's meditations short-circuited the "energy force," because shortly after their gathering the world encountered the Gulf War, the Bosnian civil war, and a plague of terrorist attacks in Europe and the Middle East. Christ is our peace! And only those who place their faith in Him have peace with God (Eph. 2:14 cf. Rom. 5:1). In addition, the blood of men will run as a river throughout the world until the *Prince of Peace* returns to establish a kingdom wherein "the increase of His government and peace there shall be no end" (Isa. 9:6,7).

> "Having the understanding darkened, being alienated from the life of God through the ignorance that is in them, because of the blindness of their heart: Who being past feeling have given themselves over unto lasciviousness, to work all uncleanness with greediness" (Eph. 4:18,19).

Inasmuch as the unregenerate have rejected the testimony of the gospel, it has left them in a state of spiritual *darkness*. Amazingly, man has walked on the moon, explored the depths of the ocean, conquered the atom, and probed the inner sanctum of the human cell. Man, indeed, thinks he is enlightened when in reality he is powerless to fulfill his greatest need—spiritual life. Sin has separated him from the life of God. If the natural man is left to himself, he will wander aimlessly through the world and never seek God (Rom. 3:11). Like Julian, the apostate, he will curse God with his dying breath.

Christ, and Christ alone, is his only hope! To complicate matters even further, Satan has blinded man's heart to the glorious gospel. Interestingly, one of his most effective tools to accomplish this end is *religion*. The truth that "man is a sinner and in danger of the hell-fire judgment to come" has been obscured by ceremonies, baptisms, rituals, and good works.

Do you recall the first time you *willfully* sinned? You probably felt so guilty about the transgression that you vowed never again to commit such a foolish act. But, then, the seductive wooing of temptation drew you into its clutches a second, third, and fourth time. Before long you were committing that sin over and over again until you became so callous to it you just didn't care anymore. This characterizes the existence of the unsaved Gentiles in the world: they are *past feeling*.

I have a piece of petrified wood sitting on my desk that at one time used to be soft and porous. However, due to "the infiltration of water and the disposition of dissolved mineral matter" this little piece of wood has become *hard* as a rock. Accordingly, sin has a petrifying effect upon those who yield to its destructive ways. In essence, the apostle is admonishing the Ephesians, and us, to never become insensitive to sin; rather, let us mortify the deeds of the flesh.

Insofar as the Gentiles habitually live in sin, they have "given themselves over to lasciviousness, to work all uncleanness with greediness." Sin had so thoroughly corrupted the Gentiles in Paul's day that *indecency* was looked upon as acceptable behavior. The obscenity of the ancient world pales by comparison to what goes on around us today. Every medium, even the new computer technology, has been infected with this filth. Then, as now, this permissiveness opened the door to uncleanness. Uncleanness encompasses a number of perversions including homosexuality. In our so-called age of enlightenment, homosexuality is referred to as an "alternative lifestyle." What men call an "alternative lifestyle" the Bible emphatically calls *sin* (Rom. 1:24-32 cf. I Cor. 6:9,10). So deplorable is this wickedness in the sight of God, that He *annihilated* the cities of the plain as a solemn warning to those who commit such things thereafter (Gen. 19). Thankfully, Christ died for this sin, too!

Little wonder, the apostle writes in another place, "I would have you wise unto that which is good, and simple concerning evil" (Rom. 16:19).

A NEW MAN IN CHRIST

"But ye have not so *learned* Christ; if so be that ye have *heard* Him, and have been *taught* by Him, as the truth is in Jesus" (Eph. 4:20,21).

Here the apostle effectively uses three verbs to convey the importance of submitting ourselves to Christ. The verb "learn" (*manthano*) denotes to "learn by inquiry or observation." "Ye have not so learned Christ," that is, our knowledge of Him will never lead us to live as the Gentiles in the previous passages. We preach Christ and Him crucified. In other words, we preach a *Person*! Thus, when we came into a personal relationship with Christ, His life and everything He stands for gave us an understanding of what is *acceptable* behavior.

The second verb "heard" (*akouo*) simply means *to hear*, but when used with an object, it denotes to "hear with perception." In connection with the phrase, "...if so be that ye have heard Him," some have sought to add the preposition "about" to teach that the Ephesians had merely heard about Christ. The record is explicitly clear, however, that they had already known the Savior for a number of years. Perhaps an illustration will help better communicate Paul's thought. I have frequently made the statement to congregations in different parts of the country: "Hear me, and hear me well!" Then I proceed to make a key point from the Scriptures. You see, it is not only essential for the listener to hear with perception, but to *apply* what Christ has said as well.

This brings us to the third verb used in this context, "taught" (*didaktos*). *Didaktos* addresses "primarily what can be taught, then, taught." So, the phrase, "taught by Him, as the truth is in Jesus" has to do with what Christ has, and is, teaching us through Paul's gospel. Remember the words of the apostle: "yea, though we have known Christ after the flesh [earthly Jesus], yet now [the present age of Grace] henceforth know we Him no more" (II Cor. 5:16). Today, we know Christ as the Lord of glory, exalted in the heavens! Consequently, if we are to be empowered to "walk not as other Gentiles," we must *obey* the commands of Christ delivered to us in Paul's epistles.

Now, the apostle gets down to the nuts and bolts of the matter as he challenges us to *put off* our former manner of life, the *old man*, and *"put on* the *new man*, which after God is created in righteousness and true holiness" (Eph. 4:22,24). Here we have what is known as the principle of replacement. Anytime God tells us to put something away, He replaces it with something infinitely better. The old nature is that which we have inherited from Adam. The following is a short list of what you are capable of: uncontrollable anger, lying, dishonesty, filthy language, hate, envy, jealousy, strife, murder, inordinate affection, etc. The old man is corrupt and *cannot* please God. In fact, Solomon informs us that even "the plowing of the wicked, is sin" (Prov. 21:4).

The Teaching of Self-Esteem

"Holding fast the faithful Word as he hath been taught, that he may be able by sound doctrine both to exhort and to convince [refute] the gainsayers" (Titus 1:9).

Satan never rests in his insatiable desire to corrupt the Word of God. A case in point is the present day teaching of *self-love, self-esteem,* and *self-worth.* The influence of this unsound doctrine has nearly permeated every strata of Christendom, including the Grace Movement. Like the beat of a drum, this theme is heard almost constantly from the pulpits of America and frequently appears on the pages of Christian literature. Beware when you hear or read: "It is important to feel good about *yourself,*" "Learn to love *yourself,*" "Probe *your* innermost self to understand why *you* think and feel as *you do,*" "God sent His Son to die for you because *you* are of great value."

On the surface these phrases may seem commendable, but in reality they are diametrically opposed to the Scriptures. The above has been weighed in the balance and found to be wanting. For example: "The heart [innermost self] is deceitful above all things, and desperately wicked: who can know it?" (Jer. 17:9). Paul concurred when he said, "For I know that in me (that is, in my flesh, [old nature or self]) dwelleth no good thing" (Rom. 7:18). The old man (self) is at *enmity* against God. He hates God and the things of God and, as we have seen, left to himself he will not seek God. The Scriptures, from beginning to end, speak with a unified voice that the old nature is rotten to the core (See Rom. 3:9-18).

Consequently, our old man (self) has been crucified with Christ. Paul made reference to this when he wrote to the Galatians, "I am crucified with Christ [i.e. his old man]: nevertheless I live [Paul's new nature]; yet NOT I [self], but

200

Christ liveth in me." We are to *put off* the old nature and *put on* the new, which is created in holiness and righteousness (Eph. 4:22-24). It is futile to try to improve one's self-image, especially since God abhors any attempt to do so. Rather, we are to conform ourselves to the *image* of His dear Son. Thus, those of the household of faith are to live accordingly:

> "Let nothing be done through strife or vainglory; but in lowliness of mind let each esteem other better than themselves. Look not every man on his own things, but every man also on the things of others. Let this mind be in you, which was also in Christ Jesus" (Phil. 2:3-5).

Self takes great pleasure in acclaim, indulgence, approval, and praise. It glories in all these things. But are we not robbing God when self is esteemed more highly than His glory? "What? know ye not that your body is the temple of the Holy Spirit which is in you, which ye have of God, **AND YE ARE NOT YOUR OWN?** For ye are bought with a price: therefore glorify God in your body, and in your spirit, which are God's" (I Cor. 6:19,20).

Shall we permit the "love of one's self" doctrine to overshadow the love of God in Christ Jesus? God forbid! May God help us to stand against this insidious teaching that essentially robs God of the glory that is rightfully due Him.

Thanks be to God that our old man has been *crucified* with Christ. If, therefore, our old man has been put to death (positionally), we no longer have to be controlled by sin. Paul says, "He that is dead is freed from sin." If a man is under the harsh taskmaster of heroin, he may try unsuccessfully to kick the habit his entire life. However, the day death taps him on the shoulder he is *freed* from the addiction. We thus conclude that if our old man has been crucified but we continue in sin, we do so of our *own volition*.

When God regenerates us, He does not transform the old nature. Rather, regeneration is the impartation of a *new nature*. Regeneration awakens us spiritually; therefore, it is our new man that desires the things of God. We should pause here to add that there is no such thing as "spontaneous generation" as some teach. All life must come from *pre-existing* life. There must be both a mother and father to be born of the flesh. In like manner, spiritually speaking, there must be a sovereign work of the Spirit for a man to be born again. He is the one who imparts eternal life to those who have believed the gospel (Titus 3:5-7).

Not long after we are saved it becomes apparent that there is a *warfare* being waged in our members. New believers often confuse this conflict with the idea that they have lost their salvation. Actually, this is a clear indication they are truly saved. Since the believer still has the old nature, this explains why some have been faithful for years but somewhere along the line fall from grace. Demas is a classic case in point; Paul recounts how "Demas hath forsaken me, having loved this present world." Thus it is imperative for us to yield to the new nature and starve the old. This is accomplished by daily disciplining ourselves in the study of the Scriptures. Only this will enable us to "walk not as other Gentiles."

CONTROLLING OUR ANGER

"Be ye angry, and sin not: let not the sun go down upon your wrath: neither give place to the devil" (Eph. 4:26,27).

Around the turn of the century, the Church was graced with an array of great preachers, but none were more tenacious and outspoken than Billy Sunday. He seemed to have a way of driving home a point. It is said that a woman once approached him after one of his meetings who was well known for her bad *temper*. She sought to defend her actions by saying: "But Mr. Sunday, although I blow up over the least little thing, it's all over in a minute." The evangelist looked her straight in the eye and said, "So is a shotgun blast!! It's over in seconds, too, but look at the terrible damage it can do."

God created us with a wide range of emotions, each of which serves a *purpose*. Yes, even anger can be good. Contrary to popular opinion, anger itself is *not* sinful. Notice how the apostle words his above statement, "Be ye angry, and sin not." In essence, Paul is saying that we are well within our rights to be angry over an injustice or unrighteous circumstances.

The present debate over "partial birth abortion" is a good example. We should be incensed by "abortion" in general and horrified by "partial birth abortions" in particular. Any procedure (usually performed at 7 or 8 months gestation) that allows the infant's head to remain in the birth canal while the abortionist forces a surgical instrument into the base of the skull to suction out the little one's brains is nothing short of first degree murder. Here a *righteous anger* is perfectly justified. In fact, there are scores of times in the Old Testament where the anger of the Lord is said to be kindled against His enemies (Num. 25:1-9; Jer. 12:13).

Surely our Lord is a prime example that anger itself is not necessarily sinful, for He knew no sin. Thus the Lord was well within the boundaries of godly behavior when He exhibited a *righteous anger* toward those who had made His Father's house a den of thieves (John 2:13-17). In the future Tribulation period those who reject God's anointed and worship the beast and his image, "the same shall drink of the wine of the *wrath of God*, which is poured out without mixture into the cup of His indignation; and he shall be tormented with fire and brimstone" (Rev. 14:10).

Carefully note, Paul adds to the phrase "be ye angry" a *warning*, "and sin not." Unbridled anger can easily turn into a fit of uncontrollable *rage* which normally leaves a path of destruction in its wake. Unchecked, anger that overflows into resentment almost always results in some form of retaliation. This may take the form of verbal attacks, threats, or even physical abuse.

In a worst case scenario, it is much like a volcano that builds pressure over a period of time and finally erupts. Whenever you watch a news report of a lone gunman who enters his former place of employment with a semi-automatic weapon and kills his supervisor and three other fellow workers, you are witnessing the *eruption* of pent-up anger. Another example is the believer who allowed his anger to get the better of him and shot an abortion doctor outside a clinic down south. With one pull of the trigger, this young man *disgraced* the name of Christ, labeled all Christians as radicals in the eyes of the world, destroyed his personal testimony, and ended up with life in prison. These are both cases where anger spun out of control with *tragic* results.

How to Deal with Anger

We are living in a day when philosophy says, "express yourself openly," "tell it like it is," "open up," "let it all hang out." However, the Scriptures counsel us to exercise *restraint*. The fruit of the spirit is "love, joy, peace, longsuffering, gentleness, goodness, faith, meekness, *temperance*: against such there is no law" (Gal. 5:22,23). As we walk by grace through faith, temperance will enable us to keep our anger under control. But how does this work out in a practical sense? Those who fly off in a fit of rage permit their anger to take control of them. Consequently, the energy emitted from this emotion is usually misdirected at someone or something.

Sinful anger *tears down*. Thus, in the heat of the moment things are often said and done which cause irreparable damage to relationships. Let's look at a hypothetical case:

Bob and Joan are a Christian couple who have been married for eight years. Things had gone smoothly with the exception of some irksome comments between them which have produced a few stress points in the relationship. One afternoon Bob phoned Joan to inform her that he was bringing the boss and his wife home to dinner. "What!!!" Joan replied, "you can't do that to me. The house is a mess, the kids need to be picked up from school, and my hair looks like I've had shock treatments. How could you be so insensitive, irresponsible, and downright selfish!!! And, by the way, Mr. Hos-pi-tal-ity, what am I supposed to prepare for dinner?"

Of course, Bob wasn't going to take this lying down. "Well, if you planned your day better maybe the house wouldn't be such a mess." Oops! Those were fighting words, which caused an all-out confrontation on the phone. Bob said some things that day he really didn't mean, but they hurt Joan deeply. Interestingly, that evening when Bob brought his boss home, everything went remarkably well. Both Bob and Joan were sweet as pie to one another in front of the boss and his wife.

Notice how both Bob and Joan brought their anger under control when the circumstances demanded it. They should have applied the same restraint earlier. But what or who was the major problem here? First, Joan was perfectly justified for being upset with Bob. Nevertheless, when she permitted her anger to run out of control, she *sinned*. And Bob's moment of *rage* landed him in the same boat. The problem was "poor timing." Rather than attacking one another they should have mutually agreed to discuss the matter later.

Since they failed to do so, however, they are now faced with additional complicating problems—hurt feelings. The solution to "poor timing" is better planning, plenty of advance notice, and respect for the responsibilities of your partner's role. Thus we must learn to direct our anger at the *problem* and not at those who are innocent victims of the circumstances. This will help strengthen the relationship rather than tearing it apart.[2]

Paul adds here in Ephesians, "let not the sun go down upon your wrath." We should never allow our anger to simmer overnight. This will only cause it to become more deeply seated. Before Bob and Joan retire for the evening, their problem should be *completely resolved*—no more silent treatment, no more dirty looks, no more raised voices. A romantic embrace and kiss good night will end the day on a *positive* note. Now they're prepared to face a new set of problems tomorrow.

"Neither give place to the devil" (Eph. 4:27). You see, if you fail to handle things in the proper manner, you may well be giving Satan an opportunity to drive a deeper wedge in your marriage. This also touches our relationships with others. Surely, we are not ignorant of his devices. Always remember, Satan is an *opportunist*.

CHRISTIAN BEHAVIOR

There is a passage of Scripture found in the Book of Deuteronomy that beautifully captures the attributes and providential care of our heavenly Father: "As an eagle stirreth up her nest, fluttereth over her young, spreadeth abroad her wings, taketh them, beareth them on her wings: so the Lord alone did lead him [that is, Jacob]" (Deut. 32:11,12). Ever since ancient times, eagles have symbolized power, strength, courage, and immortality. Although Benjamin

Franklin lobbied unsuccessfully (thankfully) to make the turkey our national symbol, our forefathers were persuaded that the eagle was a far more fitting representation.

As we know, the mother eagle normally builds her nest on the side of a sheer cliff where there is little danger of predators reaching it. When her young are old enough to leave the nest, she instinctively swoops down, hitting them with one of her wings which causes them to fall from the nest. Usually, these little ones are able to fly without any problem. However, occasionally one or two of her young will begin to tumble through the air because their wings are not fully developed. But before they can plunge to their death, the mother eagle will swoop down and safely bear them up on her massive six-foot wing span.

In similar fashion, our heavenly Father watches over His own. If we are faltering, He is able to *lift* us from the depths of despair according to the riches of His grace. Since He is infinite in wisdom and knowledge, we have an endless source of power at our disposal to perform that which is acceptable in His sight. But how do we access this *power* source so it will have a positive influence on our everyday Christian experience, not to mention the lives of those around us? Of course, there are various opinions of how this is to be accomplished, but what saith the Scriptures? And what, if any, is the importance of understanding the Word of God dispensationally when it comes to making an application of these things?

a. Stealing

"Let him that stole steal no more: but rather let him labour, working with his hands the thing which is good, that he may have to give to him that needeth" (Eph. 4:28).

I suppose we could understand these words being written to the Corinthians—but to the Ephesians? Amazing! The Ephesians were the spiritual giants of their day. They had acknowledged Paul's apostleship and message and were known throughout the world for their faith in Christ. Yet there were some among them who apparently were *stealing*. This only serves to remind us that the *old nature* is not eradicated on this side of glory. Even the most spiritually minded believer can fail and find himself lapsing back into old habits.

There is an ongoing battle raging within our members. Paul says in this regard: "For the good that I would I do not: but the evil which I would not, that I do" (Rom. 7:19). If we are honest, every believer can relate to that. Once again, the apostle admonishes the Ephesians to: "put off concerning the former conversation [behavior] the old man,[3] which is corrupt according to the deceitful lusts;...And that ye put on the new man, which after God is created in righteousness and true holiness" (Eph. 4:22,24). In short, we must yield to the *new man*. This is accomplished by obeying the Word of God. Hence the apostle's instructions: "Let him that stole steal no more."

Of course, stealing is taking something that does not rightfully belong to us. The other day I saw a news report telling of a lady who walked up to the meat counter in a major grocery chain and slipped a leg of lamb under her full-length coat. Apparently, she had somehow fastened it to the belt around her waist before attempting to leave the store. However, she was unaware that her actions were being video taped. The moment she stepped out the door the woman was apprehended by the store's security officers. Needless to say, she acted rather *sheepish* when the authorities questioned her.

While this may be the most common form of stealing, there are literally thousands upon thousands of ways to steal from our fellowman. When a lender has loaned money in good faith, if the borrower fails to pay the unpaid balance, he has stolen from the lender. Here in the Midwest a bank employee embezzled one hundred fifty thousand dollars over a ten-year period to finance her opulent life style. She is now facing forty years in prison for theft. The employee who arrives twenty minutes late for work and leaves ten minutes early every day has stolen ten hours from his employer by month's end. Those who borrow things and fail to return them to their neighbor are also guilty of stealing. Personally, I stopped borrowing things years ago, simply because every time I did, something seemed to break on the thing I borrowed, and then I was faced with the obligation not only to return it, but to repair it as well.

God has created us as creatures of *habit*. Consequently, we give little thought to the mundane things of life, because they become second nature to us over time. The years that I pastored churches, I seldom had to inquire if a particular family was in attendance. Every family had their favorite pew—if it was vacant, they were absent—simple as that! Unfortunately *sinful* behavior can become habitual as well. In order to reverse the downward spiral of sin, we must apply the Word of God to the *root* of the problem. It does work!

What is the biblical solution to the sin of stealing? Work! "Let him that stole steal no more." Notice that the apostle doesn't end here. Simply telling someone to stop stealing is like telling an alcoholic to quit drinking. He may muster enough willpower to abstain from the bottle for a week, but then finds himself back on another binge. That's why the campaign a few years ago to "Just Say No to Drugs" was such a miserable failure. You see, God's principle of *replacement* must be applied if there is to be a meaningful change in behavior.

In the case of stealing, God instructs those who struggle with this sin to "let him labor, working with his hands the thing which is good." This serves a twofold purpose: First, his time is *occupied*, drastically diminishing the opportunity to steal. The old adage: "Idle hands are the devil's workshop" is truer than we may think. Second, if he earns an honest living he can purchase what he needs or wants plus have the satisfaction of supplying for his family.

> "For even when we were with you, this we commanded you, that if any would not work, neither should he eat" (II Thes. 3:10).
>
> "But if any provide not for his own, and specially for those of his own house, he hath denied the faith, and is worse than an infidel" (I Tim. 5:8).

This would end welfare in this country as we know it. There are many able-bodied people who receive assistance from the state and federal agencies who should be earning a living (another form of stealing). Usually, they end up wallowing in the mire of self-pity and wonder why they suffer from depression. A full day's work is the remedy for this ill. It gives a sense of worth and accomplishment. Now, please don't misunderstand me, I believe there are many handicapped, indigent, and elderly who *legitimately* need this help. Even in Old Testament times God made provisions for those who had various maladies. Often they were placed by the temple gate where those who passed by could give them a gift (Deut. 15:11 cf. Acts 3:1-7).

We find it interesting that many of those whom God called into full-time service were *working* at the time of their call. Moses was *tending* the sheep of his father-in-law Jethro at

Mount Horeb when the Lord appeared to him in the midst of a burning bush (Ex. 3:1,2). Gideon was *threshing wheat* by the winepress when the angel of the Lord commissioned him to deliver Israel from the hands of the Midianities (Judges 6:11-16). David was *keeping* his father's sheep when he was called home so that Samuel might anoint him king (I Sam. 16:10-13). Our Lord called Peter and Andrew while they were *fishing*. And later that same day he appointed James and John disciples as they were *mending* their father's nets (Matt. 4:18-22). As we can clearly see, God honors the work ethic.

Before we leave this subject, Paul gives another incentive to those who are given to stealing. He adds: "that he may have to give to him that needeth" (Eph. 4:28). In other words, holding down a steady job provides the opportunity to generously share with others in need, thus keeping them from the sin of stealing also.

b. Corrupt Communication

"Let no corrupt communication proceed out of your mouth, but that which is good to the use of edifying, that it may minister grace unto the hearers" (Eph. 4:29).

I would probably question the need for Paul to address our manner of speech, except for the fact that I have frequently overheard Christians whose filthy mouths would make a sailor blush. Yes, believers, sad to say, sometimes stoop to vulgarities to be accepted by unbelieving friends and family members. They have themselves convinced that it makes them appear more macho. Actually, it *grieves* the heart of God, not to mention demonstrating their immaturity.

The apostle says, "Let no corrupt communication proceed out of your mouth." The term "corrupt" here is the Greek word *sapros* meaning "rotten, worn out, unfit for use,

211

worthless, bad." This word was closely identified with the market place where the fruits and vegetables were sometimes said to be spoiled or rotten. Corrupt speech is a direct product of a *corrupt* nature. As they say, "The apple hasn't fallen far from the tree."

James informs us: "The tongue is a fire, a world of iniquity....For every kind of beasts, and of birds, and of serpents, and of things in the sea, is tamed, and hath been tamed of mankind: but the tongue can no man tame: it is an unruly evil, full of deadly poison" (James 3:6,7,8).

Remember the last time you smashed your fingers in a door. Probably you sung a tune that you would be embarrassed to repeat. The mouthpiece of our old nature is the *tongue*. James teaches us that it is *untamable*. Man can tame lions, tigers, and bears, but the natural man will never control his unruly tongue. Our words can either be used for good or evil. Consequently, a single word from a deranged dictator can end the lives of thousands of innocent victims.

Dr. Arno Gaebelein wrote these insightful thoughts on the subject: "Tongue control? It will never be achieved unless there is first of all heart and mind control....When any Christian comes to the point of yielding to the Lord—in full sincerity, cost what it may—control of his thought life, the problem of managing his tongue will be solved, provided that such a surrender goes deeper than the intellect and reaches the emotions and will. For the Bible makes a distinction between mere intellectual knowledge of God and the trust of the heart."

As we have seen, believers are to put off the garments of sin, and put on the new man. Thus, unwholesome language is uncharacteristic of spiritually minded believers. It is unbecoming of Christ to use the vulgarities of the world. Our *speech* should be "that which is good to the use of edifying."

It should be wholesome, encouraging, and that which builds up and never tears down. With those, for example, who were struggling spiritually, Paul could have spoken down to them or criticized their lack of faith. Instead, the apostle shares how he sought to place himself *sympathetically* in their shoes that he might better communicate the gospel.

Hence, he writes these heartwarming words: "To the weak [spiritually] became I as weak, that I might gain the weak: I am made all things to all men, that I might by all means save some" (I Cor. 9:22). Paul by no means compromised his own convictions, but he was desirous (through a right attitude and manner of speech) of reaching men for Christ.

Speech that edifies may sometimes include admonition. Paul frequently found it necessary to admonish the saints, but he never sought to offend merely for the sake of offense; rather, he spoke the truth in love. As problems arose in the churches of his day, it was the apostle's custom to first *commend* the saints before he *corrected* them. Thus, Paul opens his letter to the Corinthians accordingly: "Unto the church of God which is at Corinth, to them that are sanctified in Christ Jesus, called to be saints....I thank my God always on your behalf, for the grace of God which is given you by Jesus Christ." Then he lowers the boom, regarding the divisions and contentions among them. "Now I beseech you, brethren...that there be no divisions among you; but that ye be perfectly joined together in the same mind and in the same judgment" (I Cor. 1:2,4,10).

The apostle also reminds the Ephesians that their speech ought to "minister grace unto the hearers." Our communication with those whom we come into contact with should always be characterized by *graciousness*. It is fairly easy to be gracious when others treat us with respect. The real test comes when we find ourselves the target of someone's disapproval. While others may raise their voice and say inflammatory things they will probably regret, we should never stoop to their level. My own personal observation of this over the years is telling. It has been my experience that the most mature believer during a time of crisis is the one who controls his anger and *graciously* responds in a Christlike manner (see Luke 4:22). *Question:* Is your manner of speech profitable or like the sound of chalk screeching across a blackboard? Always remember, you draw more bees with honey than with vinegar.

GRIEVING THE HOLY SPIRIT

"And grieve not the Holy Spirit of God, whereby ye are sealed unto the day of redemption" (Eph. 4:30).

There is a general consensus among parents that child-bearing would be much more enjoyable if the teen years were eliminated. Adolescence can be a turbulent time of life for some young people. In fact, a child who is wayward and always in serious trouble may bring a great deal of sorrow and grief to his parents. He may even bring shame upon the family name by his sinful actions. The same is true of the child of God. Our exalted *standing* in Christ is settled for eternity, but our *state* sometimes leaves much to be desired. Consequently, Paul instructs us to "grieve not the Holy Spirit." I guess I am an inquisitive type of person, because when I read statements like this my first thought is, *what* grieves the Holy Spirit, and *how* do we ungrieve Him or set the record straight?

Paul gives us a long list of things that grieve the heart of God. In Ephesians chapter four alone we have lying, uncontrolled anger, stealing, corrupt communication, bitterness, malice, etc. Of course, the primary goal of every believer is to walk well-pleasing unto the Lord. As we have seen, to accomplish this we must yield to the new nature that was imparted at our conversion. Thankfully, not only are we saved by grace, we also live by grace. Grace disciplines us to do that which is *right* in the sight of God (Titus 2:12).

In the Old Testament the Holy Spirit merely came *upon* the prophets, priests, and kings, only abiding temporarily with them. Today, every believer in Christ is *indwelt* by the Spirit of God. The promise of the Father according to prophecy clearly states: "Even the Spirit of truth; Whom the world cannot receive, because it seeth Him not, neither knoweth Him: but ye know Him; for He dwelleth with you, and shall be IN YOU" (John 14:17). What Israel received by promise, we receive by grace. As Paul says, we are "partakers of their [Israel's] spiritual things [blessings]," which includes the indwelling of the Holy Spirit (Rom. 15:27 cf. I Cor. 6:19).

The command to be "filled with the Spirit" today doesn't mean we can have more of the Spirit, rather it has the sense of the Spirit having *more of us*. Thus, if we allow the Spirit to take control of our lives He will make room for Christ.

> "Let all bitterness, and wrath, and anger, and clamour, and evil speaking, be put away from you, with all malice: and be ye kind one to another, tenderhearted, forgiving one another, even as God for Christ's sake hath forgiven you" (Eph. 4:31,32).

Forgiveness, like many other doctrines, must be studied dispensationally. Under the performance system of the law, forgiveness was based upon a *kindred* spirit. If one refused to forgive his neighbor a wrong after he had repented, God withheld forgiveness from the one who possessed the unforgiving spirit. Our Lord, who ministered under the law, also confirmed that forgiveness was *conditional*:

> "For if ye forgive men their trespasses, your heavenly Father will also forgive you: but if ye forgive not

men their trespasses, neither will your Father forgive your trespasses." (Matt. 6:14,15).

"In contrast, Paul's writings reveal that the believer in Christ today is working from a position of *perpetual* forgiveness from which he is free to forgive others."[4] Once again, this is a new revelation from the Lord of glory. We are to forgive others unconditionally, even as God for Christ's sake has forgiven us.

A life under the control of the Spirit will be characterized by a willingness to forgive others, knowing that it is well pleasing to God. Thus, Paul admonishes us: "Let all bitterness [bitter hatred] be put away from you." Notice, not *some*, but *all* bitter hatred. Perhaps an illustration concerning an all too common occurrence will help demonstrate the above. A godly wife has been forsaken by her husband. Doesn't she have every right to hate him with a perfect hatred? He ran off with another woman and left her without an income to raise three children on her own. The cynic will pronounce, "Surely forgiveness is inconceivable under such circumstances!"

But what saith the Scriptures? There is no question that the conduct of the husband was reprehensible. Most assuredly he will suffer the consequences of his actions at the judgment to come. God will deal with him at that day. Although this poor woman has suffered beyond measure, she is to forgive her erring husband.

By doing so she's acknowledging that she too is a sinner that didn't deserve God's forgiveness when He forgave her sins for Christ's sake. Forgiveness will also set her free from harboring bitterness in her heart that leads to resentment, which so often ends in violence. Delivered from the bondage of retaliation, she is now free to serve the Lord with a *pure* heart. Surely a great recompense of reward awaits all those at the Judgment Seat of Christ who are willing to forgive those who have wronged them. Incidentally, this would include forgiving *ourselves*, perhaps the highest hurdle of all.

10

Soaring in Freedom

"Be ye therefore followers of God, as dear children;
and walk in love, as Christ also hath loved us, and hath
given Himself for us an offering and a sacrifice to God
for a sweetsmelling savour."

—*Ephesians 5:1,2*

Have you heard the story of the man who was searching
for God's will? "He took his Bible, opened it at random, and
dropped his index finger onto the page. He assumed that the
verse on which his finger landed would tell him what to do.
But much to his chagrin, his finger fell on Matthew 27:5 which
says: Judas 'went and hanged himself.' Obviously the pages
must have stuck together, so the man thought he had better
try again. This time his finger came to rest on the admonition found in Luke 10:37: 'Go, and do thou likewise.' When he
followed the procedure the third time, his finger pointed to
John 13:27, which states: 'What thou doest, do quickly.'"[1]

This satirical narrative comes precariously close to reality.
It demonstrates how many believers approach the Scriptures
without regard to *dispensational distinctions*. How can we
ever hope to have a full knowledge of His will when passages
are taken out of context and merely applied devotionally?
Although many deny the distinctiveness of Paul's apostleship and message, it is the key that can unshackle those who
are prisoners of their own ignorance. Once we are enlightened to the glorious gospel of grace, grace teaches us the
importance of walking a *consistent* Christian walk.

IMITATORS OF GOD

"Be ye therefore followers of God, as dear children" (Eph. 5:1).

Most children have a vivid imagination. In fact, they usually toddle around the house talking to imaginary friends. Nothing passes by their general observation. These little ones seem to have a sixth sense when it comes to creatively getting into things. One Grandmother writes: "Our little rapscallion was one year old last Sunday and in the process of his birthday, I believe I just aged another ten years! I never saw a child with so much talent for making things run or quit running, and he is conveniently deaf when Grandpa and I are very loudly encouraging him to get out of things he's not supposed to be into." I guess it should not surprise us when they *imitate* nearly everything we do. For example, I was mowing the lawn one day when I turned around and there was Kevin (then 3 years old) following two steps behind me pushing his play lawn mower. He even sounded like the real thing!

Here in Ephesians when Paul instructs us to be "followers of God," he uses the Greek verb *mimetes* from which we get our English word "mimic." To put it simply, we are to be "imitators of God" as dearly loved children. But in what sense could we ever hope to imitate God, who is infinite?

When I attended Bible School everyone was required to take Systematic Theology. Most who have taken Theology will tell you it is about as dry as a mouth full of crackers. Fortunately, I had a gifted instructor who effectively guided us through this theological maze. And now, it is a matter of public record that I still remember something I learned in that class. Under the heading of *Theology Proper* is the topic of "Theism," a study of the belief that there is one true and living God. This subject includes the existence of God, names of God, trinity of God, His attributes, His eternal purpose, etc. Theologians (based on the Scriptures) divide the attributes of God into two groups: *noncommunicable* and *communicable*—this sure sounds like terminology that a theologian would come up with, doesn't it!

Actually, this is not as bad as it may sound: *noncommunicable* simply refers to those attributes that are *unique* to God. They clearly distinguish Him from His creation; consequently, we are unable to partake in them. For example, God is *omniscient*, that is, He has knowledge of all things. David says, "Thou knowest my downsitting and mine uprising, Thou understandest my thought afar off....For there is not a word in my tongue, but, lo, O Lord, thou knowest it all together" (Psa. 139:2,4). "I am God, and there is none like me, declaring the end from the beginning, and from ancient times the things that are not yet done, saying, My counsel shall stand, and I will do all my pleasure" (Isa. 46:9,10).

God is *omnipresent*. This is difficult for our finite minds to comprehend, but God is always *present*. He dwells in the heaven of heavens, yet He is present in the very room you are reading these words. While we are consoled by this wonderful truth, it must be a terrifying thought for the unsaved that they can never escape the eternal presence of God. Jeremiah writes: "Can any hide himself in secret places that I shall not see him? saith the Lord. Do not I fill heaven and earth? saith the Lord" (Jer. 23:24).

God is *omnipotent*. The Scriptures declare from beginning to end that God is *all-powerful*. He simply spoke and worlds came into being. In wisdom, He laid the foundation of the earth and by Him all things consist. As we noted earlier, nuclear scientists have absolutely no idea what holds positively charged protons together in the nucleus of an atom. Atoms are the building blocks of everything known to man.

Yet the protons within the atom repel each other with such force that it is nothing short of a miracle that everything in the universe is not blown into oblivion. The atom bomb the Allied Forces dropped on Hiroshima at the end of World War II showed the devastating consequences of nuclear fission. What holds the atom together? Who causes the planets to rotate on their axis' while orbiting the sun? The answer is really quite simple—God, by His almighty *power!* "All things were created by Him, and for Him: and He is before all things, and by Him all things consist [or are held together]" (Col. 1:16,17).

Communicable attributes are those attributes that we share with God, although not to the same degree or depth. They encompass love, kindness, forgiveness, mercy, etc. God is love! W. E. Vine states: "Love can be known only from the action it prompts." Hence, "We love Him, because He first loved us" (I John 4:19). God demonstrated His love for us by sending His only begotten Son to die for our sins.

As Paul says here in Ephesians 5:2, *"Christ also hath loved us, and hath given Himself for us an offering and a sacrifice to God for a sweetsmelling savour."* It is a solemn thought indeed that everything Christ accomplished at Calvary, He accomplished for us. He gave Himself both as an *offering* and a *sacrifice*. Interestingly, there is a subtle difference between these two great redemptive terms. When the Old Testament saint voluntarily brought his burnt offering to the door of the tabernacle, he brought it to *please* the Lord. Is it possible for poor wretched sinners like us to please the Lord? Is there anything we can possibly do to be acceptable in the sight of an infinitely holy God? In regard to this matter, Christ foreknew that there was nothing we could bring to please the Father, so He gave Himself as an *offering* on our behalf. Thus, if you come to God in Christ, the Father is as pleased with you as He is with His own dear Son. Little wonder the apostle says, "Wherein He hath made us accepted in the Beloved" (Eph. 1:6).

A *sacrifice* is that which *satisfies* God in relation to sin. Here again, Christ had knowledge of the just demands of the Father. In time past, the blood of bulls and goats temporarily withheld the judgment of God, but it did not have the efficacy to remove those sins for whom the sacrifices were made. The cost of redemption is dear. God requires *blood*! "Without the shedding of blood, is no remission [of sins]."

Christ loved the unlovely so deeply that He willingly gave Himself as that once-for-all sacrifice. Our sins were not merely laid on Him, as was the case of the lamb in the Old Testament. Rather, Christ bore our sins in His body (I Pet. 2:24). He was actually *identified* with our sins. "Knowing this, that our old man is crucified with Him, that the body of sin might be destroyed, that henceforth we should not serve sin" (Rom. 6:6). Christ's sacrificial death satisfied the righteousness of God, making it possible for the Son to bring us into the presence of the Father. Thus, we are forgiven and have *access* on the basis of His shed blood!

Perhaps you recently came to know the Lord, but shortly thereafter committed a hideous sin. Usually, such an unforeseen setback is a traumatic experience in a newborn's life. Satan normally complicates matters by posing the question, "How could a child of God have done such a sinful thing? Surely, God will have nothing to do with you now—you're lost!" But wait! Christ died for sins past, present and future. In fact, were not all of your sins *future* the day He died? It is indeed comforting to know that God has cast our sins into the depths of the sea, and put a sign over them that says: NO FISHING!

WALK IN LOVE

"And walk in love, as Christ also hath loved us, and hath given Himself for us an offering and a sacrifice to God for a sweetsmelling savour" (Eph. 5:2).

Christ Himself is our example of how to walk in love. Love gives of itself. When we came to Christ someone *cared*. Someone visited us and told us of the Savior's redeeming grace. Someone stopped by the hospital to pray for us. Someone loved us.

If we are walking in love we will *love* our neighbor. Paul says: "Love worketh no ill to his neighbor: therefore love is the fulfilling of the law" (Rom. 13:10). This touching true story illustrates the importance of loving our neighbor:

"Two farmers lived side by side on land that was divided by a shallow river. On a day in August the cows belonging to one of them got out of the pasture, crossed the stream, and ruined about half an acre of the ripened corn that grew along the bank. The man who owned the field was so angry that he corralled his neighbor's cattle and locked them in his own barn. After making the first farmer pay for everything they had destroyed, he continued to hold the animals hostage until a high ransom was paid for them.

"In the fall of that year, some hogs belonging to the second farmer escaped through a broken fence, crossed the stream, and invaded the potato patch of the man who owned the cows. The pigs rooted around his property, grunting happily, and caused great damage. Although the man was disturbed by the loss of his crop, he carefully rounded up the strays and began herding them back to their own pen. When their owner saw him coming, he expected trouble and got out his gun. But he soon discovered that his neighbor had no intention of harming him or his hogs.

"Coming out of the place where he had been hiding, he said in surprise, 'How can you be so kind to me after the way I treated you?' The man replied, 'Because I'm a Christian!' That evening the unsaved farmer and his wife paid a visit to the home of their good neighbor. Before they left, they had both trusted Christ—all because a consecrated believer refused to render 'evil for evil.'"[2]

Those who walk in love are to flee *"fornication, and all uncleanness, or covetousness, let it not be once named among you, as becometh saints"* (Eph. 5:3). We should carefully note the apostle's statement that these sins of the flesh are *"not to be once named among you."* The philosophy of the world is: "One time won't hurt anything; after all, you owe it to yourself. Who's going to find out?" Mark these words and mark them well, "That is the devil's lie!" Don't be deceived into thinking that "one time will not make any difference." *One* act of fornication outside of marriage could result in the deadly disease of AIDS. *One* illicit affair could destroy your marriage and emotionally traumatize your children for the rest of their lives. *One* snort of cocaine could leave you a vegetable. *One* dishonest act could destroy your reputation and name that took you a lifetime to build. It often takes years to earn the respect of those around us, but it only takes *one* foolish act to tear it all down.

"For this ye know, that no whoremonger, nor unclean person, nor covetous man, who is an idolater, hath any inheritance in the kingdom of Christ and of God" (Eph. 5:5). This passage and its counterpart in Galatians poses a perplexing problem for many. Some have concluded from Paul's statement that those who commit such sins will lose their salvation. But it must be remembered here that there is an underlying principle to consider. Under the law, the sacrificial system was designed to only cover sins of *ignorance.*

No provision was made for presumptuous sins, for God was unwilling to even entertain the thought that His people would ever sin against Him willingly (Num. 15:27-31).

Paul follows the same line of thought, insofar as those who walk in love and understand the sufferings of Christ would never be guilty of such sins. "For this ye know, those who live in sin are dead while they liveth," and therefore shall never inherit the kingdom of Christ.[3] However, we are the redeemed who have been forgiven in Christ—recipients of the heavenly inheritance (II Tim. 4:18). But what if a believer should fall from grace and commit one of these sins? We shall answer this query with two questions: Does not the blood of Jesus Christ cleanse from all sin? And, "Who shall separate us from the love of Christ"?

> "Let no man deceive you with vain words: for because of these things cometh the wrath of God upon the children of disobedience. Be not ye therefore partakers with them" (Eph. 5:6,7).

The name *Titanic* has come to be closely identified with tragedy. The story of this infamous ocean liner is a sad commentary on the *darkness* of the human heart. On April 10, 1912 the Titanic embarked on its maiden voyage from Southampton, England to New York. It is said that the Titanic was the largest, most luxurious ocean liner ever built by man's hands. Nothing was spared in the construction of this floating city. The length of the ship was over four city blocks, with spiral staircases and opulent chandeliers. Perhaps the most outstanding thing that set her apart from other ships of her day was the claim that the Titanic was the safest vessel afloat. The *White Star Line* that owned and built the ocean liner *boasted*, "She is unsinkable." After all, what could possibly go wrong with a ship that had a double hull with sixteen watertight compartments? In fact, one crew member went so far as to say, "Not even God could sink this ship!" Such reasoning may explain why there were so few lifeboats on board.

As the Titanic steamed across the Atlantic, her passengers had no way of knowing that the ship was headed for disaster. The sounds of merriment soon turned into cries of terror when the ocean liner struck an iceberg, tearing a 300-foot gash in its hull. As the Titanic was going down, the 1,513 passengers for whom there were no lifeboats sang together, "Nearer My God to Thee." Two and one-half hours later the vessel was resting 13,000 feet below the ocean's surface. Eva Hart, one of the last remaining survivors, recently stated: "The ship that not even God could sink is forever a monument to man's *arrogance!*"

The story of the Titanic is a regrettable commentary on the unfruitful *works of darkness*. The sins of pride, arrogance, greed and defiance of God were the seed plot for one of the worst tragedies in maritime history. Yet history continues to bear testimony that "Men love darkness because their deeds are evil."

While we witness passing glances of God's displeasure during this present evil age, the full measure of His wrath will be manifested against the children of disobedience in the coming day of the Lord, which closes with the Great White Throne Judgment. This will be the final chapter in God's triumph over sin.

DARKNESS AND THE ORIGIN OF EVIL

"For ye were sometimes darkness, but now are ye light in the Lord: walk as children of light" (Eph. 5:8).

"In the beginning God created the heaven and the earth. And the earth was without form, and void; and darkness was upon the face of the deep. And God said, Let there be light: and there was light" (Gen. 1:1-3). God is *light*, and therefore it is within His power to create light. And this is precisely what He did shortly after creating the earth on the first day. While most will acknowledge that God made the light, they would not be too quick to say that He created *darkness*. But Isaiah states, regarding this work of God, "I form the light, and create darkness" (Isa. 45:7). The absence of physical light implies darkness, but this does not necessarily suggest that darkness is always inherently evil. Moreover, it is easily substantiated that darkness was already in existence before the entrance of sin.

Evil entered God's creation sometime between Genesis 1:31 and 3:1 when Satan tempted our first parents. Upon surveying His creation at the end of the sixth day, God "saw every thing that He had made, and, behold, it was very good." God could have never pronounced His creation good, much less *very good*, had evil been present at this point in time. Therefore, *iniquity* was introduced shortly after this pronouncement. Now that we have narrowed down the time frame of the entrance of evil, is it possible to determine its origin? Theologians have wrestled with this question for centuries, so it is doubtful that we are going to address the matter to everyone's satisfaction. But we would like to offer some helpful suggestions.

We believe that *evil* originated with none other than Satan himself. Of course, it is essential to remember that God did not create Lucifer a sinful being. The very nature of God excludes any possibility that He conceived evil in any form. However, there is no question He did *permit* it, that His righteousness might be magnified to the praise of His *glory* (Rom. 3:5-7). Initially, Lucifer came forth from the hand of God a perfect being. "Thou sealest up the sum, full of wisdom, and perfect in beauty...Thou art the anointed cherub that covereth; and I have set thee so...Thou wast perfect in thy ways from the day that thou wast created, *till iniquity was found in thee*" (Ezek. 28:12,14,15).

By comparing Scripture with Scripture, we know there were five cherubims that originally graced the court of heaven. Apparently, Lucifer was the chief cherub who led the host of heaven in worship of our heavenly Father. He was the crown jewel of the angelic host, until *iniquity* was found in him. As the haze of creation began to burn away, Lucifer reasoned: "I will ascend into heaven, I will exalt my throne above the stars of God...I will be like the most High" (Isa. 14:13,14). So then, the beginning of the "great conflict of the ages" was not a choice between good and evil. Instead, it was a choice between *God's will* and *Lucifer's will*. Thus, when Satan chose to defy the will of God by reason of his wisdom and beauty, *pride* filled him with violence and he sinned against his Creator. Hence, the evil we witness about us today is a direct result of *his transgression*. When our first parents yielded to the tempter's deception, they brought death and darkness upon the whole human race. This spiritual darkness keeps men from the love of God and leads to eternal condemnation.

Darkness, then, is closely associated with unrighteousness, willing ignorance of God, and wickedness. Here in Ephesians the apostle states to his hearers, *"For ye were sometimes darkness"* (Eph. 5:8). Please notice in regard to our former manner of life that Paul did not say, "we were in darkness," although that is true too! Rather, we "were darkness." Darkness emanated from every fiber of our being. We hated God and were by nature the children of wrath. Why does a dog bark? Because it has a dog's nature. Likewise, a man sins because he is a sinner by nature. This demonstrates the importance of the sovereignty of God in salvation—without it the natural man has no hope of being saved.

THE LIGHT OF THE GOSPEL

"But now are ye light in the Lord" (Eph. 5:8). Notice, once again, that the apostle does not merely say "we are in the light" but rather we *are* light. *Light* speaks of righteousness, knowledge, and truth. As a wise old preacher once said: "God is light! In Him is no darkness and in us is no darkness, for we are light. The darkness is gone. Beloved, God is telling you what you *are*, not what you can be. If God has made you light, you don't have to try to be light."

Every form of life has its *enemies*. Birds prey on insects, but will flee to the heavens when a cat is present. Walk into a classroom of second graders sneezing and coughing and you will soon learn that those little things called germs will leave you feeling poorly. The chief enemy of the light is darkness. Your very presence in the midst of the unfruitful works of darkness will make the unbeliever *uncomfortable*. Oftentimes they will turn downright vicious when exposed to the truth of God's Word. A case in point is found in the Book of Acts, where it is said that upon entering the city of Ephesus, Paul and his companions spoke against the goddess Diana. The apostle boldly proclaimed that there are no gods made with hands. This caused "no small stir" among those who profited from selling silver shrines of Diana. The magnificence of Diana was well known throughout the world. In fact, many came from great distances to worship the image that bore her name. The craftsmen, led by a man named Demetrius, feared that Paul would turn the city against Diana and cause her downfall.

The forces of darkness were not about to take this lying down. They waged an all-out attack attempting to extinguish the light of the gospel. The opposition became so intense that the whole city was filled with confusion. "Some therefore cried one thing, and some another." This unruly mob, most of whom did not even know why they were in the streets, shouted with one voice for the better part of two hours, "Great is Diana of the Ephesians." It was only by the grace of God that Paul and his fellow companions escaped Ephesus with their lives (Acts 19:23-41).

Those who *walk in the light* show the unsaved the way to Christ. I had this very experience some years ago when I was a foreman at *Mine Safety Appliance Company* in Pittsburgh. Upon learning that I was a believer, most of those that I worked with went out of their way to avoid me. Others thought they could have a little fun using those famous titles—Holy Joe, Preacher, or The Reverend. One foreman in particular sought to be especially belligerent when I was present. He was a huge man who walked around the building chewing on nails for entertainment. The brighter my light shone in the plant the more, it seemed, the vulgarities of this man increased. I learned long ago the importance of keeping my eyes on the Lord, so for the most part I was unaffected by his ungodly conduct.

Interestingly, one evening at the close of my shift, he asked if I would stay over to assist him with a problem we were having with one of the injection molding machines. I agreed to stay and was somewhat surprised that he seemed to be guarded in his speech. About 2:00 a.m. he invited me to the cafeteria for a cup of coffee. Thinking the worst, I figured he would get me down to the loading dock and stuff me in a drum and ship me off to Topeka!

However, we no sooner sat down at the table when the tears began to stream down his face. He looked up at me and said, "Paul, I don't know how to say this, but I am not right with God. I can no longer bear the terrible guilt of my sins. I didn't know where to turn, so I was wondering if you could show me how to be right with God." After a lengthy discussion, I am happy to report that he trusted Christ as his personal Savior, and as long as I live, I shall never forget that night! That experience taught me how essential it is to always walk *consistently* in the light of God's grace.

In biblical times, Eastern caravans used lamps and torches to guide them through the darkness. The lamp was fed with oil which in turn caused the wick to burn, thus producing *light*. In like manner, the Holy Spirit illuminates us to Paul's revelation that we might walk *worthy* of our calling today.

"For the fruit of the spirit is in all goodness and righteousness and truth" (Eph. 5:9). The fruit of the Spirit—goodness, righteousness and truth are the moral results of walking in the light. When a friend inquired of Charles Spurgeon if he could write the story of his life, he responded, "Feel free to write it in the heavens, I have nothing to hide."

Beloved, could you pass the *test* of Daniel? For several months his enemies *secretly spied* on him, but the Scriptures state concerning Daniel: "they could find none occasion nor fault; forasmuch as he was faithful, neither was there any error or fault found in him" (Dan. 6:4). Daniel walked in the light; can the same be said of you?

THINGS TO REMEMBER

"Proving what is acceptable unto the Lord" (Eph. 5:10). Having shown the importance of walking as the children of light, the apostle now gives us further instructions as how to accomplish this objective to the glory of God. First, we must understand the necessity of "proving what is acceptable unto the Lord" (Eph. 5:10). Proving has the idea of putting things to a *test*. A painter who is painting the second story of a house always tests the first or second rung of his ladder to insure it is safe before he ascends thirty feet into

the air. Although we build protective hedges around these earthly tabernacles, we are often somewhat careless when it comes to our spiritual lives. How many times believers fall victim to a faulty decision making process, simply because they failed to ask the simple question, "What is God's will in this matter?"

The spiritually minded man proves all things to determine what is *acceptable* in the eyes of the Lord. This can only be achieved by having a well-rounded knowledge of the Scriptures. The Word of God is our guide to ascertain whether a thing "is" or "is not" well-pleasing to the Lord. Perhaps a few examples will help make this crystal clear. First, there are those who advocate overthrowing the government on the basis that it is *corrupt*. They claim the powers that be have no right to rule over us, since they have departed from the "letter" of the U. S. Constitution. But, is this the Lord's will?

We would do well to remember that the Lord placed Himself under the authority of Rome, which was the epitome of corruption. And He instructed His disciples to render unto "Caesar the things which are Caesar's" (Matt. 22:17-22). Paul says, "Let every soul be subject unto the higher powers. For there is no power but of God: the powers that be are ordained of God. Whosoever therefore resisteth the power, resisteth the ordinance of God....For he is the minister of God to thee for good" (Rom. 13:1,2,4). Furthermore, we are told to pray for "kings, and for all that are in authority;" Why? "that we may lead a quiet and peaceable life in all godliness and honesty" (I Tim. 2:2). There is little question that our present form of government leaves much to be desired, but the alternative is *anarchy*, such as we have seen in third world countries.

Second, young couples today seem to think that living together is a viable option to marriage, at least until they decide if they are compatible! Compatibility is a myth when we bear in mind that we must *learn* to love one another in a relationship (Titus 2:4). When problems find their way into a marriage, it will make little difference if both the husband and wife enjoy attending a soccer match. What should matter is what the Lord thinks about this arrangement. "For this is the will of God, even your sanctification, that ye should abstain from fornication: that every one of you should know how to possess his vessel in sanctification and honor" (I Thes. 4:3,4).

Thirdly, suppose for a moment that someone brutally beat you up and robbed you. What would your reaction be to this type of treatment? Probably, the word that comes to mind is, Revenge! with a capital "R". However, the Lord would have us respond accordingly: Shortly after Matthew Henry had been accosted by thieves, he wrote in his diary: "Let me be thankful first, because I was never robbed before; second, because, although they took my wallet, they did not take my life; third, because, although they took my all, it was not much; and fourth, because it was I who was robbed, not I who robbed." Sadly, I fear that many today would be seething with animosity if this were to befall them. But Matthew Henry had learned the importance of heeding the apostle's words, "In every thing give thanks: for this is the will of God in Christ Jesus concerning you" (I Thes. 5:18).

> "And have no fellowship with the unfruitful works of darkness, but rather reprove them....But all things that are reproved are made manifest by the light: for whatsoever doth make manifest is light" (Eph. 5:11,13).

Notice that the apostle does not say that it is permissible to have "some" fellowship with the unfruitful works of darkness. Rather, he states, have "no" fellowship with them! We are living in a day, however, when the "spirit of new evangelicalism" pervades the Church. It suggests that the Scriptures are no longer relevant. Thus, their philosophy is that, to win souls in these modern times, we must develop meaningful relationships with the unsaved. As we have seen, this denies the basic principle of *separation* that is taught throughout the Scriptures. God has always required that His people be separated unto Him in every age.

When God raised Israel from the quagmire of humanity, He gave her a system of laws that made her *stand out* from the other nations around her. He accomplished this through her worship, dress, diet, marriage regulations, and ceremonial laws. She was to be a *peculiar* people unto Him—a light shining in a dark place. Although we have passed from law to the dispensation of Grace, the principle of separation is still an integral part of God's plans and purposes. God says, "Be ye not unequally yoked together with unbelievers: for what fellowship hath righteousness with unrighteousness? and what communion hath light with darkness?...Wherefore come out from among them, and be ye separate, saith the Lord" (II Cor. 6:14,17). Believers are never to establish unholy alliances, partnerships, or marriages with the unfruitful works of darkness. The end result is usually heartache if we do.

Of course, we must be careful to distinguish between *separation* and *isolation*. Believers are in the world, but are not to be of the world. We are to have contact with the unbeliever, if for no other reason than to share the gospel with them. Nevertheless, we must never partake in their manner of life. Someone once asked me if I would have dinner with the unsaved. My reply—absolutely! However, should they invite me to join them for a social drink, my response is always the same: "I am sorry, but I am under the influence of the gospel, and therefore, never indulge."

We, too, are a *peculiar* people—a light shining in a dark place (Titus 2:14). As kids, it was great fun to go out behind an old barn and pick up a rotten piece of wood to see what creatures lurked below. When the *light* hits those "critters of darkness" underneath that board, they scatter like a crowd running out of a burning building!! It is much the same way with the Christian life. If a believer walks into a room filled with unbelievers, before long most of them are headed for the exit. The ones who do remain normally congregate with other workers of darkness, ignoring the fact that you are even in the room. Perchance if someone does pass by, you can be sure the conversation is going to be short and sweet. Hence, light *reproves* the works of darkness whether in action, word or deed.

> "Wherefore he saith, Awake thou that sleepest, and arise from the dead, and Christ shall give thee light" (Eph. 5:14).

Here the apostle likens the believer to one who has been lulled to sleep by the attractions of the world. He challenges the child of God to arise from the dead, that is, "from among the dead." In other words, we are not to entangle ourselves with the affairs of those who are spiritually dead. Time is too precious of a commodity to be wasted on things that have no eternal value.

When I was a little boy my grandmother used to come into my bedroom at 6:30 a.m., throw open the blinds, and say, "Rise and shine, surely you're not going to sleep the day away!" If it was up to me, I probably would have committed the unpardonable sin and slept until 11:30. Grandma was on the cutting edge of what we call today "time management."

After we believe, God wants to manage our time, since we are prone to wander through a maze of selfish pursuits.

Thus, we are to set our affections upon things above, and not upon the things of this earth. Whatever ministry God has called us to, He would have us *prioritize* our time so that as much as possible might be accomplished for the cause of Christ. The life and ministry of the Apostle Paul during the Acts period is a classic example (see Acts chapter 20). As a result of our being actively involved in the Lord's service, Paul says, "Christ shall give thee light." How? "The entrance of thy Words giveth light; it giveth understanding unto the simple" (Psa. 119:130). The Word of God, rightly divided, will direct our every step along the pathway of righteousness for His name's sake.

a. Walk Circumspectly

"See then that ye walk circumspectly, not as fools, but as wise, redeeming the time, because the days are evil" (Eph. 5:15,16).

As Paul penned these words from his musty prison cell in Rome, he knew it would not be long before a great persecution would descend upon the Church. Storm clouds were already beginning to form on the horizon. Consequently, it was only a matter of time before the Church would be tempered in the fires of martyrdom. In fact, this blood bath was to continue for nearly three hundred years and has come to be known as the *Heroic Age*. Since the days were growing more and more evil, the apostle wisely instructed the saints of that day to walk *circumspectly*. In other words, they were to walk pointedly, accurately, with precision. Vine comments, "The word expresses that accuracy which is the outcome of *carefulness*."

Our troops are often sent overseas to help keep the peace between warring factions. They soon learned that the greatest threat to their well-being isn't the harsh winters or snipers, but rather, "land mines." Our boys are taught to avoid areas where mines are known to be located. When walking along roadways they are to keep their eyes peeled for trip cords that might detonate an explosion. And the rule of thumb is to *never* pick up any object off the ground or you may find yourself in eternity.

As soldiers of the Cross, we too must be very careful regarding our every step. The ground upon which we walk must be cautiously surveyed to avoid the *perils* of this evil world system. With the close of this age nearly upon us, Paul's warning that "perilous times shall come" is poignant (II Tim. 3:1). Should we be called upon to endure another persecution as did our forebearers, the apostle's charge to walk circumspectly and to redeem the time will take on a new meaning.

> "As we have therefore opportunity, let us do good unto all men, especially unto them who are of the household of faith" (Gal. 6:10).

We should never give the devil an occasion to discredit us due to a lack of credibility on our part. Paul's letter to Philemon is a good example of walking circumspectly in action—one which we all will do well to heed.

b. Paul's Friend, Philemon

> "Paul, a prisoner of Jesus Christ, and Timothy our brother, unto Philemon our dearly beloved, and fellowlaborer" (Philemon 1:1).

Up to this point in time Paul had never visited Colosse, which indicates to us that Philemon had apparently traveled to Ephesus, where he was personally led to a saving knowledge of Christ by the apostle (Acts 19:10 cf. Philemon 1:19). The gospel transforms lives. Thus, soon after Philemon's conversion he endeared himself to Paul, who refers to his friend as *"dearly beloved, and fellowlaborer."*

Are you *involved* in some area of the Lord's work? Philemon was! When the need arose for a testimony of grace at Colosse he rolled up his sleeves and established a church in his home.

Even though he was a wealthy man, this did not deter him from carrying on a fruitful ministry among the saints. In other words, when there was a need he did something about it. What a lesson to many wealthy Christians today! Philemon was one of those saints who loved the Lord so deeply that one could not help but be encouraged when in his presence (Philemon 1:4-7). Yes, we need more Philemons today!

And now Paul is about to give his friend another opportunity to *prove* his love on the basis of a very special request.

1. Paul's Request

"I beseech thee for my son Onesimus, whom I have begotten in my bonds: which in time past was to thee unprofitable, but now profitable to thee and to me" (Philemon 1:10,11).

Philemon was probably somewhat surprised when he first learned that one of his slaves by the name of Onesimus had fled. He undoubtedly felt as a Christian that he had at least been fair with him. We are not told why Onesimus ran away from his master, although it is difficult for us to believe that Philemon was a cruel taskmaster in view of verses 4-7.

Perhaps Onesimus departed to parts unknown simply because he wanted his freedom, or could it be that he was running from the gospel that had been faithfully proclaimed by his master? It would not be the first time an unbeliever had fled from the presence of a so-called "religious fanatic." In the event that the latter is the case, Onesimus ran right into the arms of the greatest evangelist of all time—Paul! (Philemon 1:10).

For the next few moments let's place ourselves in the sandals of Onesimus: After we slip away from the household of Philemon where is a slave to go? Well, one need only to make his way to a big city, such as Rome, and get lost in the crowd so as not to be too conspicuous. But now there is a more pressing problem. How do we get a change of clothing? If we see an inmate who has just broken out of *Leavenworth* his attire singles him out as a prisoner. In Onesimus' case, the rags he was wearing cried "I'm a slave!" Before we resolve this problem though there is a more urgent matter—hunger! One could not eat at the posh restaurants of Rome without money. Therefore, the combination of being a fugitive with no income normally results in a life of *crime*.

In all likelihood Onesimus was caught stealing something, and when it was discovered he was a runaway slave it landed him in a Roman prison. It was Martin Luther who said, "we are all Onesimi [unprofitable]." In the words of one author, "we have trampled God's grace, turned from our rightful Master and spurned His love."

It isn't hard to imagine a voice from a dark corner of the prison cell inquiring of the new prisoner, "Where are you from, my son?" "I am Onesimus, a runaway slave from the house of Philemon." Coincidence? This has been the conclusion of some. However, we believe it was *providence*. The apostle implies this as well when he writes the following to Philemon: *"For perhaps he therefore departed for a season, that thou shouldest receive him forever."*

Shortly after the apostle had led Onesimus to the Lord he wrote one of his most touching personal letters to Philemon.

Paul requested of his friend to forgive his bondslave for leaving and receive him back as a brother in Christ. Furthermore, should he desire to give Onesimus his freedom to minister to the needs of the apostle, his gesture of good will would be received with thanksgiving.

2. Doing That Which is Right

"Whom [referring to Onesimus] I would have retained with me, that in thy stead he might have ministered unto me in the bonds of the gospel: but without thy mind would I do nothing; that thy benefit should not be as it were of necessity, but willingly" (Philemon 1:13,14).

In the minds of some, these days, the end justifies the means. There are those in the ministry who see absolutely nothing wrong with using deceitful means to enhance their notoriety. Surely the fulness of God's blessing will never abide with those who stoop to such things. For this cause, the Apostle Paul was very, very careful never to place himself in a position where his actions might justly be called into question.

A case in point is his decision to return Onesimus to his rightful owner. Paul could have exercised his apostolic authority, demanding that Philemon set his bondslave free for the sake of the gospel. We are sure that the apostle could have pointed to a number of reasons why it would be acceptable for him [Paul] to retain Onesimus. He felt, however, that this might be perceived as a misuse of his God-given authority. In light of the above, consider the following passage which is found in II Corinthians 8:21:

"Providing for honest things, not only in the sight of the Lord, but also in the sight of men."

"Providing for," that is, go out of our way to attend to every detail that there may be no room for even the appearance of evil. Paul practiced what he preached! Roman law mandated that fugitive slaves were to be returned to their owners without delay. The *honest* thing to do then, was to make arrangements for Onesimus to be sent back from whence he came. In so doing the apostle obeyed the governmental powers and averted circumstances which might have brought shame on the name of Christ.

Furthermore, the decision as to whether to keep Onesimus was not Paul's to make, since he was the property of someone else. The only proper thing to do was to return what did not belong to him. Such integrity is indeed refreshing, and we may be sure that Philemon never forgot the apostle's determination to do what was *right*.

> "Having confidence in thy obedience I wrote unto thee, knowing that thou wilt also do more than I say" (Philemon 1:21).

Most runaway slaves were put to death by their masters as a deterrent to others who might consider making the same mistake. But *"love suffereth long, and is kind...is not easily provoked...endureth all things."* Philemon *proved* his love once again by foregoing any type of punishment and received Onesimus with open arms as a brother beloved in the Lord. This conclusion is made on the basis that Philemon would have never permitted this letter to be made public if he had tortured Onesimus or had him put to death. In all probability he was sent back to the apostle with thanksgiving.

Far too many believers fail to see the importance of living a righteous Christian life. Like Lot, they are *"vexed with the filthy conversation of the wicked. For that righteous man dwelling among them, in seeing and hearing, vexed his righteous soul from day to day with their unlawful deeds"* (II Pet. 2:7-8). The sins of pride, lying and deceit are all too common among the Lord's people. It's becoming more and more difficult to tell the difference between the world and the Church.

Many are of the mind that only pastors are expected to live lives that are above reproach. But the Holy Spirit teaches us that this is the will of God in Christ Jesus for every believer. The Lord's standard of righteousness applies to *all*, for we must *all* stand before the Judgment Seat of Christ. Those who do "right" will have the praise of God.

c. Walk Not as Fools

> "See then that ye walk circumspectly, not as fools, but as wise, redeeming the time, because the days are evil. Wherefore be ye not unwise, but understanding what the will of the Lord is" (Eph. 5:15-17).

Paul cautions us further that we are to "walk circumspectly, not as fools [unwise]." Perhaps the simplest definition for the term "fool" in this particular passage is: an unthinking one, someone who lacks discernment. Those who live for themselves are *unwise*. The parable of the "Rich Fool" is a good example. The fields of the rich man brought forth plentifully, so much so that he decided to tear down his old barns and build bigger and better ones. He boasted, "Soul, thou hast much goods laid up for many years; take thine ease, eat, drink, and be merry. But God said unto him, Thou fool, this night thy soul shall be required of thee: then whose shall those things be, which thou hast provided?" (Luke 12:19,20).

A *fool* is one who reasons that abundance is security. He flatters himself with all of his achievements, but fails to remember that life is as the flower of the field. The unwise man's possessions are his life. Of course, there is nothing wrong with having material possessions. The problem arises when they *possess* you! Essentially, the apostle is admonishing us to make sure we have our *priorities* straight. Those who walk circumspectly desire to live for the Lord, not themselves. The things of this world hold little attraction to those who are fully surrendered.

d. Redeeming the Time

Time is a very precious commodity—here one minute, gone the next! It is said that Jonathan Edwards wrote in his diary at the age of twenty: "Resolved, never to lose one moment of time, but improve it in the most profitable way I possibly can." If we were to paraphrase "redeeming the time," it would probably come out something like this: "Making wise use of the opportunities we are given." This, of course, transcends every area of our Christian experience.

Here's a case in point. I was returning from special meetings down south recently when I met with an unexpected delay. I will spare you the details, only to say that it was a day after my original departure time before the airline re-routed me through Indianapolis to Milwaukee. Usually, I take these types of things in stride, concluding they are all in the providence of God. Shortly after our departure, I struck up a conversation with the gentleman sitting beside me. He found it interesting that I was a pastor and almost immediately seemed open to spiritual things.

He shared with me that he was a corporate leader for the Chrysler Corporation and was returning to Indianapolis to straighten out a problem created by some of the company's young financial wizards. In the course of our conversation, he shared with me how he was semi-retired from the company and recently had open-heart surgery. It was obvious that eternal things were on his mind after having a near brush with death.

Turning to spiritual matters, I asked him if he was *perfect*. "Well, nobody's perfect, but I have done my best to do good, and even go to church occasionally." I responded, if you want to spend eternity with a holy and righteous God, He demands that you must be *perfect*. I continued to share with him that he could be perfect in Christ, simply by believing that Christ died for His sins and rose again. We talked for a few minutes along these lines, but it was clear that I wasn't getting through to him.

As we ate lunch, it dawned on me to use an accounting illustration with a spiritual application. After all, this gentleman was a CPA for a major corporation. I made my case, and concluded by adding this little tidbit. Look at it like this, if you believe the gospel, the *debt* of your sins will be *paid in full* from Christ's "finished work" account. Therefore, your account is *reconciled* on the basis of His shed blood. In addition, a *withdrawal* will be made from Christ's righteousness and *deposited* to your account. You now stand "complete" in Him. Without a moment's hesitation, he received Christ! When you are "redeeming the time," time flies by! (no pun intended). The next thing I knew, the plane was touching down in Indianapolis and we were going our separate ways.

We must also take advantage of the *opportunities* which come our way to tell others about the Mystery. You would be amazed at the number who have written us to share how their search for the truth came to an end when one of our "grace people" opened Paul's gospel to them. The letters usually go something like this: "I *sensed* there was something more, but I just couldn't put my finger on it until I heard the Word, rightly divided!" We tend to rationalize that our Christian friends are so entrenched in denominationalism that they would never receive this message, even if we did tell them. This may be true, but how many opportunities have been passed by, due to our reluctance to open our mouth *boldly* to make known the Mystery?

Perhaps we need to write these words anew on the tablets of our hearts: "Walk circumspectly, not as fools, but as wise, redeeming the time, because the days are evil."

BEING FILLED WITH THE SPIRIT

"And be not drunk with wine, wherein is excess; but be filled with the Spirit" (Eph. 5:18).

What high and lofty places God has called some of His humble servants to in these closing hours of the dispensation of Grace. Some of these dear saints have advanced the cause of Christ to such heights and depths that we can only shudder at our lack of interest and ineffectiveness.

The story is told of the 17th century English pastor, Richard Baxter, who preached with great intensity because he saw himself as a dying man ministering to dying people. He always spoke as if he were preaching his last sermon and as if his listeners were hearing their last message. And what a schedule he maintained for 50 years!

Every Monday and Tuesday he spent 7 hours instructing the children of his assembly, not omitting even one child. On Wednesday he went from house to house to make sure that the material needs of the widows, the aged, and the infirmed were met. During the rest of the week he prepared sermons and wrote books—a total of 160 volumes.

As a result of his ministry, the town of Kidderminister was transformed. It had been a place full of immorality and vice, but it became a village in which nearly every household honored God, read the Bible and prayed. Baxter's consuming zeal had reaped a rich spiritual harvest.[4]

It was said of John Knox of Scotland, "He preached with such power that the people actually clung to their seats in fear and trembling." When Jonathan Edwards preached his famed sermon "Sinners in the Hands of an Angry God," the unbelievers who were present literally held onto one another, fearing lest they were slipping away into the fires of hell. They even cried aloud, "What must we do to be saved?" It was not uncommon for Charles Spurgeon to preach to thousands at a time, most of whom were captivated by his vivid descriptions of the wonders of God's grace.

One life can make a difference. But how do we explain why some believers seem to accomplish so much for the Lord while others struggle to maintain their spiritual balance? It could be concluded that the Baxters, Knoxs, Edwards, and Spurgeons of the faith are placed in positions where they can achieve more. True! But position doesn't necessarily guarantee spirituality or that the cause of Christ will be advanced. We have all witnessed humble members of the Body whose knowledge of the Word, rightly divided would put most spiritual leaders to shame. The key lies with being *filled* with the Spirit.

a. The Operation of the Spirit

The operation of the Spirit today is much different from His dealings with those on the day of Pentecost. The Jewish believers at Pentecost were all *supernaturally* filled with the Holy Spirit. Thus they were under the complete control of the Spirit, which enabled them to speak in tongues, heal the sick, and raise the dead. These miraculous manifestations were accomplished under the auspices of the *Great Commission*. This commission with its signs, miracles, and wonders would have evidently ushered in the millennial kingdom had the leaders in Israel believed. However, with the setting aside of Israel, the sign gifts of the Acts period have ceased.

During the present administration of Grace, we are instructed "to be filled with the Spirit." This is a *goal* the Lord has set before us that may be attained through Bible study and prayer. When the apostle states, "And be not drunk with wine, wherein is excess, but be filled with the Spirit," he is *not* implying that the effects of being filled with the Spirit are going to be the same as someone under the influence of alcohol. Being led by the Spirit doesn't leave one in a spiritual stupor. Nor will it cause erratic behavior that would be unbecoming of Christ.

Paul is merely seeking to strike a *contrast* between the *flesh* and the *Spirit*. It may seem shocking at first that the apostle would need to remind believers that excessive drinking is a sin, yet many still struggle with this problem today. "Wine is a mocker, strong drink is raging: and whosoever is deceived thereby is not wise" (Prov. 20:1). The drunkard staggers around out of control, usually muttering things that are unintelligible. By contrast, those who are led by the Spirit will always bear the fruit of the Spirit, which is love, joy, peace, long-suffering, gentleness, goodness, faith, meekness, and *temperance*. Both are powerful *influences*—one destroys relationships while the other strengthens them.

We learn from I Corinthians chapter six that our body is the temple of the Holy Spirit, which dwells within us. As we saw earlier, being filled with the Spirit has nothing to do with having more of the Spirit; He already abides within. Rather, it involves the Spirit possessing more of us. Essentially, it is allowing Him to take control of our thoughts, actions, and manner of speech. If we make room for the Spirit, He will make room for Christ.

Normally, we rarely go into the grammatical structure of a passage for fear of losing some of our readers. But in this particular case we are going to make an exception, since it will help enrich our understanding. Bear with us for a moment and we think you will agree.

A.T. Robertson[5] points out that Paul's phraseology here in Ephesians 5:18 is in the *imperative mood*. The imperative mood simply means that the thing stated is emphatic or urgent. In other words, "be filled with the Spirit" isn't a suggestion, but a *command* of Christ. The believer, then, is responsible to *yield* to the Spirit so that He might bring honor and glory to God through him. For example, Paul was bold as a lion in his defense of the gospel, yet he spoke the truth in love (Acts 26:1-32). He was never sarcastic or demeaning with those to whom he spoke. These are the fruits of the flesh. Those under the influence of the Spirit live according to the command: "Let your speech be alway with grace, seasoned with salt, that ye may know how ye ought to answer every man" (Col. 4:6).

Moulton[6] adds that the verb "be filled" is *plural*, which indicates the filling of the Spirit is available to *all* members of the Body of Christ. It isn't reserved merely for a select few who claim to have received the so-called second blessing of the Spirit. The second blessing is alleged to be a special anointing which endows the recipient with power from on high. While there are many sincere believers (though sincerely wrong) who feel they have been supernaturally empowered by the Holy Spirit, there are also many *deceivers* among us.

Some of our present day televangelists are a good example. They claim to be a lightning rod in the hand of God, often working their audiences into an *emotional* frenzy. With a hotline to heaven, they intuitively know the names of individuals in their audience whom they have never met. This display of supernatural insight is normally followed by the evangelist swaying back and forth with his eyes closed. Ostensibly moved by the Spirit, he now begins to reveal the various afflictions of those that he called out by name, healing them on the spot, or so he would have us believe.

Hear these words and hear them well, this is not the operation of the Spirit during the administration of Grace. Incidentally, the deception of these unscrupulous men was recently exposed out West. It was discovered that as unsuspecting souls entered the auditorium they were asked to fill out a card with their name and why they attended the meeting. Of course, those who had ailments naturally wrote them down and requested prayer. Since the evangelist is usually on the platform when the people file in they are easily drawn into the scam.

After an hour or so of hand clapping, singing, prayer, and emotional testimonies the evangelist steps forward to draw his listeners into the trap. The hotline to heaven was actually the evangelist's wife whispering by remote control into her husband's earpiece the first and last names of those who wrote down their afflictions. Surely we are living in the last days! As we know, the apostle has warned us: "evil men and seducers shall wax worse and worse, deceiving, and being deceived" (II Tim. 3:13).

b. Manifestation of the Filling of the Spirit

"Speaking to yourselves in psalms and hymns and spiritual songs, singing and making melody in your heart to the Lord" (Eph. 5:19).

Those who allow the Spirit to become a part of the fabric of their lives always desire to *worship* the Lord. The phrase, "speaking to yourselves" suggests that we are never to forsake the assembling of ourselves together with those of like-precious faith. Since God blesses on the basis of His Word, the *central* point of our worship must always be the preaching of Jesus Christ according to the revelation of the Mystery. This includes the singing of "hymns and spiritual songs, singing and making melody in your heart to the Lord."

Interestingly, the apostle says we are to make a *melody* in our heart, which stands in opposition to the music of the world. When Moses came down from the mount after receiving the Ten Commandments, Joshua met him and said: "There is a noise of war in the camp. And he [Moses] said, It is not the voice of them that shout for mastery, neither is it the voice of them that cry for being overcome: but the noise of them that sing do I hear" (Ex. 32:17-18). The beat and rhythm of heathen music echoed throughout the valley. Such music is *sensual* and turned Israel's attention away from the living God to the wickedness of Egypt.

God would have us to understand that the things which "were written aforetime were written for our learning." In order to avoid committing the same errors of those in time past, we must never attempt to integrate the world's music into the Church. Furthermore, we have always been an advocate that not only should we preach the truth, we must also *sing* the truth. It seems terribly inconsistent to sing the hymn *Marching to Zion*, then have the speaker stand up and declare we have a heavenly hope and calling. Imagine attending a worship service where the pastor brings a stirring message on the "One Baptism" and the song leader closes the service with, *"In Jordan's Stream."*

While there are many contemporary songs that glorify the Lord, most Christian music today is *subjective*. It emphasizes *self*—what I did for the Lord. Thus pronouns like *I, me,* and *my* are prominent throughout the song. Here are a few examples: "**My** Place in This World," "**I'll** Be on **My** Knees," "**People** Need the Lord," "Sing **Your** Praise to the Lord." In contrast, almost all of the great hymns of the faith are *objective*. That is, the object of the hymn is God, who He is, and what He has accomplished for us. For example: "A Mighty Fortress is Our **God**," "How Great **Thou** Art!," "Great

251

is **Thy** Faithfulness," "Wonderful Grace of **Jesus**," "Glory to **His** Name," etc.

The reader will recall that when Paul and Silas were put into prison they "prayed, and sang praises unto God: and the prisoners heard them" (Acts 16:25). Only the Spirit-filled believer would be able to sing songs of praise in the face of such adversity. Clearly Paul and Silas preached the gospel to those weary sinners incarcerated with them. Then they *sang* songs of praise in the night, praises to God, which reverberated throughout the cold, damp halls of the dungeon.

To demonstrate the power of the gospel in word and song, when the earthquake shook the foundations of the prison "immediately all the doors were opened, and everyone's bands were loosed. And the keeper of the prison awaking out of his sleep, and seeing the prison doors open, he drew out his sword, and would have killed himself, supposing that the prisoners had been fled. But Paul cried with a loud voice, saying, Do thyself no harm: for we are all here." Apparently this small band of prisoners was *saved* through Paul's testimony and decided that the right thing to do was remain with the apostle. The Philippian jailer was so moved by the experience that he too was saved.

"Giving thanks always for all things unto God and the Father in the name of our Lord Jesus Christ" (Eph. 5:20). Those who are guided by the Spirit will always give thanks for all things. "All things" here involve both the *physical* and *spiritual* blessings God has bestowed upon us. Paul gave thanks for physical healing, food, traveling grace, God's providential care, spiritual enlightenment, etc. (Phil. 2:25-30; I Tim. 4:3-5; Rom. 1:8-12; Phil. 1:12-20; Eph. 1:15-18).

Like the Apostle Paul, the Pilgrim fathers firmly believed in the providence of God, and were *grateful* for it, as we should

252

be. In regard to what has come to be known as the "First Encounter" with the Indians, William Bradford recorded these words in his journal:

"Thus it pleased God to vanquish their enemies and give them deliverance; and by His special providence so to dispose that not any one of them were either hurt or hit, though their arrows came close by them and on every side of them. [Many of their coats which hung on the barricade were shot through and through]. Afterwards they gave God solemn thanks and praise for their deliverance, and gathered up a bundle of their arrows and sent them into England afterward by the master of the ship...."

"Submitting yourselves one to another in the fear of God" (Eph. 5:21). Although there are many other areas of walking in the Spirit, Paul closes with the need to *submit* to one another in the fear of God. The question frequently arises within the local assembly as to who's in charge. Of course, it's the Lord's work, therefore we are serving Him. But God would have us do all things decently and in order. Humanly speaking, then, both the pastor and the elders are charged with the oversight of the church under God (I Tim. 5:17). They must submit to one another as they strive together to keep the ministry in the center of God's will.

It is important to remember that there is always *accountability* in the Lord's work. The missionary is accountable to the mission board, the president to his board of directors, the pastor to the elders, and the elders to the congregation. Even Paul, the apostle of the Gentiles, reported to the elders at Antioch at the close of each of his apostolic journeys.

"And when they [leaders at Antioch] had fasted and prayed, and laid their hands on them [Paul and Barnabas], they sent them away" (Acts 13:3).

"And when they had preached the word in Perga, they went down into Attalia: and thence sailed to Antioch, from whence they had been recommended to the grace of God for the work which they fulfilled. And when they were come, and had gathered the church together, they *rehearsed* all that God had done with them, and how He had opened the door of faith unto the Gentiles" (Acts 14:25-27).

"And be not drunk with wine, wherein is excess; but be filled with the Spirit." The filling of the Spirit today is a *continual* appropriation of the fruit of the Spirit, that we might walk worthy of our calling. Once again, it is allowing Him to take control of our life to the praise of God's glory.

11

Keeping the Home Fire Burning

"Submitting yourselves one to another in the fear of
God. Wives, submit yourselves unto your own husbands,
as unto the Lord. For the husband is the head of the
wife, even as Christ is the Head of the Church: and He
is the Saviour of the Body."

—*Ephesians 5:21-23*

It has been correctly said that there is a vast difference
between a Christian home and place where Christians dwell.
Simply because a number of family members know the Lord
does not necessarily mean that there is peace, harmony, and
a spiritual climate in that home. Unfortunately, we are witnessing some very troubling trends today when it comes to
the Christian home. Let's face it, many marriages are in
trouble and much of the ungodly counsel given by the world
is *unsound*.

Mr. James Weed of the *National Center for Health Statistics* has determined that newlyweds today have a greater than
50% chance of being divorced at some point in the future.
Although studies differ, the current rate of marriages ending
in divorce is estimated to be as follows: First year of marriage–61.6% end in divorce, five years–51.9%, and ten years–
40%. Those are sobering statistics, that should cause each of
us to ask the question: What can be done to turn the tide?

The solution is really quite simple; we must submit ourselves to the Author and Finisher of our faith, who *designed*
marriage in the beginning. Of course, the skeptic is quick

to point out that there are no easy answers to deeply rooted marital problems. We've all heard it said: "You don't understand." Well, after twenty-some years of counseling couples, it boils down to this: pride, stubbornness, carnality, and a *failure* to apply God's roles in the marriage relationship.

The goal of every married couple, indeed, every Christian home, should be to make Christ the Head, the Counselor, and the Guide. Barbara B. Hart has captured the very essence of this in her hymn entitled, *"A Christian Home."*

"O give us homes with godly fathers, mothers,
   Who always place their hope and trust in Him;

Whose tender patience turmoil never bothers,
   Whose calm and courage trouble cannot dim;

A home where each finds joy in serving others,
   And love still shines, tho days be dark and grim.

"O Lord, our God, our homes are Thine forever!
   We trust to Thee their problems, toil, and care;

Their bonds of love no enemy can sever,
   If Thou art always Lord and Master there:

Be Thou the center of our least endeavor—
   Be Thou our Guest, our hearts and homes to share."

Notice that the Christian home is far from being a perfect environment. Why? Imperfect sinners live there—sinners who are saved by the grace of God. It should be a place where husbands and wives desire to be conformed to the image of Christ and when problems do arise, and be assured they will, they go to the Word of God *together* to find a biblical solution.

GOD'S ORIGINAL BLUEPRINT

"Submitting yourselves one to another in the fear of God. Wives, submit yourselves unto your own husbands, as unto the Lord. For the husband is the head of the wife, even as Christ is the head of the Church: and He is the Savior of the Body. Therefore as the Church is subject unto Christ, so let the wives be to their own husbands in every thing. Husbands, love your wives, even as Christ also loved the Church, and gave Himself for it" (Eph. 5:21-25).

Let's suppose for a moment you own an old Chevy truck that you've been having problems with. You consult the next door neighbor, who's a backyard mechanic, but he's completely baffled. So you take it to the garage where you have most of your repairs done. However, they, too, are at a loss as to the problem. Finally you call the GM dealership, where you purchased the vehicle. The dealership represents the company that designed and built the truck. Therefore, they quickly resolve the matter, simply because they engineered and assembled the parts that originally went into the vehicle.

Since God designed the institution of marriage, wouldn't it be prudent to consult Him concerning the *blueprint* of the marriage relationship? God has established roles within the relationship that, if obeyed, will ultimately bring marital bliss. Although this may seem rather simplistic, most marital problems can be traced back to a failure to follow these guidelines. Thus, husbands and wives must ask themselves if they are *fulfilling* their God-given role.

Husbands are to love their wives with a sacrificial love, and in so doing they emulate the love of Christ for His Church. Wives on the other hand are to submit themselves to their husbands, which symbolizes the Church's submission to Christ. As we shall see, this does not mean that she is to grovel at the feet of a husband who may have confused his role with that of a tyrant. Before we enter into this discussion further, perhaps we should examine a few general principles that God has established in regard to the marriage relationship.

a. God's Creative Genius

"And God said, Let us make man in our image, after our likeness....So God created man in His own image, in the image of God created He him; male and female created He them. And God blessed them, and God said unto them, Be fruitful, and multiply, and replenish the earth, and subdue it: and have dominion over the fish of the sea, and over the fowl of the air, and over every living thing that moveth upon the earth" (Gen. 1:26-28).

That man was created in the image of God is significant for a number of reasons. First and foremost, God is a *trinity*—Father, Son, and Holy Spirit. When God molded man from the dust of the earth and breathed into his nostrils the breath of life, He created him a trichotomous being—body, soul, and spirit. Second, God possesses the characteristics of *personality*; therefore, when man came forth from His hand, He created Him with an *intellect, emotions,* and *will.*

In these two senses, generally speaking, it might be correctly said that the man and the woman are created *equal.* The woman as well as the man is a trichotomous being. Furthermore, she possesses a personality. But here is where equality gives way to diversity. In many ways, men and women are as different as snowflakes. With regard to the roles that God gave to the man and woman to uphold in marriage, they are equally important, but they are *not* one and the same.

With this in mind, we should note from the above passage that "in the image of God created He him; male and female created He them." In other words, the woman is *also* created in His image and to abuse her in any way, whether physically or emotionally, is to show *contempt* for the image of God.

Peter says: "Likewise, ye husbands, dwell with them [your wives] according to knowledge" (I Peter 3:7). It is the responsibility of the husband to *know* everything there is to

258

know about his wife. He should be familiar with everything she fears and be especially astute concerning her likes and dislikes. A husband should also be sensitive to his wife's *emotional* make up, which is considerably different than his own.

She often wears her emotions on her sleeve and can be brought to tears simply by reading a sad novel. That's how God made her! Husbands who callously snap, "Get a hold of yourself, you're being ridiculous!" are gluttons for punishment. Such insensitivity will usually leave a husband searching for the right words of apology later. A word to the wise here should be sufficient. A woman's memory is like an elephant's— she never forgets those unthoughtful words and unkind actions. A husband will be old and gray, only to be reminded from time to time of how insensitive he was thirty years ago! Emotional scars, like physical scars, are *permanent*.

Peter adds that husbands are to honor their wives "as unto the weaker vessel" (vs. 7b). I know this isn't politically correct today, but a woman is not equal to a man physically. God never intended her to bench press two hundred pounds. Thus, husbands need to be cognizant of the fact that when they expect their wives to pull their part of the load, it doesn't mean she should be pushing a wheelbarrow full of concrete at a construction site. Nor should she be expected to throw a fifty-pound bag of potatoes over her shoulder and carry it to the basement. The woman's gifts and abilities lie in a completely different area.

You will recall that when God placed our first parents in the Garden, He gave *them* "dominion over the fish of the sea, and over the fowl of the air, and over every living thing that moveth upon the earth." This indicates that the woman is just as *intelligent* and capable of making decisions as the man. But it is helpful to understand that men and women think differently. Although the jury is still out, medical science has discovered that men tend to think with only one-half of their brain at a time, whereas women use both hemispheres.[1]

This may explain why men are so *focused*. Ladies, have you noticed when your husband is reading the newspaper it's like talking to a brick wall? Dear, how was your day at the office? Fine! Did you call your sister today about dinner this weekend? No! Your son fell out of a tree today and broke his leg. That's nice! *He's focused!!*

The mind of a woman is like a *scanner*. She can handle three or four things at one time and do them all well. If we are planning a trip, I'm usually studying the road atlas, oblivious to everything else going on around me—I'm focused! Then there's my wife; she's washing dishes, on the phone with the dog kennel, and pointing to our youngest not to forget his homework on the counter. She runs through the preparations for the trip in her mind every hour on the hour. I must admit though, that upon arriving at our destination, I'm usually the first to say, "I think I forgot my razor!" To which my wife softly replies from the other room, "It's in the back compartment of the blue suitcase." She's good!

So then, if a wife understands that her husband is not necessarily ignoring her, but merely being focused, it will save her a tremendous amount of *frustration*. She must learn the importance of getting his attention first, before addressing world issues. Next, the husband who helps his wife with the mental list of things she needs to accomplish will soon win her affection. This may seem like a small matter to some, but if husbands and wives are *attentive* to the fact that they function on different wave lengths, it will greatly ease tension within the marriage relationship.

---

b. Leaving and Cleaving

"And the LORD God caused a deep sleep to fall upon Adam, and he slept; and he took one of his ribs, and closed up the flesh instead thereof. And the rib, which the LORD God had taken from man, made he a woman, and brought her unto the man. And Adam said, This is now bone of my bones, and flesh of my flesh: she shall be called Woman, because she was taken out of man. Therefore shall a man leave his father and his mother, and shall cleave unto his wife: and they shall be one flesh" (Gen. 2:21-24).

Upon removing a rib from Adam's side, God created the woman. Interestingly, the Hebrew word "rib" here is *plural* and literally denotes "Adam's side." In short, God removed *both* bone and flesh from the man's side and created the woman. Hence Adam states: "This is now bone of my bones, and flesh of my flesh: she shall be called Woman." Adam (Heb. man *Ish*) recognized the woman (Heb. *Isha*) was taken from him, and like him, she, too, was a *person*. Thus, the woman was a suitable help fit for the man, one who would be a perfect *complement* to him. In the very fullest sense of the word, she completes the man physically, emotionally, and spiritually. We should also note here that, by order of creation, the man is given the position of *headship*.

In addition to God's creative genius, He ordained the institution of marriage. Marriage was not a product of primitive man who is often portrayed dragging a woman by the hair with one hand and carrying a club in the other. Of course, the evolutionist believes this to be the beginning of a monogamous relationship. Mankind has indeed established many institutions; however, marriage isn't one of them.

It was God who designed the marriage relationship and gave us the regulations to govern it. In fact, God Himself walked the first bride down the aisle ("and brought her unto the man") and presented her to her husband-to-be. Thus, marriage is "not to be entered into unadvisedly or lightly; but reverently, discreetly, advisedly, and in the fear of God."[2]

> "For this cause shall a man leave his father and mother, and shall be joined unto his wife, and they two shall be one flesh" (Eph. 5:31).

This particular quote by the Apostle Paul is taken directly from the Book of Genesis. Although we are living in the dispensation of Grace, the Holy Spirit reminds us that the blueprint of marriage remains the same. The first rule of thumb for beginning the marriage relationship on the right foot is what has been called the "leaving and cleaving" process. The Lord is very clear that the man and the woman are to *leave* their father and mother, that is, they are no longer directly responsible to them.

On the basis of this passage, my wife and I consistently instructed our children when they came of age, that they are more than welcome to remain at home as long as they so choose. However, the day they marry, they are no longer permitted to live at home. Of course, if their house were to burn down, they would be more than welcome to return home until they could make other living arrangements. We are speaking of permanently returning home to live. And of course, they are always welcome to visit.

This may seem rather harsh, but there are two good reasons for this rule. First, once a young adult experiences his or her independence, they are less inclined to obey the wishes of their parents if they return home. In short, it teaches them *responsibility*. Second, it gives them more *incentive* to make their marriage work if they understand they can't come running home at the first sign of a problem.

262

When newlyweds come together in the holy bonds of matrimony, they are creating a *new* home. Therefore, the best wedding gift mothers and fathers can give their children on their wedding day IS TO LET GO!! They will always be Mom and Dad, who deserve love and respect, but they must never interfere. There will be times when newlyweds will naturally seek the counsel of their parents, and parents should stand ready to help. But they must also be prepared to accept the fact that their children may feel the counsel they are given is inappropriate for their home.

The three most common areas of marital problems that young couples face during the first five years of marriage center around *family, finances,* and *intimacy.* Sometimes it is difficult to stand back and see your children heading for a crash course with reality, but it is always best, as a parent, to follow the guidelines of God's Word, even though experience can be a hard taskmaster.

A HIGH AND HOLY CALLING

A short time ago, I came across an amusing story about a four year old little girl by the name of Suzie. Suzie attended nursery school and one day she was told the story of *Snow White* for the first time in her life. She was so excited she couldn't wait to get home to tell her mother.

Suzie gave a stunning theatrical performance as she retold the story of how Prince Charming arrived upon his white horse and kissed Snow White back to life. Suzie then paused a moment and said: "Then, do you know what happened?" To which her mother replied, "Yes, they lived happily ever after." "No, they got *married!*" Suzie touched upon a profound truth. Namely, getting married and living happily ever after are not necessarily synonymous. But they can be if we merely *apply* the counsel of God's Word.

Within the marriage relationship God has established roles to ensure harmony. Husbands are instructed to *love* their wives, while the wife is given the role of *submission*. Although these roles are *equally* important, they are not one and the same. The husband, by order of creation, is given the position of headship. In other words, he was created *first*. Thus, the head of the woman is the man.

The Scriptures clearly state: "For the man is not of the woman; but the woman of the man. Neither was the man created for the woman; but the woman for the man" (I Cor. 11:8,9). Pastor Stam once shared with me, after fifty years of service, that it was his observation that "spiritual Christian women have absolutely no desire to wrestle from the man his God-given authority and responsibility. They want him to take the lead."

In addition, when the evil one appeared in the garden to tempt Eve, it is customarily portrayed that Adam was taking a leisurely walk among the trees of the garden, far beyond earshot. However, a closer examination of the narrative reveals that he was standing *beside* his wife (Gen. 3:6). The tempter completely pulled the wool over the woman's eyes, *deceiving* her into thinking she was doing the right thing by eating the forbidden fruit. Adam on the other hand was not deceived, but *willfully* sinned against God. He wanted to be like God, to know the difference between good and evil.

Thus, the woman is more likely to be drawn into a *deceptive scheme* than the man is. This is not to say that men cannot be deceived, but, more often than not, the man will see through a deception. So then, a godly wife who understands the Fall, which adds another dimension to the man's headship, will find a divine safeguard built into her husband's leadership.

a. Submission

"Submitting yourselves one to another in the fear of
God. Wives, submit yourselves unto your own husbands,
as unto the Lord. For the husband is the head of the
wife, even as Christ is the Head of the Church: and He
is the Savior of the Body. Therefore as the Church is
subject unto Christ, so let the wives be to their own
husbands in every thing" (Eph. 5:21-24).

We are about to tread upon ground where most pastors
fear to tread. The ground we speak of is the woman's role of
submission. The term "submit" Gr. *hupotasso* is "primarily
a military term, which denotes to rank under or to arrange."
Of course, the Church has been so influenced by the world
that it has buckled under to the philosophy that any form of
submission is demeaning. We are told today that the woman's
role of submission makes her inferior and therefore her role
is less important. Hence the struggle for equal rights. Actually, nothing could be further from the truth. The problem
lies with our understanding of the term submission.

For example, every time you attend a worship service,
you're *submitting* yourself to a pastor's ministry. Every time
you walk through the door where you are employed, you're
placing yourself *under the authority* of another. Every time
you drive down the highway, you're submitting yourself to
the laws of the state. Every time you pay your federal income taxes, you're submitting to the governmental powers
that be.

Question: Does the above suggest that you are inferior,
that is, less intelligent, less adequate, or less worthwhile?
No! You see, submission has to do with *order*. It's the *lubri-
cation* that cuts down the friction between relationships. It
causes things to run smoothly in the home, the Church, the
government, and society. Imagine if a large group within a

265

congregation desired to preach every Sunday morning. The *confusion* would soon cause the assembly to close its doors. As you can see, submission plays a very important role in our lives.

Although a wife may be just as capable as her husband regarding matters at home, she is instructed by God to place herself under his watchful care. We doubt that there is a Christian wife reading these lines who would dispute Christ's Headship over the Church. As members of the Body of Christ we have *willingly* placed ourselves under His authority. "Therefore as the Church is subject unto Christ, so let the wives be to their own husbands in every thing" (Eph. 5:24). Thus, the wife's role of submission to her husband is a divine *representation* of a much higher truth.

I am sure I'll be burned at the stake for this, but in a Christ-centered home, the woman's *first* responsibility is to her family. Paul says: "The aged women likewise, that they be in behavior as becometh holiness...teachers of good things; That they may teach the young women to be sober, to love their husbands, to love their children, to be discreet, chaste, keepers at home, good, obedient to their own husbands, that the Word of God be not blasphemed" (Titus 2:3-5).

The role of *homemaker* is a high and holy calling. Here is another area where the world has led the Christian community down the *wrong* path. Sadly, when Christian mothers find themselves questioned about their livelihood, the moment they give their professional title as "homemaker," they're almost immediately *belittled*. "You mean you don't work?" "How do you folks make end's meet?" "Have you ever worked?" "Surely you plan to help out sometime?" These are unfortunate statements that reflect a trend away from a biblical parameter, which always has consequences.

If careers, two family incomes, day care centers, latchkey children, and more possessions are normal by today's humanistic standards, then why are broken homes, abuse, crime, and violence overrunning our country? Obviously, something is terribly wrong with this type of philosophy. The moment a mother is removed from her *primary* God-given role as a homemaker, it is akin to removing the hub from the center of a wheel. At our home, for example, if I'm down sick, or one of the kids has a fever, everything appears normal around the house. If my wife is sick, we call 911! The house usually looks like a tornado just passed through and no one can recall the last time they had a wholesome meal.

The apostle instructs the older women (mothers, grandmothers, great grandmothers, aunts, etc.) to teach the younger women "to be keepers at home." In other words, how to cook, sew, clean, organize, and raise their little ones in the nurture and admonition of the Lord. Most young women today couldn't tell you the difference between "baking soda" and "baking powder," even if their lives depended upon it. If the woman fails to uphold her role or becomes disobedient to her husband, she places the Word of God in jeopardy of being blasphemed. Ladies, never give the unsaved the occasion to point their finger of accusation at you with the charge of *rebellion*.

A Mennonite pastor once said: "A woman can fill no greater role than preparing the next generation for life's responsibilities....Naturally, mothers are often best suited for this role because God has endowed them with the *tender qualities* needed for the job. God expects mothers to guide the house (I Timothy 5:14), and He alone can enable them for the rigor of homemaking."

A woman has the unique ability to make a cold, plain house a home. A house is a place where we sleep. A home is

267

an *atmosphere*. It is where our children are raised in the presence of parents who show *affection* toward one another. A habitation where children are loved, taught, and nurtured in the things of the Lord. We've repeatedly said over the years that if mothers fail to bring their children up in the nurture and admonition of the Lord, when our present congregations lie in the dust of the earth, the pews will be *empty*. Incidentally, we are not speaking about religious churches, but rather sound Bible-believing assemblies where the *blood of Christ* is preached. As the old axiom says: "The hand that rocks the cradle is the hand that rules the world."[3]

By now, someone is reading these lines thinking, "Boy, is he out of touch with the real world." Actually, I did a reality check before I wrote this chapter. Beloved, simply because the world says, "Everyone is doing it, therefore it must be right," doesn't make it right! Society generally accepts *abortion* these days as a viable option for birth control.[4] Does this make it morally right? "But everyone's doing it!"

What saith the Scriptures? They clearly state that life begins at *conception*, therefore to intentionally terminate a pregnancy is nothing short of *murder* (Psa. 51:5,6; Jer. 1:4,5 cf. Gen. 9:5,6; Rom. 13:9). The Lord has also established guidelines for the Christian home, but the question we must ask ourselves is, are we following them?

b. The Workplace

While the Scriptures do give *liberty* for the woman to work outside the home, it is preferable if she doesn't, especially if little ones are involved. A mother is only given *one* opportunity to have a positive impact upon her young. Those early developmental years are *critical* as the personalities of these little ones are being molded. The question is, do you want someone raising your children that may not share your moral or spiritual values? Then there's the matter of discipline. Most child-care providers are very reluctant to discipline someone else's children.

Of course, we are well aware that it is becoming increasingly difficult to make ends meet on one income. In fact, the day is fast approaching when two incomes will be a necessity. Nevertheless, we feel strongly that if it is at all possible, mothers should try to avoid working outside the home until their children are grown. Some "domestic engineers" work part-time at home to help supplement the family income. The *influence* of one parent in the home at all times cannot be overstated.

The importance of the above paragraph came home to roost at a recent family gathering. During the years my wife and I served at local assemblies, we often did hospital visits together. Of course, this meant we weren't always at home when the kids arrived from school. Since the two oldest (our youngest was yet to arrive) were in Junior and Senior High at the time, we never gave it much thought, because we were ordinarily home before dinner.

As we all sat around the table reminiscing not long ago, both of the kids stated how they hated to come home from school when no one was there. The house seemed so cold and lonely. It may seem like a small thing, but it was important to them that one of us (usually mom) was at home. If a mother must work, she should attempt to arrange her schedule so it coincides with her children's school schedule.

There are a number of examples in the Scriptures where women worked both within and outside the home. As we know, the virtuous woman burned the midnight oil.

> "She considereth a field, and buyeth it: with the *fruit* of her hands she planteth a vineyard....She perceiveth that her *merchandise* is good: her candle goeth not out

269

by night. She layeth her hands to the spindle, and her hands hold the distaff[5]....She maketh fine linen, and *selleth* it; and delivereth girdles unto the merchant" (Prov. 31:16-24).

Lydia seemed to have owned her own business, traveling from place to place selling her fine-spun cloth to merchants:

"And a certain woman named Lydia, a seller of purple, of the city of Thyatira, which worshipped God, heard us: whose heart the Lord opened, that she attended unto the things which were spoken of Paul" (Acts 16:14).

Some have suggested that both Aquila and Priscilla labored together at the craft of tentmaking. If so, Priscilla probably helped with some of the sewing aspects of the trade. This would have been well within the boundaries of acceptable behavior for women of that period. Although Paul was the apostle of the Gentiles, he occasionally relied upon his occupation of tentmaking to support himself. This was especially true during his early ministry, which placed less of a financial burden upon the churches. There is an old Hebrew saying that goes something like this: A man who doesn't teach his son a *skill*, teaches him to steal.

"After these things Paul departed from Athens, and came to Corinth; and found a certain Jew named Aquila, born in Pontus, lately come from Italy, with his wife Priscilla....And because he was of the same craft, he abode with them, and wrought: for by their occupation they were tentmakers" (Acts 18:1-3).

Phebe was evidently a wealthly *businesswoman* from Cenchrea. In fact, she hand delivered Paul's epistle to the Romans, and was personally involved in the business affairs of a number of local assemblies.[6]

"I commend unto you Phebe our sister, which is a servant of the church which is at Cenchrea: that ye receive her in the Lord, as becometh saints, and that ye assist her in whatsoever business she hath need of you: for she hath been a succourer [helper] of many, and of myself also" (Rom. 16:1,2).

My hat is off to working women, both past and present, that keep up with husbands (a full-time job in itself), children, and the home. Surely a great recompense of reward awaits these godly women who make this type of sacrifice. According to the Scriptures though, working outside the home is the *exception*, not the rule, ladies. The home is the realm where you will find your greatest *fulfillment*.

Fear not, ladies, we are going to tackle the *role of the husband*. So you may want to have a highlighter ready. By the way, I'll do my best to be objective!

LOVE THAT KNOWS NO BOUNDS

"For the husband is the head of the wife, even as Christ is the Head of the Church: and He is the Savior of the Body....Husbands, love your wives, even as Christ also loved the Church, and gave Himself for it" (Eph. 5:23,25).

The role the Lord has given to the man in the marriage relationship is *headship*. Sadly, many men have confused headship with dictatorship. A dictator selfishly demands the servitude of his subjects without regard to their will. He often rules oppressively through fear and unreasonable demands. Such behavior has no place in the Christian home. The husband who tramples his wife's emotions under foot like a doormat should remember that she, too, is created in the image of God. Husbands are responsible to provide *loving* leadership for their wives to follow. In so doing, they are emulating Christ's Headship. Notice that the Lord's Headship is bound inseparably to *love*.

What is love? We are always hearing the world speak about falling in love. Unfortunately, the world has confused love with *lust*. Men and women do indeed fall into lustful situations. Love, however, does not come naturally in this sin-cursed world; it must be *learned* (Titus 2:3-5). Thus, through the pen of the apostle the Lord commands husbands to love their wives. This strongly implies that men tend to be preoccupied with themselves. When the Lord confronted Adam about his disobedience, he sought to defend himself without any regard for the welfare of his wife. "It's that woman you gave me, she's to blame." *Love* would have said, "Lord, I am the guilty party who failed to shield my wife from the words of the tempter."

The love with which the Lord instructs husbands to love their wives is defined for us in I Corinthians chapter 13:

"Charity suffereth long." Love is *patient*. Jacob labored seven years for the right to marry Rachel, only to learn that her father had deceived him. Consequently, "Jacob served [an additional] seven years for Rachel; and they seemed unto him but a few days, for the love he had to her" (Gen. 29:20).

"And is kind." Love does something special, even when there isn't a special occasion to remember. A godly husband will always take into *consideration* his wife's feelings.

"Charity envieth not." Love isn't *jealous*. It delights to see her honored or recognized.

"Charity vaunteth not itself, is not puffed up." A husband may have a college education, but he must never flaunt it before his wife. Love *never boasts*, it always finds ways to build her up and encourage her.

"Doth not behave itself unseemly." Love is *never discourteous*. It has manners. A husband who loves his wife will take great care to introduce her to those whom she may not know, and he will never neglect her while in the company of others.

"Seeketh not her own." Love is staying home from a major outing to watch the kids if your wife isn't feeling well. It's *unselfish.*

"Is not easily provoked." Love is always in *control.* It doesn't easily lose its temper and never uses *unkind* words. If a wife wrecks the family car, how should love respond? Probably most husbands would say: "You did what!!!" "How much damage was done?" "Now what are we going to do for transportation while the car is being repaired?" Needless to say, this isn't the correct reply. She's already devastated by the accident and therefore needs a large dose of *compassion.*

"Thinketh no evil." Some years ago I had an interesting counseling session with a couple who were experiencing marital problems. The husband had barely sat down when he pulled out a long list of grievances against his wife, which incidentally, included dates and times. I looked it over briefly, crumpled it up, and said: "According to I Corinthians 13:5, love doesn't keep a *ledger of wrongs.*" He's probably still recovering!

"Rejoiceth not in iniquity." Love never seeks *revenge.* A wife may make an unwise purchase without her husband's knowledge, but it only intensifies the problem if he *sinfully* runs up the Visa card, simply out of spite.

"But rejoiceth in the truth." For a marriage to abide the storms of life, it must be based upon speaking the truth in love. *Trust* and *respect* are the fruits of a relationship built upon truth.

"Beareth all things." Love *bears up* under difficult circumstances. Perhaps a husband learns that his wife has an incurable illness. Love stays by her side as they bear the burden together.

"Believeth all things." Love always accepts things at *face value*. Inasmuch as marriage is built upon a mutual trust, love should cause a couple to take each other at their word.

"Hopeth all things." Although every marriage experiences bumpy roads along the way, love has *high expectations* that things will improve as problems are resolved. It's optimistic!

"Endureth all things." Through times of tragedy, death, and unforeseen circumstances, the head of the family should be like a mighty fortress. He understands that God is sovereign and "He doeth according to His will in the army of heaven, and among the inhabitants of the earth: and none can stay His hand, or say unto Him, What doest thou?" (Dan. 4:35).

While most marriages begin smoothly, they have a tendency to lose some of their splendor after the first year or two. In other words, the honeymoon's over, now it's down to the nuts and bolts of every day married life. Acts of thoughtfulness, affection, concern, and gifts begin to wax and wane under the load of responsibility. Usually this trend begins with the husband, who fails to *consistently* apply the love chapter. We recently came across a story that appeared in the *Washington Post* entitled: "The Seven Ages of the Married Cold," which drives home the point:

The first year: "Sugar dumpling, I'm really worried about my baby girl. You've got a bad sniffle and there's no telling about these things with all this strep going around. I'm putting you in the hospital this afternoon for a general checkup and a good rest. I know the food's lousy, but I'll be bringing your meals in from Rossini's. I've already got it arranged with the floor superintendent."

The second year: "Listen darling, I don't like the sound of that cough. I've called Doc Miller and asked him to rush over here. Now you go to bed like a good girl, please, just for papa."

The third year: "Maybe you'd better lie down, honey: nothing like a little rest when you feel lousy. I'll bring you something. Have you got any canned soup?"

The fourth year: "Now look, dear, be sensible. After you've fed the kids, washed the dishes, and finished the floors, you'd better lie down."

The fifth year: "Why don't you take a couple of aspirin?"

The sixth year: "I wish you would just gargle or something instead of sitting around all evening barking like a seal."

The seventh year: "For Pete's sake, stop sneezing! Are you trying to give me pneumonia?"

According to the eternal purpose of God, Christ loved the Church and gave Himself for it. To which the apostle adds: "That He might sanctify and cleanse it with the washing of water by the Word, that He might present it to Himself a glorious Church, not having spot, or wrinkle, or any such thing; but that it should be holy and without blemish." When the trump sounds, the members of the Body of Christ will have the unique honor of being *presented* to the Lord. Think of it, sinners saved by grace, sanctified by grace, and delivered to glory by grace, will be displayed before the host of heaven as the trophies of His grace! This will one day be a reality because Christ loved us with a sacrificial love. In this same context the apostle states:

"So ought men to love their wives as their own bodies. He that loveth his wife loveth himself. For no man ever yet hated his own flesh; but nourisheth and cherisheth it, even as the Lord the Church" (Eph. 5:26-29).

Husbands are to love their wives with a *sacrificial love*. The husband is to care for his wife and protect her, even as Christ does the Church. He is to *cherish* her as he does his own body. It is common knowledge that men normally pamper themselves if they have been injured in some way. If a woman cuts her finger in the kitchen, she'll put a bandage on it and never break stride. When a man cuts his finger, he'll probably require stitches, faithfully change the dressing, take regular doses of aspirin to curb the pain, and more than likely miss a day's work for fear of bumping the injured finger!

Paul is illustrating that, if a husband pays this type of *attention* to his wife, she will naturally reciprocate by following his leadership. A wife should be treated like a fine piece of china—precious and easily broken!

HEADSHIP

As we have seen, according to Ephesians 5:23, the husband is "the head of the wife." Headship means leadership, that is, leadership governed by love. Sad to say, we have all witnessed families where the husband has brashly declared: "I am the head of this house," and all must bow in fear and trembling. Consequently, the household is run like a military camp where there's a strict code of discipline for every infraction. This isn't biblical headship. Biblical leadership involves responsibility, *management*, love, and compassion.

Interestingly, when Paul wrote to Timothy concerning the qualifications for those who desired to be an elder, he states: "One that ruleth well his own house, having his children in subjection with all gravity; (for if a man know not how to rule his own house, how shall he take care of the church of God?)" (I Tim. 3:4,5). The term "ruleth" used here has the idea to care for, preside over, to manage. He is to effectively *manage* his home.

The man is ultimately responsible to provide food, clothing, and shelter for his family. While a wife may volunteer to help bear the burden, the Scriptures clearly teach: "But if any provide not for **his** own, and specially for those of **his** own house, **he** hath denied the faith, and is worse than an infidel" (I Tim. 5:8).

Although most men fare pretty well at providing the physical needs of their home, far too many fail to set a good example in *spiritual things*. Godly leadership includes studying the Scriptures, devotions, prayer, and making sure the family has a regular place to worship. It provides an atmosphere wherein each member of the family can grow in the grace and knowledge of our Lord Jesus Christ. Children that see *both* parents on their knees seeking God's direction will be far less likely to end up juvenile delinquents.

There is an old saying that still rings true: "Two heads are better than one." Seeing that the woman is also created in the image of God, she adds many things to the marriage relationship—grace, intelligence, ideas, etc. Therefore, a husband is well served if he and his wife make decisions *together*. A wife's counsel, suggestions, and warnings should be weighed very carefully in the decision making process. Moreover, they should be implemented if they have *merit*.

As a rule, a husband and wife will ordinarily agree upon what course of action should be taken to resolve a problem. But there may be times when they will not see eye to eye on a particular matter. In such cases the husband should make the final decision, since he will be held *accountable* at the Judgment Seat of Christ for everything that transpired in the home (II Cor. 5:10 cf. Eph. 5:23).

Those who work at the corporate level understand the importance of matching an employee's skills with the job description they are seeking to fill. That's called good management. Along these same lines, it is the better part of wisdom if a husband makes wise use of his wife's God-given *abilities*. She can be a real *asset* in the affairs of the home. For example, my wife is a whiz working with figures. Our checkbook looks like the ones you see in textbooks. In fact, we were at the bank one day to have an error corrected—that they had made on our checking account statement—when the vice president came over to ask my wife if she wanted a job! He was looking for someone who could teach the bank's younger customers how to balance a checkbook.

Of course, you already know what I'm about to say. Since my wife could be employed at the First National Bank, I've turned all of our finances over to her. She writes all the checks, reconciles the accounts, pays the bills, and believe it or not, enjoys it. As the head of the family, could I keep the books? Yes! But I have chosen to *delegate* the responsibility to her. Sometimes when she's unsure of what to pay, due to unexpected expenses, we sit down *together* to work it out.

Headship also includes planning, *goals*, decisions, sensitivity, and accountability. As we saw earlier, the Scriptures declare that husbands should dwell with their wives "according to knowledge" (I Pet. 3:7). But it is also prudent for wives to do the same. Men and women function with *different* operating systems. That's how God created us. Men are *goal* oriented. Whether it's a project around the house or a trip across the country, they have to *conquer*!

Ladies, the next time you attend a family reunion, merely wander over to where the men have gathered and you'll see what I mean. The conversation will probably go something like this: "Yep, Ned, I made it in 7 hours and 22 minutes this trip." "Why that's 20 minutes faster than last time." To which Grandpa adds: "I remember the time when it took two days to travel that many miles." So then, when your husband is striving toward a goal, it doesn't necessarily indicate he's neglecting to pay attention to you, he's merely meeting his objective!

The Holy Spirit deemed it necessary to instruct husbands to dwell with their wives "according to knowledge," simply because men have a tendency to be *insensitive*. This is further confirmed by Paul's admonition to the Colossians: "Husbands, love your wives, and be not bitter against them" (Col. 3:19). Insofar as a woman oftentimes thinks with her emotions, she has to feel at ease with herself before entering into important decisions. This is why most husbands experience a high level of *frustration* when they go shopping with their wives.

A short time ago upon returning home from a particularly lengthy trip, I said to my wife that I was dedicating an entire day to her—sightseeing, lunch, shopping, or any other way she would like to spend the day! She had been wanting to pick up a new blouse, so after lunch we made our way to a department store to look around. After searching through a couple of racks she finally found something that caught her eye. She tried it on, but decided she didn't really care for it.

Twenty minutes later she held something up and asked me what I thought. Fabulous! Trying to be helpful, I said, "There's a checkout counter right over here, dear." However, she was still a little unsure about the selection, so she carried it around with her as we browsed a while longer. Of course, when I go shopping it's directly to the aisle where the wrenches are located, then straight to the checkout—8 minutes flat! But shopping with my wife, who is guided by another principle, I knew I needed to be *patient*. By the way, we left the store that day without making a purchase!

Bob Jones Sr. once said, "You can't move without creating friction." In short, if you move forward with a particular conviction, you're going to create *friction*. With regard to the marriage relationship there would be a great deal less friction if husbands and wives lived within the guidelines of their roles and sought to understand one another more fully.

12

The University of Life

> "For we are members of His Body, of His flesh, and of His bones. For this cause shall a man leave his father and mother, and shall be joined unto his wife, and they two shall be one flesh. This is a great mystery: but I speak concerning Christ and the church."
>
> —*Ephesians 5:30-32*

The *home* is the foundation of society, government, and the Church. If the home is under attack, whether from within as a result of sin or from without due to Satan, it will adversely affect every strata of human relations. For those who may question this, simply consider the ills of our own nation—immorality, abuse, AIDS, abortion, welfare, juvenile delinquency, teen suicide, etc. Even the fall of Rome can be traced to a *moral* decay from within. The world is an infirmary of sorrow. Sadly, however, many of these same problems also plague Christian homes.

This reminds me of the time Vince Lombardi, the legendary coach of the Green Bay Packers, held a football high into the air before his championship team and said: "Gentleman, this is a *football*!" In other words, it's back to the basics. Great advice! Perhaps someone needs to stand up before the household of God and hold a Bible into the air and shout: "Brethren, this is a *Bible*!" Of course, the point would be to challenge believers to get back to the *fundamentals* of the original blueprint God established for the home.

"Now concerning the things whereof ye wrote unto me: It is good for a man not to touch a woman. Nevertheless, to avoid fornication, let every man have his own wife, and let every woman have her own husband" (I Cor. 7:1,2).

MARRIAGE AND CELIBACY

To say that the Apostle Paul had his hands full with the Corinthians would be an understatement. They were into more trouble than a little one going through his terrible two's. The phrase: "Now concerning the things whereof ye wrote unto me" suggests the apostle had spent the better part of six chapters dealing with the carnal actions of these members of the Body of Christ. With those matters set to rest, Paul now addresses their questions regarding marriage and the issue of things offered to idols.

Apparently there were some in this assembly who condoned the practice of *fornication,* which alarmed some of the brethren—and justifiably so. Although immorality was commonplace among the Greeks, this was unacceptable behavior for a believer in Christ. Fornication is normally associated with premarital relations, but the original Greek word *porneia* goes far beyond this meaning to include every type of sexual perversion imaginable. It extends from incest to homosexual relationships and everything illicit in between. For example:

"It is reported commonly that there is *fornication* among you, and such fornication as is not so much as named among the Gentiles, that one should have his father's wife. And ye are puffed up, and have not rather mourned, that he that hath done this deed might be taken away from among you" (I Cor. 5:1,2).

"Even as Sodom and Gomorrha, and the cities about them in like manner, giving themselves over to *fornication*, and going after strange flesh, are set forth for an example, suffering the vengeance of eternal fire" (Jude 1:7).

God's answer to this sin is *marriage*. Thus, to avoid fornication, the apostle clearly states: "let every man have his *own* wife, and let every woman have her *own* husband." Marriage provides a safeguard against temptation, disease, and feelings of guilt. From the beginning God has always intended one man for one woman. But how do we explain the fact that Abraham, Jacob, Moses, and David had multiple wives? Solomon had a large harem, which included seven hundred wives and princesses, and three hundred concubines, most of whom served as wives.

Here we have a matter of the directive and permissive will of God. While a strong case could be made from eastern culture for having more than one wife, the fact remains that the Lord Himself states: "And he answered and said unto them [Pharisees], Have ye not read, that he which made them at the beginning made them male and female, and said, For this cause shall a man leave father and mother, and shall cleave to his wife: and they twain shall be one flesh? Wherefore they are no more twain, but one flesh. What therefore God hath joined together, let not man put asunder" (Matt. 19:4-6).

Notice the Lord uses the singular form "wife" not "wives." This is also confirmed through His apostle here in Corinthians, "let every man have his own wife." Although God *allowed* the practice of having more than one wife in time past, those who stepped into these treacherous waters normally lived to regret it. These arrangements almost always inflamed the fires of *jealousy*. In some cases, they even caused a departure from the known will of God.

When Hagar conceived Ishmael, Sarah was *enraged*: "And he [Abraham] went in unto Hagar, and she conceived: and when she [Sarah] saw that she had conceived, her mistress was despised in her eyes" (Gen. 16:4).

Probably a large percentage of Solomon's marriages were politically motivated, which means some of his wives were in name only. Nevertheless, when he foolishly married outside the house of God, his *Gentile* wives caused him to depart from the ways of the Lord. "For it came to pass, when Solomon was old, that his wives turned away his heart after other gods: and his heart was not perfect with the LORD his God, as was the heart of David his father....And Solomon did evil in the sight of the LORD, and went not fully after the LORD, as did David his father" (I Kings 11:4,6).

In spite of the shortcomings and failures of the patriarchs and prophets, God often used their circumstances to further His plans and purposes. So even through our imperfections He will ultimately be glorified. But for our sakes, it is always preferable to remain in the *center* of His will.

> "For I would that all men were even as I myself. But every man hath his proper gift of God, one after this manner, and another after that. I say therefore to the unmarried and widows, It is good for them if they abide even as I. But if they cannot contain, let them marry: for it is better to marry than to burn" (I Cor. 7:7-9).

Paul's statements: "For I would that all men were even as I myself," and, "It is good for them [the unmarried and widows] if they abide even as I [i.e. single]," have caused some to conclude that the apostle viewed marriage with contempt. We know, however, this charge is totally without merit. There is a general consensus that prior to receiving his apostleship Paul had been married, but prematurely lost his wife. This assumption is based upon his declaration that he had been a *Pharisee*. According to historians it was mandatory for one to be married to belong to this sect.

The issue here is why Paul seems to be encouraging the believers at Corinth to remain *unmarried*. The solution to the problem is found in verses 26-28:

> "I suppose therefore that this is good for the present distress, I say, that it is good for a man so to be. Art thou bound unto a wife? seek not to be loosed. Art thou loosed from a wife? seek not a wife. But and if thou marry, thou hast not sinned....Nevertheless such shall have trouble in the flesh: but I spare you."

The key phrase here is *"the present distress."* Paul admonishes them as a father that under the circumstances it was in their best interest not to marry if they were unattached. The blood of the martyrs had already begun to run through the streets of the ancient world and the apostle knew that the *persecution* would soon intensify. History bears witness that many Christians even sought refuge in the catacombs.[1] Back then it cost something to name the name of Christ, as seen in Paul's words to the saints at Thessalonica: "So that we ourselves glory in you in the churches of God for your patience and faith in *all your persecutions and tribulations that ye endure"* (II Thes. 1:4).

Paul knew the heartache couples would experience when Christian husbands were taken and cast to the lions. So during times of persecution, it is better to remain *unmarried*. Thus wisdom says: "Art thou loosed from a wife? seek not a wife." Paul adds, "But if they cannot contain, let them marry: for it is better to marry than to burn," that is, with *lustful* desire. Interestingly, those who do marry at such times have not sinned. But they do leave themselves susceptible to suffer trouble in the flesh at the hands of evildoers (I Cor. 7:9,27,28).

So then, Paul is not the ogre some make him out to be; he was simply concerned about the welfare of the saints. The apostle held the institution of marriage in the highest esteem, referring to it as a *gift*. "But every man hath his proper gift of God, one after this manner, and another after that" (I Cor. 7:7). For the most part, we believe it is God's will for men and women to marry. Of course, there are exceptions to the rule.

Paul says, "one after this manner, and another after that." In other words, some have the gift of marriage while others have the gift of celibacy. Those who have the latter gift are given a special measure of grace to remain *single*. As we know, celibacy has always been closely associated with paganism and religious monks who live cloistered lives. However, if those who piously participate in these religious orders do not have the gift of celibacy, it will inevitably end in *immorality*. The past ten years or so have only served to highlight the accuracy of this last statement as one scandal after another has made headline news.

True celibacy is a *gift* from God. Those who possess this gift have no desire to be married. This also applies to those who never remarry after the death of their partner. They find their sufficiency in Christ and normally are perfectly content to live alone. The Scriptures say in this regard, "The unmarried woman careth for the things of the Lord, that she may be holy both in body and in spirit" (I Cor. 7:34). While the married woman has contentment through a Christ-centered marriage, the unmarried woman finds fulfillment by consecrating herself *wholly* to the things of the Lord.

I had an aunt who epitomized the above. She was as pure as newly fallen snow. The day my wife and I were saved, we rushed to visit our families, convinced that everyone would be as excited about our conversion as we were. Of course, most of them thought we had a concussion from some type of fall. My aunt's response was *jubilation*, followed by these words: "I have been praying for you and Vicki every day for three years that you would come to know Christ." Those weren't idle words, she meant it! She added, "Now I am going to pray that God will call you into full-time service." Well, I guess you might say we are the fruits of my aunt's prayer life.

But how does one determine if he has the gift of marriage? Since celibacy is the exception to the rule, this is relatively easy to ascertain. Those who have this gift *desire* to be married. They are uncomfortable with the thought of being single the rest of their life. Singles customarily spend a lot of time dreaming (rightly so) about one day having their own home and eventually a family. And both young men and women will almost always feel life is passing them by if they aren't married by age 22. In short, those who have the gift of marriage are usually *consumed* with the thought.

PREPARATIONS FOR MARRIAGE

Normally the procedure for choosing the right partner for life begins on the wrong foot. The counsel of the world goes something like this: appearance, compatibility, education, and financial status. Unfortunately, the Church has been so influenced by this concept that believers seem to also have the idea that these factors insure a happy marriage relationship.

Consider *appearance* for a moment. It will matter very little at 2:30 a.m. that a husband is tall, dark, and handsome when the firstborn is screaming at the top of her lungs. And it's about this same time that the vision of beauty he married with long, flowing hair down to her waist has it cut short for practical considerations. Well, isn't *compatibility* surely a must? Isn't it essential to have the same likes and dislikes? But what profit is there if both a husband and wife are computer literate or enjoy playing tennis, when the breadwinner comes home to inform his wife that he lost his job because the company downsized?

Now please don't misunderstand me, there's nothing wrong with having the same interests or a good education or being financially responsible. These things are indeed commendable, but *believers* who make them the foundation of their marriage relationship are like the man who built his house upon the sand. "And the rain descended, and the floods came, and the winds blew, and beat upon that house; and it fell: and great was the fall of it."

Believers in Christ should begin their search for Mr. or Miss Right according to the pattern of God's Word. The four essentials for a Christ-centered marriage are: salvation, spirituality, convictions, and a willingness to solve problems biblically. Salvation is the first essential, simply because believers are not to be unequally yoked to unbelievers. It is God's will that believers only marry *in the Lord*.

> "she is at liberty to be married to whom she will; only in the Lord" (I Cor. 7:39).
>
> "Be ye not unequally yoked together with unbelievers: for what fellowship hath righteousness with unrighteousness? and what communion hath light with darkness?" (II Cor. 6:14).

Those who violate these clear injunctions will only heap *sorrow* upon themselves. A young lady may have good intentions that she will reach her fiancé for Christ after they are married, but this is seldom the case. The fact is, the unbeliever normally draws the believer away into the things of the world. Through the years, I have had a number of godly women share with me that the thing they regretted most in life was being married to an unbeliever. Nearly all said, it wasn't that their husbands were not good providers; they were, but there was *no* fellowship with them in the gospel. Disobeying the Word of God always has consequences!

Although it is not a biblical prerequisite that a marriage partner has the other three spiritual graces, they do provide the means through which the relationship will function more smoothly. For example, if a young woman is a Grace believer and marries a dyed-in-the-wool Baptist, he naturally has very strong *convictions* that they should attend a Baptist Church. In his words, he was born a Baptist, raised a Baptist, and will die a Baptist. Of course, the issue is only complicated a hundred-fold when the little ones come along. What should they be taught—Baptist or Grace doctrine?

The wife could compromise, but this runs contrary to her convictions, which are as deep as her husband's. They could attend different churches, but this divides the family. Another option would be to stay at home; however, the Scriptures teach us that we shouldn't forsake the assembling of ourselves together. I rest my case!

MARRIAGE, DIVORCE, AND REMARRIAGE

"Nevertheless let every one of you in particular so love his wife even as himself; and the wife see that she reverence her husband" (Eph. 5:33).

A discourse on the institution of marriage would be incomplete without addressing the subject of *divorce* and *remarriage*. Sometimes the saints find themselves in a set of circumstances that are beyond their control. For those who may be reading these lines that are divorced, we want you to know God loves you, and that it is His will for you to continue to live a *productive* Christian life to the praise of His glory.

The last thing someone needs who has gone through a painful divorce is to be criticized or neglected by the local assembly, although sadly, this is often the case. They are already brokenhearted over the matter. What they need is our *compassion* and a helping hand to pull their lives back together.

> "And unto the married I command, yet not I, *but the Lord*, Let not the wife depart from her husband: but and if she depart, let her remain unmarried, or be reconciled to her husband: and let not the husband put away his wife" (I Cor. 7:10,11).

a. The Christian Marriage

Here, it is imperative to remember that we are no longer under the law, but under grace. As we know, God raised up a new apostle and commissioned him to go to the Gentiles. Thus, we must look to the Apostle Paul for our marching orders today. In his epistles we have the commands of Christ concerning the *regulations* for the marriage relationship, which should be of particular interest to those of us who rightly divide the Word of truth. Having dealt with the issue of celibacy, Paul now presents various dilemmas the members of the Body of Christ could find themselves embroiled in, along with the *proper* response.

With the change in dispensations the Lord imparted a new revelation to the apostle in regard to believers in Christ. When a *saved* man and woman have been united in holy matrimony, they are bound together until death according to verses 10 and 11. Since couples who know the Lord are equally yoked together, it is the *directive* will of God that they never divorce. This is why it's essential that young couples who are contemplating marriage make sure that they are prepared to enter into a lifelong commitment. May we remind the reader again of the solemn words of the traditional wedding ceremony that marriage is "not to be entered into unadvisedly or lightly; but reverently, discreetly, advisedly, *and in the fear of God."*

But what if a serious problem arises in the marriage? For example, if a wife finds herself in an abusive relationship she has every right to *separate* from her husband until he gets help. She should never place herself or her children in harm's way. A wife isn't a punching bag; she's created in the image of God. Mark these words and mark them well, a husband who strikes his wife is striking the image of God. In the event her husband refuses the counsel of a godly pastor, and continues in his sinful behavior, the wife can remain *separated* until a time of repentance. However, she is not permitted to divorce him.

When marital problems arise, it is always preferable for both the husband and wife to attend counseling sessions *together*. There still must be contact between the couple, in a controlled environment, if they ever hope to resolve the problem. A counselor is indispensable at such times since he serves as an *impartial* mediator. God has given him the tools to find a biblical solution to the problem.

If her husband comes to the point where he sees the error of his ways and repents, she should be more than willing to *reconcile*. Grace will always *forgive* the erring party. As the apostle says: "Forbearing one another, and forgiving one another, if any man [or woman] have a quarrel [complaint] against any: even as Christ forgave you, so also do ye" (Col. 3:13).

As we continue, suppose for a moment that a believing wife commits adultery with another man. She's trapped in the snare of Satan and habitually living in sin. In order that she might understand the gravity of her sinful lifestyle her husband should immediately separate from her until a time of *repentance*. Once again, divorce is not an option for the believer in Christ. Although the experience may be painful, the wounds deep, *grace* will follow the instructions of the Spirit: "And be ye kind one to another, tenderhearted, forgiving one another, even as God for Christ's sake hath forgiven you" (Eph. 4:32).

In both of the above cases, Christian couples who experience unforeseen problems have one of two options, either *separate* or be *reconciled* to one another (I Cor. 7:11).

But what about Christian couples who have divorced and one or both the husband and wife have *remarried*? Perhaps they were unaware of these instructions. This matter falls under the realm of the *permissive* will of God. Since past actions "belong to the ages" our counsel is always the same. Paul states: "Brethren, I count not myself to have apprehended: but this one thing I do, **forgetting those things which are behind, and reaching forth unto those things which are before**, I press toward the mark for the prize of the high calling of God in Christ Jesus" (Phil. 3:13,14).

In other words, you cannot change the past, but you can apply the above marital regulations to your *present* marriage. God's forgiveness extends to broken relationships. The believer may not be perfect in this life, but he is *forgiven*.

Those who find themselves in these circumstances have often shared with us that while they are somewhat reluctant to hold positions of leadership, the Lord has used them greatly in other areas of service. Indeed, there are ten thousand things that need to be accomplished for Christ and every member of His Body should be helping in the cause, including those who are picking up the pieces of a shattered relationship. Our prayer is that God will burden our local assemblies to *actively* pursue ways to make these weary souls feel a part of the ministry.

b. The Unequally Yoked Marriage

"But to the rest speak I, not the Lord: If any brother hath a wife that believeth not, and she be pleased to dwell with him, let him not put her away. And the woman which hath an husband that believeth not, and if he be pleased to dwell with her, let her not leave him. For the unbelieving husband is sanctified by the wife, and the unbelieving wife is sanctified by the husband: else were your children unclean; but now are they holy" (I Cor. 7:12-14).

Paul's phrase, "But to the rest speak I, not the Lord" isn't any less authoritative than that which has gone before. The inspired apostle is merely showing that in the previous passages he had received a direct revelation from the Lord. Now in light of these *new conditions*, Paul addresses another marital issue under the direction of the Holy Spirit (vs. 40).

Here we are introduced to an *unequally yoked* marriage. "The woman which hath an husband that believeth not, and if he be pleased to dwell with her, let her not leave him." This may be a case where two unbelievers have married but in the course of time one of them comes to know Christ as their personal Savior. Some might conclude that since they are now unequally yoked the believing partner should forsake the marriage. However, just the *opposite* is true. If the unbelieving partner is willing to continue the relationship the believer is *not* to depart.

According to the Scriptures, "the unbelieving husband is *sanctified* [i.e. set apart to the marriage, not salvation] by the wife...else were your children unclean; but now are they holy." In short, God honors the marriage for the sake of the believer. Moreover He classifies any children born of the relationship to be legitimate. Thus, every attempt should be made, by God's grace, to make the marriage work.

This arrangement serves a twofold purpose. In addition to the children having the opportunity to be raised by their *natural* parents, the unbelieving husband may be won to the Lord. Paul poses the question: "For what knowest thou, O wife, whether thou shalt save thy husband?" (I Cor. 7:16). Of course, a believing wife has no power to save her husband, but she may deliver him from the judgment to come through her faithful testimony. The likelihood of her husband being converted to Christ is much greater since he is repeatedly exposed to the gospel.

Perhaps a word of caution should be added here for those who may be living with an unsaved loved one. Never badger an unbeliever with the gospel; this will only serve to alienate him from the Lord. We recently read about one lady who stuffed her husband's newspapers with tracts. Every time he opened them he was showered with the gospel. When this didn't work she tuned his car radio to the Christian radio station every morning. While these are ingenious methods, an unbelieving husband will sooner be won to Christ through the godly *example* of his wife. Peter gives us these insightful words:

> "Likewise, ye wives, be in subjection to your own husbands; that, if any obey not the word, they also may without the word be won by the conversation [behavior] of the wives; while they behold your chaste conversation [behavior] coupled with fear" (I Pet. 3:1,2).

c. Remarriage

There are many pastors who feel that remarriage is *impermissible* under any circumstances. While we hold their convictions in high regard, we believe that the apostle gives liberty to *remarry* under certain circumstances. Let's suppose that a believing wife has sought to be faithful to her husband, but he's fed up after two or three years with all this "religion." He hadn't bargained to be married to a "religious fanatic" who will no longer participate in drunken binges or cheat on their taxes—he wants out! Thus there is a willful desertion on *his* part. Under these circumstances the apostle gives the following counsel.

> "But if the unbelieving depart, let him depart. A brother or a sister is not under bondage in such cases: but God hath called us to peace" (I Cor. 7:15).

It seems clear to us from this passage that if the *unbeliever* files for a divorce, "let him depart." Insofar as the circumstances are beyond the believer's control "a brother or a sister is not under bondage in such cases." Some have concluded that the *bondage* here is a reference to the bondage of sin. However, the immediate context isn't addressing the sin question, but marriage. It is our firm conviction that the believer is *not bound* to the unequally yoked marriage. The opposite of bondage is liberty; therefore, the believer is at liberty to *remarry*, but only in the Lord (I Cor. 7:39). But how do we reconcile what the apostle says here in I Corinthians with Romans?

> "Know ye not, brethren, (for I speak to them that know the law,) how that the law hath dominion over a man as long as he liveth? For the woman which hath an husband is bound by the law to her husband so long as he liveth; but if the husband be dead, she is loosed from the law of her husband. So then if, while her husband liveth, she be married to another man, she shall be called an adulteress: but if her husband be dead, she is free from that law; so that she is no adulteress, though she be married to another man" (Rom. 7:1-3).

First of all, we must remember that Romans and I Corinthians were both written during Paul's early ministry. Since Paul received a special revelation from the Lord concerning the marriage relationship under grace (I Cor. 7:10-16), this means that the passage under consideration in Romans 7 would have to be interpreted in light of Corinthians.

Of course, Paul uses the marriage relationship to show that we are free from the law just as a wife would be free from the law of marriage if her husband passed away. Here it must be remembered that the Scriptures were primarily written to *believers*; therefore, it seems clear that the apostle has those in mind that were equally yoked together in the bonds of holy matrimony. However, he gives us a *further* revelation on the matter and goes into far more detail in I Corinthians 7 where an unequal situation may arise.

God always begins with the *ideal*. As we have seen, under the law He only made a provision in the sacrificial system for "sins of ignorance." Surely His chosen people would never sin against Him willingly (Lev. 4:27-29). But, in reality, they committed every sin under the sun, time and time again. Thus God graciously instituted the Day of Atonement to cover the sins of the nation. With regard to marriage, the standard has always been one man for one woman (Matt. 19:4-6). Nevertheless, under the law God permitted divorce because of the hardness of Israel's heart.

Today, grace is to forgive the erring party that a reconciliation might take place. Furthermore, in the case of an unequally yoked marriage a new regulation has been added. If the unbeliever *abandons* the marriage the believing party is permitted to remarry, but only in the Lord (I Cor. 7:15,39). Essentially, God has called us to *peace*.

Although marriage is taken lightly these days, those of us who know the Lord should hold it in high esteem. These matters must be taken more seriously for the Lord's sake, lest the Word of God be blasphemed. It is essential to teach our young people at an early age that they should only date and marry believers. "But that's so narrow!" Be that as it may, but I've sat across the counseling table with too many shipwrecked lives. The stories are heartbreaking. It won't seem so narrow if your daughter comes home from college and says she's fallen madly in love with an unsaved young man who has a history of drug abuse.

Christian parents and local assemblies must begin to work in tandem to curb the increased divorce rate due to unequally yoked marriages, that is, those that are entered into *knowingly*. Those who have will usually be the first to tell you it's an extremely difficult situation.

We've all heard parents say that their son or daughter's involvement with an unsaved dating partner is purely platonic. But why encourage them to become *emotionally* involved in a relationship that can never be brought to fruition? When the time comes to break off the relationship, the unbeliever simply won't understand, no matter how much explanation is given. Sadly, those who entangle themselves in this way usually end up in unequally yoked marriages.

The Scriptures present a clear line of teaching on this matter: "Be ye not unequally yoked together [partnerships, marriage, etc.] with unbelievers: for what fellowship hath righteousness with unrighteousness? and what communion hath light with darkness?" (II Cor. 6:14). God merely wants what is *best* for us. Our marriages can indeed stand the test of time if we will only obey the counsel of His will.

A GREAT MYSTERY

"For we are members of His Body, of His flesh, and of His bones. For this cause shall a man leave his father and mother, and shall be joined unto his wife, and they two shall be one flesh. This is a great mystery: but I speak concerning Christ and the Church" (Eph. 5:30-32).

297

Although we are unable to fully comprehend the mystical union that believers share in Christ, the apostle uses Adam and Eve, by way of *comparison,* to help our understanding.

1. *In the beginning God **created** the first man and woman.* "So God created man in His own image, in the image of God created He him; male and female created He them" (Gen. 1:27).

1. *We are a **new creation** in Christ.* "Therefore if any man be in Christ, he is a new creature [creation]; old things are passed away, behold, all things are become new" (II Cor. 5:17).

2. *Eve received her **life** from Adam.* "And the LORD God caused a deep sleep to fall upon Adam, and he slept: and He took one of his ribs, and closed up the flesh instead thereof; and the rib, which the LORD God had taken from man, made he a woman, and brought her unto the man" (Gen. 2:21,22).

2. *As members of the Body of Christ we receive our **life** from Christ.* "When Christ, who is our life, shall appear, then shall ye also appear with Him in glory." "I am crucified with Christ: nevertheless I live; yet not I, but Christ liveth in me" (Col. 3:4; Gal. 2:20).

3. *Since Adam was first formed then Eve, the **head** of the woman is the man.* "But I would have you know that the...head of the woman is the man" (I Cor. 11:3).

3. *Christ is the **head** of the Church, which is His Body.* "And He is the head of the Body, the Church...that in all things He might have the preeminence" (Col. 1:18).

4. *God **called** their name Adam.* "This is the book of the generations of Adam. In the day that God created man, in the likeness of God made he *him*; male and female created He them; and blessed them, and called their name Adam, in the day when they were created" (Gen. 5:1,2). Thus, we have Adam (*him*) without Eve called *Adam* and both Adam and Eve called *Adam.*

4. *According to the determinate counsel of God we are **called** the Church, the Body of Christ.* "For as the body is one, and hath many members, and all the members of that one body, being many, are one body: so also is Christ" (I Cor. 12:12). As one mighty warrior of the faith has expressed it: "We have Christ without the Church, and Christ and the Church as *Christ.*"[2]

5. *When God brought Adam and Eve together the two became **one flesh**.* "And Adam said, This is now bone of my bones, and flesh of my flesh: she shall be called Woman, because she was taken out of Man. Therefore shall a man leave his father and his mother, and shall cleave unto his wife: and they shall be one flesh" (Gen. 2:23,24).

5. *The members of the Body of Christ are said to be of **one flesh** with Him.* "For we are members of His Body, of His flesh, and of His bones." "So we, being many, are one Body in Christ, and every one members one of another" (Eph. 5:30; Rom. 12:5).

While Adam and Eve had no knowledge of what God had planned and purposed before the foundation of the world with regard to the Body of Christ, they nevertheless are used as a divine illustration of a wonderful truth. Namely, "they two shall be one flesh. This is a *great mystery*: but I speak concerning Christ and the Church."

THE BRIDE OF CHRIST

"Husbands, love your wives, even as Christ also loved the Church, and gave Himself for it; that He might sanctify and cleanse it with the washing of water by the Word. That He might present it to Himself a glorious Church, not having spot, or wrinkle, or any such thing; but that it should be holy and without blemish.

"So ought men to love their wives as their own bodies. He that loveth his wife loveth himself. For no man ever yet hated his own flesh; but nourisheth and cherisheth it, even as the Lord the Church: for we are members of His Body, of His flesh, and of His bones. For this cause shall a man leave his father and mother, and shall be joined unto his wife, and they two shall be one flesh.

"This is a great mystery: but I speak concerning Christ and the Church. Nevertheless let every one of you in particular so love his wife even as himself; and the wife see that she reverence her husband" (Eph. 5:25-33).

Bible teachers both past and present have debated as to whether or not the apostle taught that the Body is the *Bride of Christ*. Those who say we are, usually turn to this portion of Scripture to support their position.

Although this matter falls under the classification of a "secondary issue," the very nature of the subject has a profound effect upon how certain passages are interpreted.

Being mindful of the gravity of these *eternal issues*, I have sought to weigh the evidence very carefully under the microscope of Paul's gospel. After bringing everything into focus, I am more convinced than ever that the Body of Christ is *not* the *Bride, the Lamb's wife*. To me it seems terribly inconsistent to make distinction after distinction between Israel and the Church and then turn around and say that the Body is a *part* of the Bride of Christ. Of course, some teach that the "Body" is the Bride, not Israel, but this is simply not supported by the facts. One thing is clear, the opinions of men are inconsequential in view of the eternal question, "What saith the Scriptures?"

a. Words and Phrases

In our quest to rightly divide the Word of truth, certain "words" and "phrases" are identified with the Prophetic Program while others are associated with the Mystery. Interestingly, the "Bride of Christ" is an *unscriptural* phrase that is foreign to both programs of God. It is merely a theological expression that originated in the futile mind of man, to describe those who will be present at the *marriage of the Lamb* preceding the kingdom (Rev. 19:7-9). The exact phrase used in prophecy is only found in the Apocalypse where one of the seven angels said to John: "Come hither, I will show thee the bride, the Lamb's wife" (Rev. 21:9).

The terms "bride," "Lamb," and "wife" (in relation to the marriage of the Lamb) are woven throughout the pages of prophecy. For example: "He that hath the bride is the bridegroom" (John 3:29 cf. Jer. 2:32). "Behold the Lamb of God, which taketh away the sin of the world" (John 1:29 cf. Isa. 53:7). "...for the marriage of the Lamb is come, and His wife hath made herself ready" (Rev. 19:7 cf. Isa. 54:4-7).

One will search in vain to find any of this terminology in Paul's epistles. In fact, Paul frequently makes reference to Christ as Savior, Lord, and Head, but he never speaks of Him as the *Lamb of God* and for good reason. In prophecy, God had graciously imparted the sacrificial system which foreshadowed the once-for-all sacrifice. Thus, Christ was the sinless, spotless Lamb of God who satisfied the righteous demands of the law. He was consistently portrayed as the innocent *victim*—a lamb being led to the slaughter (Lev. 4:32-35; Isa. 53:3-8). With the introduction of a new dispensation, Christ is portrayed in a completely different light by the Apostle Paul. Today, He is the *Lord of glory*, the mighty *victor* who has conquered sin through His death and resurrection (I Cor. 2:8; 15:20-23).

b. The Bride in Prophecy

Who is the Bride of the Lamb? Thankfully, we do not have to rely upon our own human reasoning for an answer to this perplexing question. The Scriptures are explicitly clear that the "Bride" is *Israel*. When John the Baptist was asked why all men sought the Master while his ministry was fading in glory, he responded: "He that hath the bride is the bridegroom: but the friend of the bridegroom, which standeth and heareth him, rejoiceth greatly because of the bridegroom's voice: this my joy therefore is fulfilled. He must increase, but I must decrease" (John 3:29,30).

Working in reverse order, clearly the "friend of the bridegroom" is John the Baptist. John states that it was cause for rejoicing upon hearing the voice of the bridegroom. "This my [John the Baptist's] joy therefore is fulfilled." The "bridegroom" is none other than Christ Himself. In the previous verse John stated that he was "not the Christ, but that I am sent before Him" (vs. 28). He then confirms this by applying the illustration of the bridegroom. John was merely the forerunner to prepare the way for the Messiah. Hence, "He [Christ] must increase, but I [John] must decrease" (vs. 30).

Bearing in mind that the gospel according to John is a record of the earthly ministry of Christ, the "bride" is obviously *Israel*. Thus John the Baptist plainly declares in this record: "And I knew Him not: but that He should be made manifest to Israel, therefore am I come baptizing with water" (John 1:31). Did not our Lord instruct His disciples to "Go not into the way of the Gentiles....But go rather to the lost sheep of the house of Israel"? (Matt. 10:5,6). Furthermore, did He not say concerning Himself at that time: "I am not sent but unto the lost sheep of the house of Israel"? (Matt. 15:24).

Moving farther along, in the gospel according to Matthew, we have the parable of the ten virgins (Matt. 25:1-13). Here we learn that only *believing* Israel will participate in the actual marriage of the Lamb. You will recall that there were five wise virgins and five foolish. When the bridegroom delayed his coming the lamps of the unwise virgins ran out of oil as they slumbered. Therefore, the five foolish virgins, representative of the unsaved, were unprepared when the midnight cry came: *"Behold, the bridegroom cometh!"* While they went to purchase oil, the Bridegroom came "...and they [five saved virgins] that were ready went in with him to the marriage" (vs. 10). In addition, this portion teaches us that the *marriage* will take place when our Lord returns in His glory at the close of the Great Tribulation (vs. 13).

The above is confirmed by the Apostle John in the Book of Revelation.

> "Let us be glad and rejoice, and give honor to Him: for the marriage of the Lamb is come, and His wife hath made herself *ready*. And to her was granted that she should be arrayed in fine linen, clean and white: for the fine linen is the righteousness of saints" (Rev. 19:7,8).

Here in the context of the Second Coming of Christ, believing Israel is said to make herself *ready*. This is in keeping with the Prophetic Program, insofar as the kingdom saints did not have the assurance of their salvation. Consequently, they were instructed to *overcome, seek* and ye shall find, *endure* to the end, etc. (Matt. 6:33; 24:13; I John 4,5). Surely, this cannot be said of the Church, the Body of Christ. We are not only eternally secure, we have the assurance of it. As members of His Body we are *accepted* in the Beloved and therefore *complete* in Him (Eph. 1:6; Col. 2:10).

It should also be noted that John refers to Israel as the "wife" of the Lamb. Of course, this excludes the Body of Christ as participants in this ceremony inasmuch as Paul always addresses us in the *masculine* gender. Christ is our Head, not our groom. But in what sense is Israel the "wife" of the Lamb if she is to be united to the Messiah in the holy bonds of matrimony? The answer lies in the law of the *betrothal* (Deut. 22:23-25).

In days of old, when a man and woman came together before a rabbi, they were betrothed to one another. Similar to our present day engagement, the betrothal was a binding agreement wherein the parties were actually classified husband and wife. Upon completion of the ceremony, the couple returned to their respective homes for one year. This period was to give the husband an opportunity to *prepare* a home for his bride-to-be. It was also to ensure that the woman had been *faithful*, and was not with child. As we know, it was during this time that Mary was found with child before she and Joseph had come together in the intimacy of the marriage relationship (Matt. 1:18-25).

In this regard, Christ has returned to heaven to prepare a place for His bride in the kingdom. Since this aspect of the kingdom of heaven will be brought to the earth, it will be like heaven on earth. The millennium will have rebellion, crime, and punishment, etc., though in reduced degree because justice will be swift and accurate.

As the Tribulation period runs its course, Israel will be observed to determine who among them have been faithful to the commands of Christ contained in the kingdom gospel. This is why she is instructed to *occupy* until He comes (John 14:1-3 cf. Luke 19:11-27).

It is imperative that we glean from all of these principal passages that the marriage of the Lamb will occur on the earth when Christ returns to set up His kingdom. Following the wedding, the Apostle John was instructed to write:

> "Blessed are they which are called unto the marriage supper of the Lamb" (Rev. 19:9).

These guests are undoubtedly the kingdom Gentiles who will be invited to enjoy the blessings of the coming Golden Age (Matt. 25:31-46; Luke 14:15-24).

c. The Bride and Paul's Epistles

It is essential we keep in mind that the Church, the Body of Christ was *hid in God* from ages and generations past. Thus with the advent of the administration of Grace a number of *new* metaphors are applied to the Church, such as: Body, stewards, ambassadors, etc. Some seem to think that Paul also speaks of us as the Bride of Christ here in Ephesians chapter 5. But they have failed to distinguish between Paul's usage of a *metaphor* and a *simile*. A well-respected theologian from the turn of the century writes:

"The confounding of the Church as the Bride in Ephesians 5 has resulted from not seeing that the Figure of Speech used throughout the passage is that of *Simile*, and not *Metaphor*: 'Metaphor' places one thing for another. It is representation. 'Simile' is but resemblance. We must therefore not say when comparing one thing with another that that one thing is another. Observe the continued comparison between Christ and the Church of His Body, and the conduct of wives and husbands. Note the presence of simile in every instance, and the absence of metaphor."

"Wives, submit yourselves unto your own husbands, AS UNTO THE LORD" (Eph. 5:22).

"For the husband is the head of the wife, even AS CHRIST IS THE HEAD OF THE CHURCH"(vs. 23).

"Husbands, love your wives even AS CHRIST ALSO LOVED THE CHURCH, and gave Himself for it" (vs. 25).

"For no man ever yet hated his own flesh; but nourisheth and cherisheth it, even AS THE LORD THE CHURCH" (vs. 29).

So then, the apostle by using a *simile* instead of a metaphor is desiring to show the resemblance between the marriage relationship and Christ and His Church. Paul points to the *love relationship* to demonstrate that "as Christ loved the Church," husbands should love their wives. In like manner, wives are to emulate the Church by submitting to their own husbands. Nowhere in the portion under consideration does the apostle use the metaphor of a bride. In fact, just the opposite is true: "and He is the Savior of the BODY" (vs. 23). "For we are members of His BODY, of His flesh, and of His bones" (vs. 30).

> "For I am jealous over you with godly jealousy: for I have espoused you to one husband, that I may present you AS A CHASTE VIRGIN TO CHRIST" (II Cor. 11:2).

Since the Corinthians had a propensity to live carelessly, the apostle again uses the marriage relationship to show the importance of living a godly life in Christ Jesus. Marriages are built on trust, fidelity, and purity of heart and life. Paul was challenging the Corinthians to be *faithful* to the one who called them into His grace. We should add that since the apostle uses the pronoun "you" in this context it would seem to indicate that he was limiting his words to this local assembly of believers, and not the whole Body of Christ. Paul had established this assembly and naturally had a godly jealously over them as their spiritual father. Of course, we would do well to heed the apostle's admonition lest we too follow in the footsteps of the Corinthians.

It is our firm conviction that the Body of Christ is not the Bride, the Lamb's wife. We believe to teach otherwise is to bring a kingdom truth into our program where it is not only unnatural, but a forced interpretation as well. May God in His grace give us a Berean spirit to study to see if these things are so.

13

The Art of Admonition

> "Children, obey your parents in the Lord: for this is right. Honour thy father and mother; (which is the first commandment with promise;) that it may be well with thee, and thou mayest live long on the earth."
>
> —*Ephesians 6:1-3*

In addition to companionship, marriage provided the means through which the human race could *propagate* itself. Adam and Eve were to "be fruitful, and multiply, and replenish [Heb. *to fill*] the earth." This command has never been rescinded. In fact, following the flood it was reaffirmed with Noah and his family upon their arrival in the New World (Gen. 9:1).

In the days of Nimrod, when the whole earth was of one language, men sought to unite under the banner that there is strength in unity, that is, apart from God. As men attempted to build a city *contrary* to God's command, lest they "be scattered abroad," He confounded their language, scattering them across the face of the earth. This resulted in the formation of the nations as we know them today.

So then, it is God's will for mankind to bear children and *fill* the earth. The Scriptures have a great deal to say about conception, birth, and how to raise our children. Although there is an impressive array of books written on these subjects, *the Book* is the final authority in all matters of faith and practice.

THE HERITAGE OF THE LORD

"In the beginning was the Word, and the Word was with God, and the Word was God. The same was in the beginning with God. All things were made by Him; and without Him was not any thing made that was made. In Him was life; and the life was the light of men" (John 1:1-4).

The moral issues of life and death have always stirred the deepest emotional responses. As the battle over the origin of life continues to rage between creation and evolution, one thing which has been lost in the discussion is the fact that only life can *generate* life. Life cannot emerge from inanimate things. The *theory* of evolution would have us believe that over billions of years "out of nothing came something" which gradually evolved into the present complex life forms on earth today.

The author of *Evolution in a Test Tube* states that life originated from inorganic (lifeless) chemicals: "This survival-of-the-fittest scenario takes place even at the level of molecules. On primordial [primeval or dateless past] Earth, chemicals with slight individual variations must have replicated themselves and competed with one another, scientists believe. The successful ones gave rise to the complex biological molecules that serve living organisms today."

George Wald, the author of *The Physics and Chemistry of Life* emphatically declares: "One has only to contemplate the magnitude of this task to concede that the spontaneous generation [i.e. life somehow generated from slime or some other inorganic form] of a living organism is impossible. Yet here we are—as a result, I believe, of spontaneous generation." Of course, evolutionists often oppose themselves, as seen in Sir Fred Hoyle's statement: "The likelihood of spontaneous formation of life from inanimate matter is one to a number of 40,000 noughts after it."

Wow! You have to admit those are some weighty statements. As I read them a passage of Scripture immediately came to mind: "Professing themselves to be wise, they became fools." Evolutionary thought lacks any *credible* evidence. It is all based upon assumptions, which have never been substantiated. Moreover, it should be noted that neither evolution nor creation can be proven scientifically. Consequently, it essentially comes down to a matter of *faith*. Either we must place our faith in the theory of evolution, that life originated in a primitive soup of chemicals, or that God created all things. Since man is fallible and frequently prone to error, we prefer to believe the biblical account of creation.

God created all things in heaven and earth in *six* literal twenty-four hour days. On the sixth day, He formed man from the dust of the earth and breathed into his nostrils the breath of life. However, that lifeless shell of clay only became a *living being* after God imparted the breath of life—"In Him was life." As a creation of God, man has the ability, as He wills, to *reproduce* life through the natural means of conception and birth. Thus, the marriage relationship provides the biological mechanism to produce offspring.

> "Lo, children are an heritage of the LORD: and the fruit of the womb is his reward. As arrows are in the hand of a mighty man; so are children of the youth. Happy is the man that hath his quiver full of them: they shall not be ashamed, but they shall speak with the enemies in the gate" (Psa. 127:3-5).

Children are the *Lord's* inheritance—they belong to Him. If He blesses us with the pitter-patter of little footsteps around the house, He expects us to raise our children to be instruments of praise and thanksgiving. Children are likened to arrows in the hand of a mighty man; they demonstrate the *strength* of our youth while advancing the fulfillment of God's purpose to fill the earth. "Happy [or blessed] is the man that hath his quiver full of them." In David's day a quiver held about twelve arrows. So, happy is the man who has *twelve* children!

a. Training Up a Child

"Children, obey your parents in the Lord: for this is right. Honour thy father and mother; (which is the first commandment with promise;) that it may be well with thee, and thou mayest live long on the earth. And, ye fathers, provoke not your children to wrath: but bring them up in the nurture and admonition of the Lord" (Eph. 6:1-4).

Notice the apostle commands children to *obey* their parents. In other words, it isn't something that comes natural to a child. That little bundle of joy has an *old nature*, which sometimes is mean, deceptive, talks back, throws temper tantrums, and can be downright obnoxious. If you're a parent, we need say no more. But how do we *train* our children to obey without hog-tying and gagging them until they're twenty-one?

The popular humanistic approach of our day says, let children *express* themselves, never spank them, simply because you may inhibit them for life. This philosophy, however, causes children to become assertive and in some cases even demanding. Today, children are running their parents for the most part. They quickly learn how to *manipulate* their parents to get their way—the old nature is crafty even at a young age!

Probably most of us have had this same experience at one time or another while shopping at a supermarket: You pass a mother leisurely pushing a cart down an aisle with a sweet little three year old enjoying the ride. The next time you pass them this little guy has turned into a Jekyll and Hyde, screaming at the top of his lungs because he wants out of the cart. Desperate, mom tries reasoning with her three year old, if that's possible: "Honey, mommy's going to tell daddy." He already knows, though, that daddy's a pushover and will only raise his voice.

As the screaming intensifies she attempts a new tactic: "If you stop crying, mommy will buy you an ice cream cone." But he normally gets his way plus the ice cream treat!! By now, most are headed for the exits as she tries the sympathy approach: "You're going to make mommy cry." Meanwhile, you're standing there thinking someone should be crying here, but it should not be mom. Embarrassed, she finally gives in and finds herself chasing her persistent little guy through the store. He has effectively *expressed* himself.

As we have seen, children are a *gift* from the Lord. Thus, they should be a blessing, not a cause for calling out the National Guard. A child must be properly trained during those early developmental years or the parents will reap a whirlwind when he reaches his teen years. The mistake most parents make is waiting to administer disciplinary action until after their son or daughter turns fifteen. The crucial period for training a child to be *obedient* is from birth to about ten years of age. There is a timeless principle found in the Book of Proverbs that if applied consistently will save parents a lot of heartache.

> "Train up a child [Heb. *na'ar*—infancy to adolescence] in the way he should go: and when he is old, he will not depart from it" (Prov. 22:6).

Interestingly, Solomon uses the term "train" here rather than teach. Of course, we teach our children the difference between right and wrong on a daily basis, but they must be trained to apply what they have been taught. The Hebrew word "train" has the idea to mold the character, drill, make obedient to orders. Parents are to establish *rules* of acceptable behavior for their children to obey, and if they fail to be obedient the proper discipline should be administered. Sadly, most times the family pet is more obedient to instructions than the children who live in the same house.

According to the Scriptures, the proper form of discipline should be the application of the *rod*. "Foolishness is bound in the heart of a child; but the rod of correction shall drive it far from him" (Prov. 22:15). In short, a good spanking at the *seat* of the matter effectively teaches the child that there are *consequences* for breaking the rules. Although most parents feel like their hearts are being torn out, it is far better for godly parents to discipline their children than the *State Department of Corrections* when they become young adults. They won't be as understanding.

Moms and dads should never allow their children to *embarrass* them in public, although it has happened to us all. The remedy at our house was always to give a spanking in the presence of others for unruly behavior. Once your children are embarrassed a couple of times, they won't be so inclined to act up. I know, I know, those crocodile tears can tug at your heart. But which would you prefer: that your children shed tears while they are growing up as result of your loving discipline, or for you to shed tears over their *rebellious* actions when they come of age?

While a child ought to be consistently disciplined, he should never be abused in any way. Children should obey out of love and respect, not fear. Paul adds: "And, ye fathers, provoke not your children to wrath: but bring them up in the nurture and admonition of the Lord" (Eph. 6:4). This phrase may seem strange at first, especially since mothers spend the lion's share of the time with the little ones. But ultimately the fathers will be held *accountable* at the Judgment Seat of Christ in regard to whether or not their children were brought up in the things of the Lord.

George Douglas writes these insightful words: "A father is neither an anchor to hold us back, nor a sail to take us there, but always a guiding light whose love shows us the way."

Since fathers have a tendency to be overbearing, Paul cautions dads to be very careful that they don't provoke or *exasperate* their children. Fathers are prone to let things slide for months until something triggers an overreaction, which results in some form of unreasonable discipline. We call this *changing* the rules.

Imagine if you attended a baseball game and every inning the rules of the game changed. Instead of three strikes and you're out, the batter is given five strikes before he's out. But when the home team comes to bat the umpire revises the rules making two strikes an out. Before long you would be so frustrated that you'd throw your hands up in exasperation. But this is oftentimes exactly what happens in the home. Once the rules are established they must be *consistently* applied. If the kids aren't permitted to swing from the chandeliers then, if they are caught doing so, they should be *immediately* disciplined.

b. Honor Thy Father and Mother

Both fathers and mothers have a God-given responsibility to *teach* their children the ways of the Lord. Not simply drilling them with the Scriptures or merely imparting a bunch of facts, but encouraging them to make the Word of God a part of their lives. Once again, the best teacher always serves as a *guide*. There's a little passage tucked away in the Old Testament that will help give us some direction:

> "And thou shalt love the LORD thy God with all thine heart, and with all thy soul, and with all thy might. And these words, which I command thee this day, shall be in thine heart: and thou shalt teach them diligently unto thy children, and shalt talk of them when thou sittest in thine house, and when thou walkest by the way, and when thou liest down, and when thou risest up" (Deut. 6:5-7).

Although these instructions were given to Israel under the law, we can glean from these passages another time-honored principle. Our walk through life gives us thousands of opportunities and object lessons to share with our children the *handiwork* of God. Here are some suggestions.

If you're sitting around a crackling fire at home, it's a great time to teach those little ones that have gathered at your feet how God delivered Shadrach, Meshach, and Abednego from the fiery furnace. Think of it, not a hair on their heads was singed. If you're walking along the rim of the Grand Canyon, what a great opportunity to share with the kids that the Grand Canyon was not carved out by the Colorado River over billions of years, as evolutionary geologists tell us. Rather, it was formed in the days of Noah when God judged the earth with a cataclysmic *universal* flood (Psa. 104:6-9).

If mom and dad pray before they retire every evening the little ones soon learn the *importance* of prayer. Challenge them to pray about what area of *full-time* service the Lord might use them some day. Around the breakfast table in the morning the conversation might go something like this: "Just think, heaven could be astir at this very moment. Perhaps today is the day the Lord will return for the Church, which is His Body."

c. A Challenge For Our Parents

Probably the most commonly asked question of a seven year old is, "What do you want to be when you grow up?"

Usually the little one is so frozen with fear that the one inquiring must resort to a form of interrogation: "a doctor, lawyer, policeman; I know, a fireman!" These are noble professions indeed, but why are children almost never encouraged to pursue the *ministry*? Is the Lord's work any less meaningful? Are the callings of pastor, evangelist, missionary and Christian counselor unworthy of our childrens' consideration? Parents do well to remember that there is no higher calling in life than the Lord's service.

Sadly, our young people are so preconditioned to aspire to worldly professions that the ministry is not even a viable option. Timothy's mother had no way of knowing whether or not God would call her son into full-time service. But to her credit, she trained Timothy from a small child in the Scriptures to *prepare* him for the things of the Lord. Shortly after his conversion to Christ, he was called into the ministry, where he delivered many from a Christless eternity (II Tim. 1:6).

During those formative years we need to encourage our young to seek the face of the Lord as to what area of *Christian service* the Lord might use them.

> "Honor thy father and mother; (which is the first commandment with promise;) that it may be well with thee, and thou mayest live long on the earth" (Eph. 6:2-3).

There are two benefits when children honor their parents. Paul begins by stating, "that it may be well with thee." In short, if a child honors his parents he will have a *good conscience* that he has done right by them and also glorified God. The second benefit is the *promise* of prolonged years made reference to by the phrase: "thou mayest live long on the earth." This does not mean that all young people who die at an early age necessarily dishonored their parents. It does mean they will *escape* many of the pitfalls of life that could shorten their lives.

For example, a young man who heeds the warning of his parents that speed kills, will never lose his life because he was driving too fast. If a daughter obeys her parents never to get into a car with a stranger, the likelihood of her being a murder victim is greatly diminished.

Every parent should consider taking their ten, eleven, and twelve year olds to a rescue mission. I have preached a number of times at the *Pacific Garden Mission* in Chicago and came away profoundly touched by the experience. You witness firsthand how the sins of immorality, alcoholism, gambling, and drug abuse destroy lives. Thankfully, many of these poor souls have come to know Christ, but they must live with the consequences of their *disobedience*.

DELIVERANCE IN CHRIST

"Servants, be obedient to them that are your masters according to the flesh, with fear and trembling, in singleness of your heart, as unto Christ;

"Not with eyeservice, as menpleasers; but as the servants of Christ, doing the will of God from the heart; with good will doing service, as to the Lord, and not to men:

"Knowing that whatsoever good thing any man doeth, the same shall he receive of the Lord, whether he be bond or free.

"And, ye masters, do the same things unto them, forbearing threatening: knowing that your Master also is in heaven; neither is there respect of persons with Him" (Eph. 6:5-9).

The term "servants" used here by the apostle is the Greek word *doulos* or *bondslave*. According to historians there were approximately six million slaves throughout the Roman Empire at the dawn of Christendom. Paul left *slavery* where he found it. This is not to insinuate that he sanctioned it, nor do we. Slavery was so firmly entrenched at the time that any attempt to uproot it would have brought the full wrath of the pagan world against the Church. We do feel, however, the apostle surmised that Christianity would eventually *eradicate* this oppressive system from the face of the earth. A recent article that appeared in a Christian periodical entitled, *Abolishing Slavery in the British Empire* serves as an example:

"On June 22, 1772, Lord Mansfield, chief justice of the King's Bench, handed down his famous decision that effectively eliminated slavery on the soil of the British Isles. Although slavery had gradually died out in Europe after the introduction of Christianity, it was not officially prohibited, and occasionally a slave-owner from overseas would bring slaves with him to Britain. In his celebrated decision, Mansfield held that a slave automatically became a free man by setting foot in Britain. But this decision did not have the slightest effect on slavery in the overseas colonies.

"Not until 1811 did William Wilberforce—who had been deeply influenced by John Newton [himself a former slave-trader before he came to Christ], author of *'Amazing Grace'*— succeed in getting the Parliament to ban the slave trade. In 1833 the decision was reached to abolish slavery throughout the British Empire over a six year period."[1]

Until Christianity gained a greater influence in the world, Paul dealt with the matter of slavery according to the precepts of the gospel. Basically there were three ways to become a slave in biblical times. You could be made a slave by a conquering nation, be born into it, or by selling yourself into slavery to pay a debt. Although the cruelties of slavery are incomprehensible, Paul instructed Christian slaves to obey their masters with fear and trembling. They were to do so with "singleness of heart," that is, not with *duplicity*—appearing to be serving faithfully on one hand, but plotting to escape on the other. Nor were they to serve with "eyeservice, as menpleasers," which has the idea of only working when the master was present.

Rather, Christian slaves were to labor as unto the Lord. The gospel message lifted the slave out of the doldrums of slavery and raised him to *new* heights. In essence he was to place himself in a completely *different* mindset. Whatever he was called upon to do, he was to view it as being done for Christ. Thus, as servants of the Lord they were "doing the will of God from the heart." But there was also an added *incentive*: If they did that which was right and faithfully served their masters, the Lord would *reward* them accordingly at that day (vs. 8).

The apostle addresses the *masters* as well. "And, ye masters, do the same things unto them, forbearing threatening." The Christian master was to follow the same instructions. He was to treat those under his authority with *love* and *compassion* as the Lord does the Church. Furthermore, masters were admonished to forbear threatening, simply because not all those under their dominance knew the Lord. If a master was cruel and abusive, it would be unlikely that a slave would have respect for what he said about the gospel. They were to remember that one day they, too, would stand before their Master, which is in heaven.

We have often said that the Word of God is *timeless*. These practical instructions that were delivered to slaves and their masters nearly 2,000 years ago can also be applied to Christian labor and management today. Thus, we too are well served if we heed these warnings and work together to the glory of God. Perhaps the following story will help illustrate the importance of *working together* to further the cause of Christ.

THE CARPENTER'S TOOLS

"The carpenter's tools had a conference. Brother Hammer was in the chair. The meeting had informed him that he must leave, because he was too noisy. But he said, 'If I am to leave this carpenter shop, Brother Drill must go too. He is so insignificant that he makes a very little impression.'

"Little Brother Drill rose up and said, 'All right, but Brother Screw must go also. You have to turn him around and around again and again to get him anywhere.'

"Brother Screw then said, 'If you wish, I will go; but Brother Plane must leave also. All his work is on the surface; there is no depth to it.'

"To this Brother Plane replied, 'Well, Brother Rule will also have to withdraw if I do, for he is always measuring folks as though he were the only one who is right.'

"Brother Rule then complained against Brother Sandpaper, and said, 'I just don't care; he is rougher than he ought to be, and he is always rubbing people the wrong way.'

"In the midst of those discussions the Carpenter of Nazareth walked in. He had come to perform His day's work. He put on His apron, and went to the bench to make a pulpit from which to preach the gospel to the poor. He employed the screw, the drill, the sandpaper, the saw, the hammer, the plane, and all the other tools.

"After the day's work was over, and the pulpit was finished, Brother Saw arose and said, 'Brethren, I perceive that all of us are laborers together with God.'"[2]

Every member of the Body of Christ is important in the eyes of God. He gives each of us enabling gifts whereby we might carry on the work of the Lord in His absence. Let's never count a thing too small to be done for the Lord. As it has been said, "That little thing that is to be done may, after all, be the important thing, and may stand out in ages to come as the most important of all."

14

The Great Conflict

"Finally, my brethren, be strong in the Lord, and in the power of His might. Put on the whole armor of God, that ye may be able to stand against the wiles of the devil."

—Ephesians 6:10,11

History bears witness to an endless stream of conflicts between the nations of the world. Those who fought in these campaigns affirm that *war* is nothing short of mass *confusion*. The army with the most comprehensive plan of attack to minimize confusion is usually victorious.

When the Allied Forces prepared to liberate Europe in World War II, Hitler's forces, under the command of General Rommel, armed for the conflict. Relatively sure the attack would be along the coast of Normandy Beach, the German army wasted no time strategically placing their machine gun nests along the cliffs of the beach. The army stationed on higher ground is always in an enviable position. Thus, fate appeared to be on Hitler's side, simply because it would be a suicide mission to attempt a landing at Normandy.

On the day of the invasion, the weather had turned inclement. As providence would have it, General Rommel concluded that the Allied Forces would never attack under such conditions; consequently, he left his post and returned home to celebrate his wife's birthday. As dawn broke, the Allied Forces, under the command of General Eisenhower, came ashore and caught the German army off guard, but it did not take them long to regroup. The battle was intense and casualties were high on both sides. Once Eisenhower's troops managed to scale the rugged cliffs, they broke through the front-lines of Hitler's main defensive position. This caused *confusion* throughout the German ranks. No commanding officer dared to call for reinforcements without the approval of Hitler or Rommel, neither of whom was able to be reached. Historians agree that the Allied landing at Normandy Beach, commonly known as "D" Day, was the turning point of the Second World War.

If we compare our *spiritual warfare* with the above, there are many uncanny similarities. Satan has a well-devised plan of attack to cause confusion in our ranks. His plan is twofold: First, he is tireless in his attempt to blind the minds of the unsaved that they might not receive the light of the gospel of salvation (II Cor. 4:3,4). Perhaps his most effective tool to accomplish this end is *religion*. Yes, you read that correctly—religion! Only the Judgment to come will bear witness as to how many have been swept into a Christless eternity on the basis of this blind guide (Col. 2; Rom. 10:1-4; Gal. 2:16). Second, the god of this age is well aware that he is unable to rob believers of their salvation (Rom. 8:35-39), but he can, and often does, defeat the child of God, thus causing him to suffer great loss. Of course, Satan has a special hatred for those who have come to see the preaching of Jesus Christ according to the revelation of the Mystery. For those who may think otherwise, simply consider the *Grace Movement*; he has successfully broken us into pieces, and the pieces that remain are one by one being shattered by *new evangelicalism* or *extremism*.

A CALL TO ARMS

"Finally, my brethren, be strong in the Lord, and in the power of His might. Put on the whole armor of God, that ye may be able to stand against the wiles of the devil" (Eph. 6:10,11).

Before a country enters into a war, it must ready its army in *advance*. Picture in your mind's eye for a moment a battlefield with barbed wire strewn about, bombs exploding and bullets whizzing everywhere. Now imagine a young soldier hunkered down in a foxhole asking his squad leader, "Sarge, how do I load this gun?" This may seem rather absurd, but it is a fairly accurate assessment of how unprepared most believers are to do battle with the enemy. Upon the commencement of a spiritual conflict, we must be *prepared* beforehand to effectively defend the faith and wield the Sword of the Spirit to the glory of God. Those who fail to do so are either lost in action or they are the spiritual casualties you see lying about on the battlefield.

As Paul calls us to a state of readiness, he says, *"Be strong in the Lord."* A similar phrase is found in the Book of Joshua. "Be strong and of a good courage: for unto this people shalt thou divide for an inheritance the land, which I sware unto their fathers to give them. Only be thou strong and very courageous, that thou mayest observe to do according to all the law, which Moses my servant commanded thee: turn not from it to the right hand or to the left, that thou mayest prosper whithersoever thou goest" (Josh. 1:6,7).

Through Abraham, God had promised His chosen people that they would *inherit* a land flowing with milk and honey. This massive piece of real estate called the *Promised Land* rightfully belonged to Israel—all she had to do was *claim* it. But there were enemies in the land, some of whom were giants. Hence, Jehovah's charge to Joshua, "Be strong and of a good courage." In other words, God would go before them as a mighty man of war to do battle on behalf of His people. *If* they obeyed the Word of the Lord, they would be more than conquerors. In addition, the physical and material blessings of God would flow from Zion like a mighty river.

With the change in dispensations, God is making known His manifold wisdom through the Church, the Body of Christ. Via the revelation committed to the Apostle Paul, we understand that the members of Christ's Body have a *heavenly* hope and calling. Unlike Israel, we have been *unconditionally* blessed with all spiritual blessings in the heavenlies. The apostle has spent the better part of three chapters here in Ephesians explaining our *position* in Christ and the spiritual blessings that flow from it.

It is advantageous for every member of the Body of Christ to not only familiarize himself with these blessings, but more importantly, to understand the *significance* of each. You see, the battle scene has shifted from the earthly to the *heavenly* realm. But this realm is presently occupied by Satan and his fallen angelic host (second heaven). And be assured, he is not about to relinquish any of his authority or territory without a fight.

Throughout the ages Satan has sought to hinder, and in some cases, overthrow the plans and purposes of God. Arno Gaebelein was the first to call this hostility, "The conflict of the Ages." In the days of Noah, he attempted to *corrupt* the human race. When God turned from the nations and set His affection on Abraham, Satan targeted the children of Israel, causing one *calamity* after another. Now that Israel has been set aside in unbelief and God has turned to the Gentiles, we are the objects of his wrath. The powers of darkness would like nothing better than to discourage, corrupt and defeat every member of the Body of Christ. Little wonder, the apostle challenges us to "be strong in the Lord." Why? Because we are up against a formidable foe, one who knows us better than we know ourselves. We must never enter this conflict in our own strength, for if we do, it will be one sorrow after another.

The only way the believer will ever endure the malicious attacks of this enemy is to put on the whole *armor of God*, stand firm, and rely solely on the *power of His might*. We must defend our *position* in Christ much like a goalie does on a hockey team. The goal tender has to consistently be on his guard—vigilance is his middle name! As the puck enters his end of the ice, the goalie must react quickly to the deceptive maneuvers of his opponent. Although it may be tempting for him to skate down the ice with the puck, if he strays out of position the opposition usually regains possession and scores the game-winning goal. Consequently, both he and his teammates would suffer a humiliating loss. We, too, must know everything there is to know about our position in Christ, defend it, and never forsake it. The victory is ours if we follow the marching orders of the Commander in Chief!

THE POWER OF HIS MIGHT

> "and in the power of His might....For we wrestle not against flesh and blood, but against principalities, against powers, against the rulers of the darkness of this world, against spiritual wickedness in high places" (Eph. 6:10,12).

As we enter into the battle, we must do so "in the power of His might." As we mentioned earlier, in the Old Testament when God chose to demonstrate His almighty power, He did so by pointing to His miraculous parting of the Red Sea. With the breath of His nostrils He caused the waters of the Red Sea to stand up as a heap on the right and on the left, and the children of Israel crossed to the other side on dry ground. Interestingly, in these end times, God points us to the *resurrection* of His dear Son as an exhibition of His omnipotence.

Thus, Paul's reference to the "power of His might" refers us back to Ephesians chapter one: "And what is the exceeding greatness of His power to us-ward who believe, according to the working of His mighty power, which He wrought in Christ, when He raised Him from the dead" (Eph. 1:19,20). Of course, God is not permitting outward manifestations of this power today, such as raising the dead. However, we do have at our disposal an endless source of *spiritual* power from which to draw *strength* in times of temptation, discouragement, depression, mourning, etc. This will help us withstand the shock of the conflict. It is also important to remember that God delivered others from the hand of the enemy and the same promise applies to us in the administration of Grace (II Tim. 3:11,12 cf. 4:17,18).

We should add that there is another dimension to this phrase "the power of His might." If we continue with the apostle's train of thought in Ephesians 1:20, not only did God the Father raise Christ from the dead, He also "set Him at His own right hand in the heavenly places, far above all principality, and power, and might, and dominion, and every name that is named, not only in this world, but also in that which is to come: And hath put all things under His feet" (Eph. 1:20-22). Christ is indeed all that He claimed to be, therefore the Father has highly exalted Him. All things are *subject* to Him in both heaven and earth. He is seated far above all these various realms of angelic authority, and they humbly render servitude to Him who is above all others. The Scriptures clearly record that God does everything decently and in order. Heaven is a place of *organization*. For example, the elect angels are ranked accordingly:

Cherubims: Defenders of God's holiness (stationed around the throne) (Gen. 3:23,24 cf. Rev. 4:6-8).

Seraphims: Champions of God's righteousness (stationed above the throne) (Isa. 6:1-8).

Seven Spirits of God: Attendants of highest service (stationed before the throne) (Rev. 1:4 cf. Luke 1:19).

Principalities: Supreme rulers (similar to our Cabinet Members) (Eph. 3:10).

Powers: Delegated authority (similar to our Joint Chiefs of Staff) (Eph. 3:10).

Mights: Battalions (similar to our Armed Forces—Army, Navy, etc.) (Eph. 1:21).

Thrones: Seats of authority over a territory (similar to our Governors) (Col. 1:16).

Dominions: Enforcement agencies (similar to our local authorities—Police, etc.) (Col. 1:16).

Host: Populace (similar to our various stations in life) (Psa. 148:1,2 cf. Neh. 9:6).

In the beginning when Lucifer sinned, one-third of the angelic host defected with him in rebellion against God (Rev. 12:3,4 cf. 12:9). As he assumed his fallen position as the *archenemy* of God, Satan arranged his workers of darkness in a similar pattern as the authority structure of heaven. But, here, something is often overlooked. Satan and his unseemly cohorts are also *subject* to Christ. He has power over these "forces of evil" as seen in the gospel according to Luke. As our Lord ministered the good news of the kingdom on earth, there was a flurry of demonic activity. Like any well-trained general, Satan knows when and where his attacks will prove to be most effective. Of course, since it was the Lord Himself ministering the Word, the battle was unbelievably intense.

Shortly after the Master miraculously calmed the raging storm on the Sea of Galilee, He came to the country of the Gadarenes. As He prepared to preach, a man by the name of Legion, who was demon possessed, withstood Him.[1] Those under the control of a devil, in this case devils, as his name implies, usually tend to be lewd, violent, and have unusual strength. Legion was all this and more; he was *exceedingly fierce*, so much so that all men feared him. Naked, he threw himself down at the feet of the Master, and a demon within this poor prisoner of darkness said, mockingly: "What have I to do with Thee, Jesus, Thou Son of God Most High?" Even the demons acknowledge the Deity of Christ! But the next two statements uttered by this devil are telling. "I beseech Thee, torment me not....And they besought Him that He would not command them to go out into the deep." These workers of darkness knew that the Son of God had *authority* over them. In fact, they trembled at the thought that He would chain them in the sides of the pit where they would live in torment until the future Judgment (Luke 8:26-39).

Satan and the demonic host probably roll in laughter when a believer pridefully exclaims in his own strength, "Get thee behind me, Satan!" However, "in Christ," as we put on the gospel armor in the *power of His might*, they head for cover! Why? Because they know that they are already defeated. When dawn broke on the morning of our Lord's crucifixion, Satan had successfully manipulated all of the powers that be to condemn Christ. As the sound of the hammer hitting the nails echoed off the surrounding hills of Calvary, the demonic host looked on intently, they had Him right where they wanted Him! Suddenly, an eerie hush fell over heaven as the skies darkened and the hour drew near. Then, the moment of triumph—He's dead! We've won the conflict of the ages, evil shall now prevail! They probably bowed themselves before the great one who brought them to this glorious victory—Lucifer!

But three days later they were singing a different tune. Imagine their surprise when the seal of Christ's tomb was broken and they beheld the Son of God *rise* from the dead! It was their worst possible nightmare. The party was over and they knew they were helpless. Paul says: "And having spoiled principalities and powers, He made a shew of them openly, triumphing over them in it." This is a picture of the mighty ancient warrior who *surprises* his enemy, conquers, and parades his subjects through the streets of his homeland. Victory!!! Satan and his fallen host had absolutely no idea that when Christ died that day, He was dying for the sins of the world! He had purchased with His own blood the eternal salvation of all those who would hereafter believe on His death, burial and resurrection. Satan and his entourage may attempt to intimidate us, but we are more than conquerors in Christ.

THE WILES OF THE DEVIL

"Put on the whole armor of God, that ye may be able
to stand against the wiles of the devil" (Eph. 6:11).

The definition of *illusion* is: "The state or fact of being intellectually deceived or misled." Perhaps the most well-known illusionist of our day is David Copperfield. News reports were rampant when he supposedly made the *Statue of Liberty* disappear in New York harbor. Millions looked on as he raised a black curtain in front of the statue and when it was lowered, Lady Liberty was gone! Even those who were present that evening could not believe their eyes. Many walked away muttering to themselves, "How'd he do that?" The answer is "elementary Watson," it was merely an illusion. Things are not always as they appear to be.

The same may be said of the world's perception of Satan, who is the *master* of illusion. Caricatures of the evil one often portray him as a red, grotesque being with horns, tail, and a pitchfork in his left hand. According to popular opinion, the devil spends his time stoking the eternal fires of hell awaiting those who have been condemned. Of course, this is nothing more than a *fabrication* of Satan. In reality, Lucifer can appear as an angel of light, perfect in beauty and wisdom (Ezek. 28:17 cf. II Cor. 11:14).

We would venture to say that if Satan were to transform himself into human form, which is well within his means, he would probably be handsome, intelligent, articulate and have enough charisma to mesmerize the masses. Although he is light years away from God in knowledge, wisdom, and power, he does possess an unbelievable *aptitude* far beyond any human capability. For example, he supernaturally flashed all the kingdoms of this world before Christ in a moment of time. Furthermore, he will also empower the Anti-Christ to perform miracles in the coming Tribulation period (Luke 4:5,6; II Thes. 2:8,9).

While "hell" was originally created for the devil and his angels, they have yet to be cast there. Consequently, Satan is alive and well, roaming about "seeking whom he may devour." Interestingly, he is not confined to the earth nor stoking the fires of hell as some suppose. His realm is in the heavens where he *presides* over the rulers of darkness.

THE FALL OF SATAN

> "How art thou fallen from heaven, O Lucifer, son of the morning! how art thou cut down to the ground, which didst weaken the nations!" (Isa. 14:12).

Based on this passage and other related ones in Ezekiel and the gospel according to Luke, many have surmised that

God has cast Satan out of heaven to the earth where he now dwells. Actually, this passage here in Isaiah and its counterparts are merely prophecies regarding the devil's *future* expulsion from his heavenly realm.

God's ways are not man's ways. He sees the end from the beginning and frequently speaks of events yet to be fulfilled in the *present* tense. Paul states, God has "raised us up together, and made us sit [present tense] together in heavenly places in Christ Jesus" (Eph. 2:6). He presently sees us seated with Christ in the heavenlies. However, our current address is good old "planet earth." So then, insofar as God's sovereign purpose can never be frustrated, He views all things from the standpoint of its ultimate consummation.

Shortly after God pronounced His creation very good on the sixth day, Lucifer *fell*. Once the holiness of God was violated by Satan's transgression, he was *expelled* from the third heaven, experiencing the first of several *demotions* (Ezek. 28:16-19). As one author has expressed it, he has gone from "walking up and down in the midst of the stones of fire [the presence of God] to the lake of fire" [which is his ultimate end] (Ezek. 28:14 cf. Matt. 25:41). By the decree of God, Satan now inhabits the *first* and *second* heavens. He will occupy this domain until Michael and his angels cast him to the earth in the middle of the coming Tribulation.

> "And there was war in heaven: Michael and his angels fought against the dragon; and the dragon fought and his angels, and prevailed not; neither was their place found any more in heaven.
>
> "And the great dragon was cast out, that old serpent, called the Devil, and Satan, which deceiveth the whole world: he was cast out into the earth, and his angels were cast out with him....Woe to the inhabiters of the earth and of the sea! for the devil is come down unto

you, having great wrath, because he knoweth that he hath but a short time" (Rev. 12:7-9,12).

As the Apostle John was supernaturally transported to the future day of the Lord, he actually saw this literal fulfillment of Isaiah's prophecy concerning Satan's *fall* from heaven. Then, three and one-half years later, John witnessed the devil being bound and cast into the *bottomless pit* for one thousand years (Rev. 20:1-3). The final phase of his demotion comes at the close of the millennial kingdom. Satan will be loosed from prison and go forth to turn the nations of the world against the true and living God. But his reign of terror is only momentary as he is taken and cast into the *lake of fire* (Rev. 20:10). The final chapter in this saga will be entitled, the *abolition* of evil.

Most pastors have witnessed, at one time or another, Satan destroy those he methodically entangles in a web of *pride*. Sadly, others usually see the fall coming long before the victim knows what is happening. They can't see the forest for the trees, until it's too late. Consequently, we must keep a *watchful* eye for his crafty ways, always being mindful of the apostle's words: "Wherefore let him that thinketh he standeth take heed lest he fall." It is a frightening thought when Satan is cast to the earth that he will be consumed with "great wrath." Little wonder, the latter part of Jacob's Trouble is called the *Great Tribulation*. Between the wrath of God and the rage of Satan this world will be an asylum of heartache.

Although Satan has access to the earth today, his primary base of operations is the *heavens* (first and second). From here he *controls* the kingdoms of this world that were initially handed over to him by Adam (Luke 4:5-8). In addition, this is the strategic location from which he launches attacks against the household of God. Hence, "we wrestle not against flesh and blood, but against principalities, against powers, against the rulers of the darkness of this world, against spiritual wickedness in *high places* [the heavenlies]." When things go poorly between believers, the enemy is *not* our brothers and sisters in Christ, rather, it is the evil influences behind the scenes that we are contending against, as seen from the preceding passage.

THE STRATEGIES OF THE DEVIL

"Put on the whole armor of God, that ye may be able to stand against the wiles of the devil" (Eph. 6:11).

The illusionist obviously doesn't have the ability to make things disappear, therefore he must resort to *trickery* to deceive his audience. Interestingly, the term "wiles" in the original language means, "strategies or sly *tricks* of the devil." Since he does not possess the power or authority he would have us believe, the devil must use various forms of trickery to accomplish his end. "Wiles" is also the terminology from which we receive our English word, "method." To illustrate this term, picture if you would, a mountain lion stalking its prey. He carefully observes it, then cautiously moves alongside, but is never seen or heard. He astutely watches for just the right moment to attack. Thus, we must constantly be monitoring every area of our spiritual lives for an unexpected invasion.

Perhaps we should consider some of the *strategies* that Satan employs in order to prepare us for the battle. As the apostle says, "we are not ignorant of his devices," although we are unsure whether most believers are aware of his devices today.

a. Temptation

Temptation is an effective tool the enemy uses against us to erode our credibility. James states in this regard, "But every man is tempted, when he is drawn away of his own lust, and enticed" (James 1:14). The Scriptures are very clear that God is never responsible for tempting anyone to do evil. This would be contrary to His nature. Satan, on the other hand, is a master at the art! Those who become entangled in the snare of temptation have no one to blame but themselves. True, Satan may dangle something enticing before us, but we are drawn away of our *own* desire to partake of a particular forbidden fruit. The word "enticing" used here by James is a fishing term which denotes "to lure by a bait."

For example, our family spent a few days at a small fishing camp not long ago in northern Wisconsin. Our youngest, Timothy, loves to fish! In fact, he had spent some of his birthday money on a fluorescent green fishing lure that could be seen 50 yards away under water! We arose early the second morning and arrived at the lake at the crack of dawn. Of course, Timmy was confident his new lure would produce immediate results, but Dad was somewhat skeptical.

This fluorescent "green thing" barely hit the water when a 28-inch Northern Pike was *enticed* to swallow it whole. Covered with fishing tackle and barely awake, I managed to grab the net and wrestle the monster into the boat. After showing Mom the catch back at camp, I asked Timmy if he wanted to eat his trophy or mount it, to which he exclaimed, "Dad, let's throw him back so someone else can have some fun." It was a memorable moment indeed. That fish, unlike many who yield to temptation, had a second chance.

It is a time-honored fact that the course of temptation always follows the *same* path. The first step involves the flesh, or Satan drawing the victim into the trap through *enticement*. Forthwith, he is carried along by his *own desire* to have that which is forbidden. "Then when lust hath conceived, it bringeth forth *sin*: and sin, when it is finished, bringeth forth death" (James 1:15). That is, separation from God and His subsequent judgment.

The end result of this slippery path is plainly seen in the life of King David, when he sought to *number* the children of Israel. "And Satan stood up against Israel, and *provoked* [Hebrew, *enticed*] David to number Israel" (I Chron. 21:1). The foundation of this particular temptation was *pride*. King David was a mighty man of war. Under his leadership, David's armies sent their enemies scattering in seven different directions. Satan merely placed the thought before the king that he had accomplished these mighty feats in his own strength. Consequently, David's *desire* to number the children of Israel was an attempt to intimidate his enemies. He was making it known that the armies of Israel were invincible. And who would receive the recognition and glory for amassing such a formidable force? David!

Enter sin! "And David said unto God, I have sinned greatly, because I have done this thing: but now, I beseech Thee, do away the iniquity of thy servant; for I have done very foolishly" (I Chron. 21:8). As we know, sin always has consequences, and in David's case the Lord permitted him to choose his own poison. He had to choose between one of three judgments: three years of famine, three months to be destroyed before Israel's foes, or three days of pestilence throughout the coast of Israel (I Chron. 21:12). David chose the latter, wherein seventy thousand men suffered a horrible death.

b. The Spirit of Fear

Another effective weapon Satan has in his arsenal is *fear*. When we faithfully obey the Word of God, the devil will try to *alarm* us, that is, literally scare the wits out of us. He ingeniously attempts to *threaten* us with his evil consequences for our obedience to God. Peter is a good example. As our Lord revealed to His disciples how He would suffer at the hands of evil men and subsequently be put to death, Peter rebuked Him. "Be it far from Thee, Lord: this shall not be unto Thee" (Matt. 16:22). A valiant stand, indeed; he was determined to be *obedient* and fight to the end if necessary. "Then said Jesus unto His disciples, if any man will come after me, let him deny himself, and take up his cross, and follow me" (Matt. 16:24).

This passage is usually approached from a *devotional* viewpoint to show that a little rain is going to fall into every Christian life. Therefore, faithful believers are going to daily be called upon to bear various crosses in the form of criticism, rejection, verbal abuse, etc. Actually, our Lord's words are pointed here insofar as, if His disciples followed Him from that hour forward, they must *deny* themselves and quite literally be willing to take up their own cross and die for Him. To live for the Lord back in those days could cost you something—your life! Peter was willing to pay the ultimate sacrifice, or so he thought. "Lord....I will lay down my life for Thy sake," to which the Master replied: "Verily, verily, I say unto thee, The cock shall not crow, till thou hast denied me thrice" (John 13:37,38).

Satan honed in on Peter's words like radar on an incoming aircraft. After the authorities apprehended the Lord at Gethsemane, they brought Him to the house of the High Priest. "And Peter followed afar off" (Luke 22:54). Why? Because he was gripped by *fear*. Then, Satan tightened the noose, "But a certain maid beheld him as he sat by the fire, and earnestly looked upon him, and said, This man was also with Him." Peter swallowed hard fearing for his life, and said, "Woman, I know Him not." This incident was followed by a second and a third *denial*: "Then began he to curse and

336

to swear, saying, I know not the man. And immediately the cock crew" (Luke 22:54-62 cf. Matt. 26:69-75).

Satan is merciless in his assault to *frighten* us away from the truth, even to the point of denying the Lord. The narrative goes on to add, "And he went out, and wept bitterly." Guilt undoubtedly weighed heavy upon him for a number of days, but by the grace of God Peter recovered from this eye-opening defeat. The wiles of the devil give us plenty of reasons to put on the *whole* armor of God. Only with the protection that this panoply offers can the Christian ever hope to withstand the attacks of the evil one.

15

The Panoply of God

> "Wherefore take unto you the whole armor of God,
> that ye may be able to withstand in the evil day, and
> having done all, to stand."
>
> *—Ephesians 6:13*

Those who thoughtfully study Paul's epistles soon learn
that they are rich with metaphors. As the apostle pondered
the believer's warfare, his mind may have well wandered
back to young David as he prepared to face Goliath. After
David convinced King Saul that he was up to the challenge,
Saul gave him his suit of *armor*. This would have been hi-
larious to see, if it had not been such a solemn occasion.
Imagine this lionhearted young lad putting on a mighty
man of war's accouterments. He probably looked like Charlie
Brown in his father's coat and hat! In fact, the armor was
so heavy, he was unable to move. David, the diplomat that
he was, graciously said to the king, "I cannot go with these;
for I have not proved them." Thus he went forth with the
armor of God and conquered the giant!

As Paul prepared to challenge the Ephesians in this regard, it must also be remembered that the apostle was quite
familiar with the attire of his captors. Day in and day out,
he observed the changing of the guard and the various pieces
of equipment the Roman soldiers wore. Whatever the case
may be, the Lord *inspired* the apostle to write:

> "Wherefore take unto you the whole armor of God,
> that ye may be able to withstand in the evil day, and

having done all, to stand. Stand therefore..." (Eph. 6:13,14).

Here again we have the *sovereignty of God* and *human responsibility* running side by side like two rails of a railroad track that when viewed at a distance merge together. God has not called us into the heat of battle without first providing the necessary *gear* to protect and defend ourselves. On the other hand, it is our responsibility to "take" or "put on" the armor He has provided for us.

There are two lines of thought the Holy Spirit would have us follow as we consider God's provision. First and foremost, six pieces of armor are introduced: belt, breastplate, shoes, shield, helmet, and sword. Interestingly, all six pieces are *defensive* in nature. Only the sword of the Spirit serves as both a defensive and an *offensive* weapon. Consequently, we are going to find ourselves "digging in," as it were, a greater percentage of the time to *defend* the faith that has been delivered unto us. This is what the apostle means when he states: "Stand therefore, having your loins girt about with truth." In short, maintain the ground that has been *won*—defend it—don't give an inch! In addition, we must faithfully wield the sword of the Spirit, *offensively*, to advance the cause of Christ. This is done by winning lost souls to Christ, teaching the fundamentals of the faith, and sharing the Word, rightly divided, with others.

Second, the armor of God is divided into two sets of three. Paul undoubtedly observed that those who were guarding him never took off their belt, breastplate, or shoes for obvious reasons. Should an enemy launch a surprise attack, there was no time to be fumbling around with strapping on a bulky breastplate. One who was so foolish to be this unprepared would probably find himself a casualty of the conflict. The apostle introduces the next set of three with the words, "above all, *taking*" implying that the shield, helmet and sword could be temporarily set down and taken up as needed. These pieces of armor were never far from reach. In the event a clamor of war echoed through the camp, a Roman soldier was ready for battle before the sound of the trumpet faded in the distance. By the time his opponent appeared on the scene, he was facing a well-trained fighting machine. It is said that a Roman soldier's arm strength was such that he could cut a man in half with one swing of the sword.

These general observations will prove to be most helpful as we examine more closely the various characteristics of the panoply of God.

THE BELT OF TRUTH

"Stand therefore, having your loins girt about with truth" (Eph. 6:14).

In biblical times, the soldier's leather belt served a two-fold purpose. Garments back in those days were loose fitting which could impede movement, therefore they would tuck them under their belt. This enabled them to react quickly without fear of becoming entangled in their clothing, especially since other things were attached to it, such as the sheath and sword. It has been noted that another purpose for the belt was to give "a feeling of inner fortitude and strength when tightened." Of course, the lesson here is that the Roman soldier was always in a state of *readiness*.

In regard to the armor of God, we must gather up the *truth* and bind it on tightly. The belt of truth gives the believer inner strength and confidence when he confronts the "father of lies." It's too late to put on the truth once we enter the theater of war. The believer must be prepared beforehand. Thus, it is imperative that we *equip* ourselves with a well-rounded knowledge of the *whole* counsel of God. In short, we must be able to defend all the cardinal doctrines of the Christian faith. Sadly, many are woefully ignorant in this area. When they should be teachers, they have need to be taught again the first principles of the Word of God.

If the cultist tries to plant the seeds of doubt in the mind of a new believer concerning the Deity of Christ, could you defend His Deity? For example, normally, the cultist will agree that the "child" spoken of in Isaiah 9:6 is a reference to the birth of Christ. In fact, they use this passage to prove that He is the one who will bring the kingdom to the earth. Hence, "the government [Theocracy] shall be upon His shoulder." Thus, they will acknowledge that Christ is the Son of God, a great teacher, prophet, priest and king, but *not* God. But what saith the Scriptures? Read on!! This very same passage continues: "and His name shall be called Wonderful, Counselor, THE MIGHTY GOD, THE EVERLASTING FATHER, The Prince of Peace." Paul gives affirmation to this as well: "Whose are the fathers, and of whom as concerning the flesh Christ came, who is over all, GOD blessed for ever. Amen" (Rom. 9:5).

On another front, if the *extremist* begins to attend your assembly, could you Scripturally dismantle his argument that God doesn't love the world and Christ only died for the sins of the elect? Theologically, this view is called "limited redemption." Here caution must be exercised, simply because those who hold this position are quick to point out that "all" does not always mean "all without exception." For example: "*All* are invited to attend our special meetings this weekend." Obviously, the term "all" is not referring to everyone in the world, but is limited to those whom I am addressing. Thus the very nature of the term requires that the context be closely observed to determine whether everyone is meant or only a select group.

We firmly believe that God loves the world and Christ died for *all*. The apostle says: "For the love of Christ constraineth us; because we thus judge, that if one died for *all*, then were *all* dead" (II Cor. 5:14). Now I must ask, is there anyone among us who does not believe that "*all* have sinned, and come short of the glory of God" and therefore, "death passed upon all men because *all* have sinned"? I seriously doubt it! (Rom. 3:23; 5:12; Eph. 2:1-3). Everyone is in agreement that the "all" here is *without exception*. This is precisely Paul's argument: "we thus judge, that if one died for *all* [without exception, we conclude] then were *all* dead [without exception]" (II Cor. 5:14).

> "Even the righteousness of God which is by faith of Jesus Christ unto *all* and upon *all* them that believe: for there is no difference" (Rom. 3:22).

Once again, we have before us a passage that there is no getting around. The apostle clearly shows here the two usages of the word "all." Hence, the righteousness of God is available *unto all* without exception, for all have sinned. But it is only *upon all* them that believe. A provision has been made for all mankind, but it only *benefits* those who believe on the Lord Jesus Christ. Dear friend, have you placed your *faith* in Christ, that He died for your sins, was buried, and rose again? "Without faith it is impossible to please Him." Some time ago I came across the following story that adequately illustrates the importance of distinguishing between mere mental assent and true *faith*:

"A person was standing on one side of Niagara Falls watching a man who could not only walk over the Falls on a tightrope, but who could trundle a wheelbarrow across as well. He turned to the man standing by and said: 'Do you believe that I can not only take a wheelbarrow over to the other side but that I can also take it across with a man sitting in it?'

'Yes, I do' said the man. 'Well,' he replied, 'take your seat in the barrow!' But the onlooker would not."

You see, it is not enough to merely give an intellectual assent to the historical fact that Christ died on a Cross nearly two thousand years ago, and then try to do your best. Faith believes the message that Christ died for you *personally*. It gets into the wheelbarrow and allows the Savior to take you over to the other side. Faith is placing your full *confidence* in Him that He will forgive your sins on the basis of His shed blood and grant you the free gift of eternal life. "Believe on the Lord Jesus Christ and thou shalt be saved" (Acts 16:31).

Moving on, how would you handle the *liberal* who calls into question the *bodily* resurrection of Christ, claiming that only His "spirit" rose from the dead? This very thing is presently being taught by a segment of Christendom. Incidentally, the Lord Himself drives the death nail into this unsound teaching. The reader will recall that shortly after our Lord's resurrection, He appeared to His disciples in the upper room. They were visibly shaken by all that had been transpiring the past few days and bolted the door, fearing for their lives.

As they discussed among themselves the events of that day, the Lord passed through the door into their presence. The disciples were so startled by His appearance, they were frozen with *fear*, supposing they had seen a spirit (Luke 24:37). The fainthearted of their number were probably thinking, where's the smelling salts? As they were searching for their composure, the Master consoled them with these words: "Behold my hands and my feet, that it is I myself: handle me, and see; FOR A SPIRIT HATH NOT FLESH AND BONES, AS YE SEE ME HAVE" (Luke 24:39). Surely there could be no doubt that Christ rose *bodily* from the dead from this statement alone! The apostles actually handled the Word of life and beheld the nail prints in His hands and feet. Although they could not believe their eyes, nevertheless it was true, He had risen from the dead!

Peter shows us that the bodily resurrection of Christ was in fulfillment of David's prophecy of long ago: "He [David] seeing this before spake of the resurrection of Christ, that His [Christ's] soul was not left in hell [Gr. *Hades*, the unseen world], neither His flesh did see corruption" (Acts 2:31). Notice that the soul of our Lord is said to have descended into Hades (Paradise) after His death. For the next three days His *body* laid in the tomb, but did not see *corruption*. Why? God the Father raised Him from the dead (Acts 2:32). Moreover, Paul states: "For in Him dwelleth all the fulness of the Godhead *bodily*" (Col. 2:9).

THE BREASTPLATE OF RIGHTEOUSNESS

"Stand therefore, having your loins girt about with truth, and having on the breastplate of righteousness" (Eph. 6:14).

As dawn broke across the eastern skies of the city of Rome a new day sprang to life. But suddenly the stillness of the morning was disrupted by the changing of the guard. As Paul arose from his bed he saw a towering Roman soldier enter the room; it was a scene with which he was all too familiar. "Another routine day," grumbled the guard as he leaned his sword and shield against the clay wall. He then proceeded to take off his tarnished helmet, placing it on a nearby table.

The apostle noticed, however, that no member of the watch ever removed his breastplate—for obvious reasons. Should an enemy descend upon the city, or should a prisoner try to escape, there would be no time to wrestle with a cumbersome breastplate.

This observation provided Paul with a fertile field of thought from which he draws the likeness of the Christian soldier. Since believers are engaged in a spiritual warfare, with a very real enemy, we are instructed to *put on* the whole armor of God, that we *"may be able to withstand in the evil day."* To avoid becoming a spiritual casualty in the heat of battle we must never be without the "breastplate of righteousness." Just as this piece of armor protected the vital organs of the Roman soldier, in like manner it shields us against being *"pierced through with many sorrows."* Incidentally, those who stand uncompromisingly for the preaching of Jesus Christ according to the revelation of the Mystery are the prime targets of the fiery darts of the wicked one (See Eph. 6:11-17).

The *breastplate* is to be put on and never removed, as implied by the phrase "and *having on.*" This particular piece of armor protected the vital organs. Here in Ephesians, the breastplate illustrates the role of *righteousness* in our lives. Since there are different classifications of "righteousness" addressed in the Scriptures, it will be necessary for us to ascertain which righteousness the apostle has under consideration.

While many revel in their self-righteous ways today, Paul sets forth some impressive credentials in his attempt to establish his own righteousness. "Circumcised the eighth day, of the stock of Israel, of the tribe of Benjamin, an Hebrew of the Hebrews; as touching the law, a Pharisee" (Phil. 3:5). But once Christ became the object of his faith, he says, "But what things were gain to me, those I counted loss for Christ....And be found in Him, not having mine own righteousness." Paul's denunciation of his own self-righteousness leaves little doubt that this is not the breastplate.

Some have suggested it is the "imputed righteousness of God" that is received upon conversion. "For He hath made

Him to be sin for us, who knew no sin; that we might be made the righteousness of God in Him" (II Cor. 5:21). This righteousness, however, is never said to be *put on*, suggesting that it could be taken off. Furthermore, the believer bears the responsibility to take up this piece of armor, whereas God in His sovereignty imputes the righteousness of Christ to us *instantaneously*. Thus it is unlikely that Paul had this in mind.

We believe the breastplate is a "practical righteousness" which emanates from the *new nature* that is said to be "created in righteousness and true holiness" (Eph. 4:24). The breastplate has to do with our morality, that is, performing that which is *right* by living a life of good works. Paul charges us, "In all things showing thyself a pattern of good works: in doctrine showing uncorruptness, gravity, sincerity, sound speech, that cannot be condemned; that he that is of the contrary part may be ashamed, *having no evil thing to say of you*" (Titus 2:7,8).

Perhaps you will recall an eye opening experience Daniel had in the Old Testament. Shortly after Media-Persia overthrew Babylon, Darius set Daniel over the whole realm. This decision enraged the upper crust of the kingdom who felt they were in line for the position. Consequently, they devised a scheme to find an indiscretion in the life of Daniel whereby they might *discredit* him before the king. So they secretly followed Daniel day and night with a long checklist: lying, payoffs, greed, fornication, stealing, favoritism, or any other sordid thing. But to their dismay, after months of trailing the prophet, the Scriptures declare: "Forasmuch as he [Daniel] was faithful, neither was there any error or fault found in him" (Dan. 6:4). Daniel's enemies could find "none occasion against him"—he was squeaky clean!! How would you fare if you were placed under such *scrutiny*? Would those observing you find a different person behind closed doors? Are your actions and manner of speech the same in private as in public?

The breastplate of righteousness is a safeguard against the enemy's attempts to discredit us and the message we proclaim. Of course, the adversary is always quick to point out our *inconsistencies*. But if we never remove this piece of armor, his accusations will be without foundation.

We tend to view the armor of God here in Ephesians 6:10-18 as six distinct pieces of divine protection. Of course, there is a sense that this is true. But Paul's phrase, "Put on the *whole* armor of God" strongly suggests that the armor is to be viewed as an *ensemble*. The term "whole" conveys the thought of completeness. God's provision is *complete*. We are covered, as it were, from the crown of our head to the soles of our feet. And who better to equip us for the conflict than the Lord Himself? He has walked among us on the plain of the battlefield and was "touched with the feeling of our infirmities."

Needless to say, a suit of armor is of little benefit if one piece is missing. Suppose for a moment that your neighborhood is experiencing a rash of burglaries. What profit is there if you lock all your doors and windows, but *carelessly* forget to repair the broken lock on the side door? The house is secure with the exception of that one door. Every line of defense you sought to put into place is meaningless due to your failure to repair that lock. It may seem like a small matter, but a burglar is sure to take advantage of your *negligence*.

Imagine a company of Roman soldiers reasoning that their helmets were unimportant. The cry of the enemy echoing through the valley would be chilling—aim for their heads! Should we be so foolish to think that it is any different in the spiritual realm? Surely, the enemy will attack us where we are the most *vulnerable*. In addition, each piece of armor must be *equally strong* in every point. For example, we might give a great deal of attention to the belt of truth while neglecting to fasten the breastplate of righteousness properly. Should the breastplate *slip*, it could leave the warrior of the faith exposed to danger. Hence, the criticism, "your actions are speaking louder than your words." Satan repeatedly discredits the believer on the basis of his inconsistent behavior.

The following true story illustrates the above: "A non-Christian lawyer attended a church service and listened incredulously to the testimonies of some who were known to him for their shady deals and failure to meet their honest obligations. 'How did you like the testimonies?' a man asked him at the close of the service. He replied, 'To a lawyer there is a vast difference between testimony and *evidence*.' Words are cheap, and it is perilously easy to give a fine sounding testimony for Christ, but quite another matter to demonstrate evidences of God's purifying power in our lives through Christ."

DO YOU HAVE YOUR SHOES ON?

"And your feet shod with the preparation of the gospel of peace" (Eph. 6:15).

In these words we have another piece of armor that is to be put on and never removed. The proper footwear gave ancient armies the ability to march long distances across rugged terrain. In fact, the military successes of both Alexander the Great and Julius Caesar have been attributed to their troops marching for days to *surprise* an enemy. The sandals of the foot soldier were made of a stiff leather with iron studs embedded in the soles. This gave him mobility to move about freely. These types of shoes also provided stability so that the foot could easily be planted to withstand the vicious blows of the opponent.

But there was another reason for wearing the *correct* shoes. In those days, the enemy would oftentimes bury sharp sticks in the pathway of an approaching army. Since these objects were camouflaged, if they were stepped on with worn sandals, it could easily disable those on the frontlines. Thus, the watchword here is vigilance.

Interestingly, as the children of Israel prepared to leave Egypt, God instructed them to observe the Passover with their *shoes on* (Ex. 12:11). They were to be ready in a moment's notice to march through enemy territory or stand still as God miraculously delivered them. Throughout the forty years that the Israelites wandered in the wilderness, these shoes never "waxed old" (Deut. 29:5). Amazing! It would be a mother's dream to buy shoes for her children that would never wear out. But even more incredible, as the feet of the younger Israelites grew, their shoes apparently *expanded!*

If our feet are shod with the *preparation of the gospel*, as we grow in the faith, we find a greater length, width, and depth in the gospel to meet our spiritual needs. We never outgrow these shoes simply because "they are always a perfect fit for our changing conditions."[1]

The "preparation" of the gospel of peace has to do with our *readiness* to rise to the occasion. But what is the significance of our feet being shod with the gospel of peace? First of all, the subject here is *not* evangelism as some have supposed. This conclusion is often drawn from Paul's words: "How beautiful are the feet of them that preach the gospel of peace and bring glad tidings of good things" (Rom. 10:15). Although the phraseology is similar, it must be remembered that the context here in Ephesians is the *believer's warfare* with the adversary.

Peace manifests itself in various forms in Paul's epistles—"grace and peace from God the Father," "peace with God," "He [Christ] is our peace," "the peace of God which passeth understanding," etc. It is a well-established fact that if we are at *peace* with God, we are at *war* with the devil. Most would agree, however, that this is a positional truth. Thus, Paul has in mind the *state* of the believer. He pictures us in the heat of battle, fighting the good fight of the faith. Each day brings a new danger. Each day brings another conflict. Each day brings a different set of circumstances. Hence, the apostle charges us—have your shoes on, be ready with the *gospel of* peace, that is, whatever you are called upon to face, let "the peace *of* God, which passeth understanding...keep your hearts and minds through Christ Jesus" (Phil. 4:7).

A short time ago, a Christian family from Chicago was traveling through Milwaukee. It was a trip that would change their lives forever. Somehow a piece of steel broke loose from the undercarriage of a tractor-trailer traveling in front of them. The force in which the metal slid under their van punctured the gas tank. The van was instantly engulfed in flames, trapping its occupants. Severely burned, dad and mom managed to rescue one of their sons from the vehicle, but tragically their other five children perished in the fire. The next day the child they heroically rescued also died.

Approximately two weeks later, these godly parents held a news conference. They shared how words were inadequate to describe their loss. As a hush fell over the pressroom, they expressed their *gratitude* to God for the time that He gave them together. The father went on to say that he knew his children were in heaven because each of them had trusted the Lord. And although they were unable to fully understand

351

why this tragedy happened, they knew God had a plan and a purpose, and that He was working all things out according to the counsel of His will. The media was so moved by the event that there wasn't a dry eye in the place.

This godly couple had their feet shod with the gospel of peace. They weren't bitter or resentful, nor did they blame God for the accident. After all, it was by one man's disobedience that sin, death, and sorrow entered in the first place. But how could they possibly hold up under the weight of such a heavy burden? You see, they knew beforehand that God is *sovereign* and in control of all things. "And He doeth according to His will in the army of heaven, and among the inhabitants of the earth: and none can stay His hand, or say unto Him, What doest Thou?" (Dan. 4:35).

Thus, the peace of God, which passeth all understanding, held them steady through a tumultuous time. There is little solace in the empty words of men at such times, but in Christ we find true *comfort*. When the final brush strokes are applied to the canvas of this dispensation, then we will see the full panorama of God's plans and purpose. In the end, all things will work together for our good and to the praise of His glory.

Those who fail to have their feet shod with the peace of God often sound like Job's wife. You will recall the entry in Job's journal of affliction of how he lost his children, possessions, and his health practically overnight. Mrs. Job was devastated! Everything she loved in this life was gone. Sadly, her judgment had been severely impaired by the things of this world. Consequently, she said to Job: "Dost thou still retain thine integrity? curse God, and die." But Job viewed his circumstances through the eye of faith. He chose to trust in the Lord with all his heart, and lean not on his own understanding.

Job *admonished* his wife accordingly: "Thou speakest as one of the foolish women speaketh." He then adds these insightful thoughts: "What? shall we receive good at the hand of God, and shall we not receive evil....The Lord gave, and the Lord hath taketh away; blessed be the name of the Lord. In all this Job sinned not, nor charged God foolishly" (Job 1:21,22; 2:9,10).

A crisis has a way of refining and purifying us for greater things in the Lord's work. Even though living in a sin-cursed world may sometimes be overwhelming, we must learn to ponder what God is *teaching* us. One thing about *experience*, it gives the test first and the lesson later. Before moving on, when we think of our feet and shoes, both have to do with *balance*. If this piece of armor is worn consistently, it will help us to have a balance in the Christian life. Those who have given themselves over to extremes or overemphasis of a particular doctrine usually end up losing their credibility. Many capable men over the years are no longer in the Lord's service due to their defense of an *unsound* position. We must never lose sight of that for which God has called us, namely, the preaching of Jesus Christ according to the revelation of the Mystery. *Balance* is important!

THE SHIELD OF FAITH

"Above all, taking the shield of faith, wherewith ye shall be able to quench all the fiery darts of the wicked [one]" (Eph. 6:15).

The phrase "above all" here in the English fails to convey the intent of the original language. In fact, it is somewhat ambiguous. Wuest states: "The thought in the original is, 'in addition to all,' that is, in addition to all the equipment just mentioned, the Christian should add" the shield of faith, helmet of salvation and the Sword of the Spirit. The first set of three: the belt, breastplate and shoes are to be put on and never removed. "In addition" introduces the second set of three—these pieces of armor could be set down, but were always kept close at hand should the enemy attack.

Probably the *shield* Paul has in mind here was about four feet in length by two and one-half feet wide. It was a large piece of wood covered with metal and came to a point on the bottom. Although the weapons of warfare have changed dramatically over the centuries, many strategies of war still remain the same.

At the Battle of Gettysburg during the Civil War, General Lee gave orders to fire over one hundred and twenty-five cannons at the North's front lines. This was done for over two hours in an attempt to dislodge the Union forces who held the *higher ground* on Cemetery Ridge. Historians agree that this was a major turning point in the battle, simply because the artillery overshot its mark. As Lee's army advanced for the main attack, even though they outnumbered the North, they were sitting ducks—the rest is history!

In the arena of ancient warfare, the enemy would launch a barrage of fiery darts prior to the main attack to confuse the opposing army. When these missiles were hurling through the air, the Roman soldier merely planted his shield in the ground and hunkered down behind it to protect himself. If he failed to do so, and one of these darts hit their mark, it caught his clothing on fire. While he was putting out the fire, the enemy was advancing. In addition, these darts were not only painful, they also caused infections which could disable a soldier for weeks. On the battlefield, the *shield* proved to be an essential piece of armor.

The shield of faith plays an important part in our spiritual warfare as well. But what is faith? "Now faith is the substance of things hoped for, the evidence of things not seen" (Heb. 11:1). Notice that faith has "substance" and "evidence." In other words, it is based on the Word of God. We do not have a hope-so kind of faith. Rather our faith finds its rest in God who cannot lie. It is placing our *full* confidence in God that He will honor His Word. Consider the faith of Abraham as one example, that what God promised, "He was able also to perform" (Rom. 4:16-21).

So when the host of darkness sends these fiery projectiles in our direction, we must be prepared to effectively use the shield of faith. These fiery darts of the wicked one are not to be taken lightly. They are meant to *distract* us. And if the shield of faith is not taken up, they will do just that. I sometimes wonder if he's using heat-seeking missiles these days! *Doubt* is perhaps Satan's favorite dart in his arsenal. Be ready when you hear this one whistling through the air.

Since you have been saved, has God seemed distant to you at one point or another? Have you ever doubted your salvation? If you have the shield of faith in hand, the promise of God found in Ephesians will be your *defense.* "In whom also after that you believed, ye were sealed with that Holy Spirit of promise, which is the earnest of our inheritance until the redemption of the purchased possession."

Then there are those darts that put you *asleep.* Read a magazine, newspaper, or a thrilling novel and you're enthralled. Pick up the Scriptures in the evening to do a little reading and you will probably find yourself slouched down in your easy chair dead to the world. Now if your studying the Scriptures or praying, the forces of evil use the dart of *interruption.* Have you ever been doing one or the other of the above and your mind begins to wander? Before you know it, there are four or five things that come to mind that need your immediate attention. Sometimes they are even ministry related. If the devil interrupts your prayer time in the morning, simply finish it later in the day. Little wonder Paul says: "Pray without ceasing."

One author defines the *shield of faith* as meaning "the quick application of what we believe as an answer to everything the devil hurls at us." We must place our total *dependence* on God "who is a present help in time of need."

THE HELMET OF SALVATION

"And take the helmet of salvation" (Eph. 6:17).

The Scriptures abound with examples of those who stood courageously for that which was right in the face of almost unbelievable opposition. They were unwilling to *compromise* their convictions under any circumstances. Courage is "the state or quality of mind or spirit that enables one to face danger with confidence and resolution." Of course, for the believer, his *confidence* is in God who is "able to do exceeding abundantly above all that we ask or think, according to the power that worketh in us."

When Shadrach, Meshach, and Abednego refused to worship the golden image erected by King Nebuchadnezzar, the king gave them an ultimatum. Either they bow to the image or be cast into a fiery furnace. To which they replied: "If it be so, our God whom we serve is able to deliver us from the burning fiery furnace, and He will deliver us out of thine hand, O king. But if not, be it known unto thee, O king, that we will not serve thy gods, nor worship the golden image which thou hast set up." And God did indeed deliver them. Incredibly, "the fire had no power, nor was an hair of their head singed, neither were their coats changed, nor the smell of fire had passed on them" (Dan. 3:17,18,27).

According to the law of the Medes and Persians, "no decree nor statute which the king establisheth may be changed."

This oath was used by those who were envious of Daniel to trap Darius in his own words. They convinced him to make a decree that "whosoever shall ask a petition of any God or man for thirty days, save of thee, O king, he shall be cast into the den of lions."

Since Daniel chose to obey the living God instead of men, Darius had no other recourse other than to place his friend in harms way. Thus, Daniel found himself standing face to face with a group of hungry lions. Early the next morning, the king came to the den of lions with haste, and cried with a lamentable voice, "O Daniel, servant of the living God, is thy God, whom thou servest continually, able to deliver thee from the lions?" After a brief pause, Daniel said, "My God hath sent His angel, and hath shut the lions' mouths, that they have not hurt me" (Dan. 6:15,20-22).

Although Satan was unsuccessful in his attempt to cause these heroes of the faith to make a concession, this is still one of his favorite weapons. Today the masks of the enemy may be many and varied, but the face of *compromise* remains the same. In fact, he has added another tactic to his arsenal to draw sincere believers away from the faith. And normally, they are totally unaware that they have departed. It is called *new evangelicalism.* New evangelicalism is a mood of toleration which says, "let's forget our doctrinal differences and simply get along." Consequently, programs, skits, testimonials, and musicals have nearly replaced sound biblical preaching.

Beware when you hear, "Is Paul's apostleship and message really that important? Would it not be far more profitable to invite other denominations in for joint services? After all, we're all Christians aren't we?" "What we need in this church is some innovative programs to attract more young couples." "We must adapt to our changing times. Sure doctrine is important, but what we need to hear are more messages on the social issues of our day." Perhaps one of the most troubling statements we've read recently comes from a nationally acclaimed evangelist: "But, as an American, I respect other paths to God—and, as a Christian, I am called on to love them."

Please notice that there is a common thread woven through each of these statements, they are all *void* of any reference to the Word of God. If there was one thing God taught us through the period called the Reformation, it was this: the preaching of the Word must be the *centerpiece* of our worship. True worship is always around the Word of God—all other things are secondary in importance. Do not be deceived by the well-meaning new evangelical who says: "We've heard enough doctrine, it's time to learn more about how to live the Christian life." This is like trying to build a house without a foundation; it simply will not stand. Both doctrine and the Christian walk must be given *equal* time.

Sadly, once an assembly or a believer starts down the slippery slope of new evangelicalism, they are rarely recovered for the truth. It is a cancer that will destroy the stand of even the most seasoned believer. Thankfully, the Word of God is always relative to the times in which we live. Little wonder, the apostle charges us to put on the whole armor of God and "stand therefore, having your loins girt about with truth." It takes a great deal of *courage* to stand against the tide of popular opinion known as new evangelicalism. Yes, you may walk through the fires of criticism or stand in the critics den, but "if God be for us, who shall be against us?" (Rom. 8:31).

The helmet of the Roman soldier was made of leather covered with strips of brass. Its primary purpose, of course, was to protect the head. As a spiritual piece of armor, it is to guard the *mind* of the believer against the ruthless attacks of the adversary. The helmet of salvation has to do with the three tenses of our salvation in Christ:

Past tense—*justification* from the *penalty* of sin.

Present tense—*sanctification* from the *power* of sin.

Future tense—*glorification* from the *presence* of sin.

In the midst of a spiritual conflict, we may find ourselves calling to remembrance one or more of these tenses at any given time. Justification simply means that we have been declared eternally righteous by God. "There is therefore now no condemnation to them which are in Christ Jesus" (Rom. 8:1). We are *beyond* the reach of judgment. So when the old serpent levels the accusation that you are unfit for heaven because you have sinned against God, your response should be: How true, BUT, I am justified freely by His grace on the basis of the shed blood of Christ.

Those who do not understand the Word, rightly divided, sometimes find themselves confronted with the thought that they have committed the *unpardonable sin*. As we know, dispensationally, this is an impossibility. But God has graciously left a safety net under those who have yet to see this wonderful truth. Namely, we are eternally secure in Christ. "Who shall lay anything to the charge of God's elect? It is God that justifieth....[And] who shall separate us from the love of Christ? shall tribulation, or distress, or persecution, or famine, or nakedness, or peril, or sword?...Nay, in all these things we are more than conquerors through Him that loved us" (Rom. 8:33,35,37).

Sanctification has to do with being set apart from the world unto God's *service*. As we approach this from the practical side, there is a sense we are being saved daily from the *power of sin* in our lives. This is what the apostle speaks of

359

when he wrote to those at Philippi: "Wherefore, my beloved, as ye have always obeyed, not as in my presence only, but now much more in my absence, work out your own salvation with fear and trembling" (Phil. 2:12).

Notice Paul instructs these saints to "work out" their own salvation. The Philippians were not to "work for" it; they already *possessed* it. Rather, they were to "work out" that inwrought salvation that God had bestowed upon them. Suppose your mother and father left you their house as an inheritance. Legally, you own it, but you must *work out* all the details with the state and local governments before they are willing to publicly acknowledge your right to claim ownership. In a sense this is true of the believer—God has saved us, but He wants us to live a transformed life that others will acknowledge we belong to Him.

As we grow in grace, our life should begin to reflect the image of Christ. The temporal things of the world that were once so important to us suddenly become meaningless. Our entire purpose in life, or at least it should be, is to *serve* Christ. Our foremost desire is to see others saved and come into a fuller knowledge of His will. Here the enemy is usually quick to point out that you are incompetent to minister in this capacity. You don't have a Bible school education. What if you mislead this poor soul? Boy, he's a fine one to make that charge!

This type of assault must be met with the understanding that we are called with a holy calling. Therefore, we are the stewards of God entrusted with the *responsibility* to make known the preaching of Jesus Christ according to the revelation of the Mystery. Beloved, it is not a prerequisite to have theological training or a Bible school diploma to be used of the Lord.

Pastor C. R. Stam, the founder of the *Berean Bible Society* only had an eighth grade education,[2] never attended seminary, but has probably accomplished more in his life than most who have PhD's or ThD's behind their names. You see, God uses those who are faithful and willing to stand for the truth of Paul's gospel. "Without faith it is impossible to please Him." Thus, as *ambassadors* for Christ each of us is commissioned from on High with the ministry of *reconciliation*.

The future state of glorification will ultimately deliver us from the very *presence of sin*. On the battlefield, every soldier at one time or another must face his own mortality. As they used to say in World War II when they saw a fallen friend, "That bullet had his name on it." As we know, there have been times throughout the history of the Church when the battle grew so intense that some gave their lives for the gospel. Many of these martyrs departed this life singing hymns while they were being burned at the stake. A proper understanding of the helmet of salvation enabled them to stare death in the face without fear because they knew God was able to *raise* them from the dead. This particular piece of armor gave them, and us for that matter, the hope of *victory*.

Of course, we may not be called upon to suffer martyrdom for the cause of Christ, but there may come a day when we are facing major surgery or the possibility of a terminal illness. At such times the enemy often causes waves of anxiety to come over us in an attempt to shake the foundations of our faith. He is a master at getting the child of God to dwell on his circumstances, better known as *worry*. Do you worry? No, I didn't think so. You see, ninety-nine out of a hundred things we worry about never come to pass and the one-percent that does is usually beyond our control.

Here again "the peace of God, which passeth understanding, shall keep your hearts and minds," in three ways. First, Paul says, "I am persuaded, that neither death, nor life...nor things present, nor things to come...shall be able to separate us from the love of God" (Rom. 8:38,39). Second, to be absent from the body is to be present with the Lord (II Cor. 5:8,9). Third, we are promised the *redemption* of our body, that is, God is going to raise and glorify this old body of humiliation (Rom. 8:23). A dear Christian friend once told me in this regard, "We have a *future!!*"

THE SWORD OF THE SPIRIT

"and the sword of the Spirit, which is the Word of God" (Eph. 6:17).

The sword of the Roman soldier was both a defensive and an offensive weapon. It had two edges and was about twenty-four inches in length. Those who would one day enter into battle were trained in the skillful use of the sword at a very young age. It is said that the son of a Roman soldier who kept losing to his sparring partner commented, "Father, my sword is too short." To which the father replied, "Take one step forward son, and it will be the right length."

As we wage an offensive campaign, we too must step forward with the Word of God to advance the cause of Christ. This begins with *evangelism.* Paul says, "Do the work of an evangelist." Every believer bears the responsibility to share Christ with others. Of course, we are well aware that various methods have been developed to win the lost to Christ. But the most effective tool we have at our disposal is the Scriptures. God uses His Word to convict the sinner of his sin.

"For the Word of God is quick [living], and powerful, and sharper than any two-edged sword, piercing even

362

to the dividing asunder of soul and spirit, and of the
joints and marrow, and is a discerner of the thoughts
and intents of the heart" (Heb. 4:12).

Notice how the Word of God is like a surgical instrument.
It is able to define and distinguish between the soul and
spirit, something never accomplished by the sciences. It
pierces straight through the hardest of hearts to allow the
glorious light of the gospel to shine in. Thus "faith cometh
by hearing, and hearing by the Word of God." The cold, hard
steel of a man-made sword is intended to end life, but the
sword of the Spirit is meant to impart life, and life more
abundantly. In physics, *centripetal force* pulls toward the
axis of rotation whereas *centrifugal force* is just the opposite, it pushes away from the axis. The gospel has the very
same effect upon us: it first draws us to Christ, then upon
belief, it gives us a burning desire to send its message forth
to others.

After an army is pushed back by the enemy they normally
reorganize their forces to advance another day. Perhaps the
time has come in the Grace Movement to regather the troops
and *charge!!!!* Stop and think! When was the last time you
used the sword of the Spirit to effectively present the Word,
rightly divided to someone else? How long has it been since
you methodically (in love) dismantled the Acts 2 position and
brought someone into the truth of Paul's gospel?

Interestingly, it is Paul who states: "And take...the sword
of the Spirit, which is the *Word* of God." Here the apostle
uses the Greek word *Rhema* instead of *Logos*. According to
W. E. Vine the term *Logos* denotes "an expression of thought...
the revealed will of God." Most times it is used in relation
to the "sum of God's utterances" (John 10:35). On the other
hand *Rhema* refers to a particular passage or portion of
Scripture which the Spirit may bring to mind in defense of

the truth. Consequently, we must use *Paul's epistles* today to defend the faith. For example:

Why did our Lord teach His disciples to go *not* into the way of the Gentiles?

Why has Israel been set aside in unbelief?

Why is it impossible to fulfill the "Great Commission" today?

Why is it wrong to preach "repent and be baptized for the *remission* of sins" in this dispensation?

Why has Daniel's seventieth week (7 years of Tribulation) not been fulfilled?

Why has the promise of Christ's coming to the earth remained unfulfilled?

Why has the millenial kingdom not been established?

Have you ever wondered, why Paul? We know that he was not one of the twelve nor did God ever intend him to be. You see, God had a secret purpose in mind called the *Mystery*. Therefore, He raised up Paul to make known the revelation of the Mystery to the Gentiles. Only those who acknowledge Paul's apostleship and message will be equipped to answer the above questions.

The "girdle of truth" speaks of the Word of God in its *broadest* sense. It is here we find our defense for the cardinal doctrines of the Christian faith—creation, deity of Christ, bodily resurrection, etc. The sword of the Spirit, which is the Word of God, points us *specifically* to Paul's revelation which gives us God's definitive will for the dispensation of Grace. May God give us grace, wisdom, and courage to *stand* for this wonderful message that was first delivered unto us through the Apostle Paul. As has been said, "The battle is the Lord's."

"Praying always with all prayer and supplication in the Spirit, and watching thereunto with all perseverance and supplication for all saints" (Eph. 6:18).

Every army has a secret weapon or strategy. In our case it's *prayer*. God would have us pray without ceasing as we fight the good fight of the faith. During Old Testament times the priest, who ministered in the things of the Lord, burnt sweet incense every morning as an act of worship (Ex. 30:1-8). As the aroma of the incense arose heavenward it symbolized the prayers of God's people. Today our prayers ascend to the Father through the Lord Jesus Christ who makes intercession for us (Rom. 8:34 cf. I Tim. 2:1-5).

So then, it is well pleasing to God when we pray "always with all prayer," that is, all *types* of prayers; including supplication, intercession, petition, thanksgiving, etc. They are to be offered up on every occasion, not only for ourselves, but also for those fellow-soldiers who are fighting alongside of us. And, we should be "watching thereunto with all perseverance and supplication for all saints." Watching for what? For God to work in their lives in answer to our prayers.

It is noteworthy what the apostle requested the Ephesians to pray "that utterance may be given unto me, that I may open my mouth boldly, to make known the mystery of the gospel." In response to their prayers, Paul *boldly* testified of the gospel of the grace of God before Caesar, which shook all of Rome (II Tim. 4:16,17).

16

A Contagious Style

> "And for me, that utterance may be given unto me, that I may open my mouth boldly, to make known the mystery of the gospel, for which I am an ambassador in bonds; that therein I may speak boldly, as I ought to speak."
>
> —*Ephesians 6:19,20*

Everyone, now and then, reminisces about the good old days. I've often wondered what was so good about those days. For one thing, I can remember when gasoline was twenty-two cents a gallon, a postage stamp cost two cents, a candy bar was a nickel, and a bottle of soda pop set you back a dime. I guess you could say that was good, especially if you were a kid! Then again, there was no cure for the crippling disease of polio, childhood diseases such as whooping cough, rubella, and mumps were rampant, and the life expectancy for an average adult was approximately forty-five years of age. In addition, there were no microwave ovens, computers, cell phones, or fax machines. It's amazing we survived! Perhaps the key to the whole matter is that they were *simpler* times before our minds became so cluttered with these technological advances. The times of our life—some were memorable while others we would probably just as soon forget.

The foregoing paragraph is a fairly accurate assessment of the Christian life as well. The goal of every believer in Christ (or at least it should be) is to "know Him, and the power of His resurrection, and the fellowship of His sufferings." As we grow in grace there are often great strides made in our understanding of Paul's gospel.

Then again, the battle can become so intense at times that the enemy turns believers against one another, and in the process causes them to lose ground that was originally won for Christ. The air often becomes so filled with tension you could cut it with a knife. Satan is a master at causing confusion and destroying the atmosphere for the effective proclamation of Christ and Him crucified. If there is one thing that we need to learn it is this: we must stop giving up hallowed ground to the enemy or we'll soon be looking down the barrel of self-destruction.

Then there are those dry spells when it seems as though we are moving along at a snail's pace spiritually. The harder we try, the deeper the hole we dig ourselves. Busy schedules, commitments, unforeseen circumstances, financial setbacks, and discouragement are only a few of a thousand things that sometimes hinder our growth.

Incidentally, my wife and I can relate to many of the above struggles. When we were in Bible School our schedule was such that it was sometimes difficult to retain things, especially the first year. At the time, I was working a full-time job (third shift), my wife was single-handedly raising our two little papooses, and we were both students at the *Berean School of Bible and Theology*. Furthermore, we crammed a four-year course into three years by taking all summer semesters. Surely God must have given us a special measure of grace, because I'm exhausted just thinking about it!!!

During my first year at school I took a class called *Dispensational Survey*. For the most part I fared pretty well, with the exception of one area. I had the hardest time (one of those times you would rather forget) distinguishing between the "gospel of the Mystery" and the "Mystery of the gospel." Call it what you will, a mental block, fatigue, or my mind so in the heavenlies that I was of no earthly good, but I couldn't keep these two phrases straight for the life of me. However, I am happy to report that before the year was out I had conquered the beast and I still enjoy the spoils of victory! These many years later, it is a privilege to share with you what the Lord has taught me on this subject and I trust that you will find it profitable as well.

THE GOSPEL OF THE MYSTERY

> "Now to Him that is of power to establish you according to my gospel, and the preaching of Jesus Christ, according to the revelation of the Mystery, which was kept secret since the world began" (Rom. 16:25).

Here Paul takes up the matter of how to be "established" or built up in the faith. This is primarily accomplished by acknowledging the good news of the *Mystery* that was initially committed to Paul. Historically, the stoning of Stephen marked a major turning point in the plans and purposes of God. As we know, the next order of business on the prophetic calendar would have been the pouring out of God's wrath upon this Christ-rejecting world. Instead, God set Israel aside in unbelief and announced His *secret purpose* for the Church, which is Christ's Body. This in a nutshell is the good news of the Mystery!

The *Mystery* is a *self-contained* program that manifests the counsel of God's will for this present age. The heavenly ministry of Christ dawned with the conversion of Paul. To him was revealed that which was kept secret from ages and generations past. Perhaps the best way to show the distinction between the two programs of God is by comparing the Great Commission given to the twelve with the commission of reconciliation committed to us. This will help us see more clearly the uniqueness of the Mystery.

The Great Commission: Since the nation Israel held a position of *preeminence* over the nations, our Lord instructed the twelve to begin at Jerusalem. Why Jerusalem? Because this was the seat of authority both politically and religiously. If the leaders in Israel rejected the Messiah there was little hope the nation would be converted. Next, they were to take the gospel to Judaea (a representation of all the tribes of Israel under Roman rule), followed by Samaria (Jews and Gentiles who had intermarried), then the uttermost parts of the world (the Gentiles who would be saved *through* Israel) (Acts 1:8).

The terms of salvation under the kingdom gospel required that the sinner confess his sins and do works fit for repentance. Since Israel had a *covenant relationship* with God, it had to be restored before she could be saved. For example, under both the Abrahamic and Mosaic covenants Jehovah demanded circumcision. Refusal to do so meant they were cut off from the blessings of God. Although circumcision did not save in and of itself, it did give them the *opportunity* to be saved. If a Hebrew family, at the time of Christ, was careless and failed to circumcise their male children, before these young men could be saved, the family had to *repent* and have them circumcised.

Repentance was followed by the need to *believe* on the name of Christ. That is, believe He was indeed the Messiah of Israel. Upon placing their faith in Messiah, they were required to be *water baptized* as an expression of faith. This symbolized the washing away of their sins, manifested Christ to Israel, and inducted them into the priesthood. Christ plainly taught His disciples: "He that believeth and is baptized shall be saved." That's God's divine order—no exceptions![1] Consequently, those who refused to be water baptized under the terms of this gospel are said to have *rejected* the counsel of God against themselves (Mark 1:4,5,14,15; John 20:31; Mark 16:16; John 1:31; Luke 7:29,30).

Interestingly, the Lord goes on to say: "And these signs shall follow them that believe." They were given the authority to cast out devils, speak with new tongues, heal the sick, raise the dead, forgive sins, etc. These miraculous manifestations *confirmed* the Word of God that Christ was the King of Israel who would one day establish His kingdom of righteousness upon the earth (Matt. 10:5-15; Mark 16:17-20; John 1:47-49; 20:21-23).

The commission of reconciliation: According to the revelation given to our apostle, we are living under a *new* set of marching orders. In this regard, Paul says: "By whom [Christ] we have received grace and apostleship, for obedience to the faith among all nations, for His name." Note that the Holy Spirit here emphasizes "all nations." This includes Israel. With the fall of Israel God has made all nations *equal*. Today, He is saving *individuals* out of the nations in spite of Israel. So then, the *good news of the Mystery* highlights the fact that Gentiles no longer have to be saved through Israel, nor do we render servitude to her as secondary citizens of the kingdom (Rom. 1:5; 11:11-13,32).

The terms of salvation in this dispensation have also changed. Since Gentiles were never the covenant people of God, we are not called upon to repent in relationship to salvation. Rather, we are to simply *believe* that Christ died for our sins, was buried, and rose again the third day. But what does God require of us as an expression of faith? NOTHING!!! Thus saith the Lord: "But to him that worketh *not*, but believeth on Him that justifieth the ungodly, his faith is counted for righteousness." We are saved by grace through faith alone (I Cor. 15:1-4 cf. Rom. 4:5).

As we know, water baptism was an ordinance. And all the Baptists said: Amen!! In biblical times, an ordinance was a *work* or something performed according to a particular set of standards. Today, the handwriting of ordinances has been blotted out by the finished work of Christ. What saith the Scriptures?

> "Blotting out the handwriting of ordinances that was against us, which was contrary to us, and took it out of the way, nailing it to His Cross" (Col. 2:14).

Those who place a water ceremony in conjunction with salvation under this dispensation make the Word of God of no effect. But some will cry that Christian baptism is an "outward sign of an inward work of grace" and should be performed immediately after our conversion to Christ. Actually, those who make such a claim do not have one shred of evidence to substantiate it from the Word of God. We have chosen rather to obey the command of Christ through our God-given apostle: "For Christ sent me not to baptize, but to preach the gospel" (Col. 2:14; I Cor. 1:17; 14:37).

"There is one Lord, one faith, *one baptism*" binding upon us during the administration of Grace. Thus, those who believe the gospel today, whether Jew or Gentile, are *spiritually* baptized by the Spirit into the Body of Christ. This not only identifies us with Christ's death, burial, and resurrection, but also with one another as members of His Body. This is the "one baptism" of Ephesians four. We are a new creation in Christ. Moreover, Christ is our Head who has promised us a place in His heavenly kingdom (I Cor. 12:13; II Cor. 5:16,17; II Tim. 4:18). The fact that we are no longer under law, but under grace is another unique feature of the good news of the Mystery.

THE MYSTERY OF THE GOSPEL

"And for me, that utterance may be given unto me, that I may open my mouth boldly, to make known the mystery of the gospel" (Eph. 6:19).

The mystery or secret of the gospel has to do specifically with *Calvary.* You might say that it is the heart of the Mystery. Of course, covenant theology and even some dispensationalists teach that Old Testament saints were saved by placing their faith in the coming death of Christ. This implies of course that they understood the significance of the Cross. But, once again, what saith the Scriptures?

It is true that the death, burial, and resurrection of Christ was foretold in prophecy. For example, the prophets prophesied His:

Death: "He was wounded for our transgressions, He was bruised for our iniquities: the chastisement of our peace was upon Him....He is brought as a lamb to the slaughter, and as a sheep before her shearers is dumb, so He openeth not His mouth" (Isa. 53:5,7).

Burial: "And He made His grave with the wicked, and with the rich in His death" (Isa. 53:9).

Resurrection: "For Thou wilt not leave My soul in hell [Hebrew—Sheol]; neither wilt Thou suffer Thine Holy One to see corruption" (Psa. 16:10).

Here we must be cautious not to *anticipate* revelation. That is, taking what we have received from the Apostle Paul and assuming that the prophets of old comprehended the finished work of Christ. Surely the words of Peter should set the matter to rest once and for all. "Of which salvation the prophets have inquired and searched diligently, who prophesied of the grace that should come unto you: searching *what*, or what manner of time the Spirit of Christ which was in them did signify, when it testified beforehand the sufferings of Christ, and the glory that should follow" (I Pet. 1:10,11).

The prophets are said to have "inquired and searched diligently." They saw the profound importance of the matter, but were unable to interpret the words they spoke and wrote. Consider the riddle: "Out of the eater came forth meat, and out of the strong came forth sweetness." The one to whom the riddle is given can surely ponder the words and may even venture a guess as to their meaning, but the interpretation lies solely with the one who gave the riddle.[2] The same is true of the prophecies under consideration. In fact, the prophets "inquired" or prayed for further light on these matters, but the heavens were *silent*. You see, the truth of the Cross was "to be testified in due time" through Paul's gospel.

They "searched what," that is, what the prophecies *meant* and when they would be *fulfilled*. While these holy men knew that a redeemer was to come, they didn't know who he would be, how he would redeem the nation, or when he would appear on the stage of the world. Peter continues by adding this interesting morsel of truth: "Unto whom it was revealed, that not unto themselves [the prophets], but unto us they did minister the things, which are now reported." If these prophecies regarding the Cross were not revealed to the prophets, then how can it be said that they understood the finished work of Christ, much less placed their faith in it to be saved?

Did the twelve understand about Christ's death, burial, and resurrection? Many seem to think so, but when our Lord told them that He would be put to death at the hands of evil men and rise again the third day, "they understood none of these things: and this saying was *hid* from them, neither knew they the things which were spoken" (Luke 18:34).

Obviously, the twelve couldn't have placed their faith in that which was hidden from them.

Paul is the first to reveal the *significance* of Calvary. In other words, Paul removes the veil from the Cross and shows us what God accomplished there on our behalf. That is, God was in Christ reconciling the world unto Himself. He also explains that at Calvary Christ gave Himself a ransom for the sins of the world; therefore, whosoever places their faith in His death, burial, and resurrection is freely justified by "His grace through the redemption that is in Christ Jesus."

Thanks be unto God that our sins were laid upon Him, who knew no sin, so that His righteousness might be *imputed* to us. Past, present, and future sins are forgiven on the basis of His precious blood. Hence, our old man was crucified with Christ, buried with Him in Joseph's tomb, and our new man has been raised with Him to walk in newness of life (Rom. 3:24; II Cor. 5:19-21; Eph. 1:7; I Tim. 2:4-6). This is the secret of the gospel.

May we, like the apostle, open our mouths *boldly* to make known the revelation of the Mystery and the heart of this message, which is the good news of Calvary!

THE AFFLICTIONS OF THE GOSPEL

"For which I am an ambassador in bonds; that therein I may speak boldly, as I ought to speak. But that ye also may know my affairs, and how I do, Tychicus, a beloved brother and faithful minister in the Lord, shall make known to you all things" (Eph. 6:20,21).

D. J. DeHaan tells the story of Horatio G. Spafford, an earnest Christian lawyer from Chicago, who put his wife and family on an ocean liner bound for France. In the mid-Atlantic the steamship collided with another vessel. Twelve minutes later it went down, carrying most of its crew and passengers with it. Among them were Mr. Spafford's four children. His wife, however, was rescued and taken to France with the other survivors. Immediately she cabled her husband in Chicago: "Saved-alone." The message struck him with full force and plunged him into deep sorrow. Some time later Mr. Spafford wrote the gospel song that has been sung by Christians around the world:[3]

> When peace, like a river, attendeth my way,
> When sorrows like sea billows roll—
> Whatever my lot, Thou hast taught me to say;
> It is well, it is well with my soul.

Whatever the trial, affliction or lot we may be called upon to bear, let us rejoice if by God's grace we can also say, *"It is well; it is well with my soul."*

a. Be Not Ashamed

"Be not thou therefore ashamed of the testimony of our Lord, nor of me His prisoner: but be thou partaker of the afflictions of the gospel according to the power of God" (II Tim. 1:8).

The Apostle Paul's life had such a profound impact upon the lives of the saints that it should teach us the importance of a godly example. If we are ashamed of Christ and His apostle, then it should not surprise us if those to whom we are ministering are ashamed as well. The old adage, "Do as I say, not as I do," falls under the category of poor counsel.

Although the apostle was in bonds when he wrote to the saints at Ephesus and later here to Timothy, he sought to challenge them not to be ashamed of the gospel on the basis that he himself had *boldly* proclaimed the message in the face of almost unbelievable adversity. The question naturally arises from our passage that perhaps Timothy was already struggling with this problem, as he ministered the gospel at Ephesus. While this is a possibility, we believe the tenor of Paul's words were meant to *encourage* Timothy never to be ashamed no matter how perilous the circumstances. Bear in mind there was much to fear at that time, not to mention the tendency to become discouraged.

First of all, Hymenaeus and Philetus were aggressively persuading many of the saints to accept the extreme teaching that the resurrection was past (II Tim. 2:17,18). In addition, Timothy knew in advance of this letter that all Asia (which included Ephesus) had departed from the *Mystery* which was committed to them by the Apostle Paul (Rom. 16:25; I Cor. 14:37; II Tim. 1:15). Moreover, Rome was rapidly turning against the Christians of that day; in fact many believers had already become martyrs for the cause of Christ.

The Apostle Paul knew that the best hope for the continuance of the gospel of grace was vested in Timothy. He also realized though, that there may be a temptation on Timothy's part not to speak out for fear of persecution.

By now the news that Peter had denied our Lord three times was a well-known fact. How could this be possible of the most fearless one of all of the disciples? Why, Peter was the one who had climbed out of his boat and walked on the water at our Lord's beckoning (Matt. 14:28-30). On another occasion when the Master spoke of His impending death at Jerusalem it was Peter who stepped forward and boldly said, *"Be it far from thee, Lord: this shall not be unto Thee"* (Matt. 16:21,22). In other words he was willing to fight to the death to protect the one he loved so dearly. Thus, it was Peter in Gethsemane who drew his sword in defense of Christ and cut off the right ear of Malchus, servant to the high priest (John 18:10,11).

However, after the soldiers had apprehended our Lord the disciples fled to the hills, as everything seemed to come crashing down around them. But Peter followed the soldiers and stood outside the door where the first interrogation took place. Standing by the fire warming himself he was questioned by some of those present, *"Art thou also one of His disciples?"* He denied it and said, *"I am not."* Had Peter lost track of his senses? This may seem like the case, however he had weighed the consequences carefully and decided to deny our Lord that no harm might come to him. Sadly, the fear of rejection is perhaps one of the leading causes of being ashamed when proclaiming the good news. This is one of the many devices that Satan frequently uses against the saints with amazing success.

Many capable men have succumbed to the fear of retaliation or rejection, thus the apostle warns us: *"...let him that thinketh he standeth take heed lest he fall"* (I Cor. 10:12). We too, are living in a time when some are seeking to distance themselves from the apostleship and message of Paul. Others, like Alexander the coppersmith, have resorted to various forms of intimidation to discourage believers from standing for the truth. But, what many fail to be mindful of is that *"we must all appear before the Judgment Seat of Christ"* (II Cor. 5:10). Therefore, may we encourage you to stand fast, come what may! *"For God hath not given us the spirit of fear; but of power, and of love, and of a sound mind"* (II Tim. 1:7).

b. How to Have Boldness

"For which I am an ambassador in bonds; that therein
I may speak boldly, as I ought to speak" (Eph. 6:20).

In our modern day there is a great demand for instant success. We read frequently of how many have risen to fame and fortune practically overnight. Seldom, however, do we hear of the hours of labor, practice, sacrifice, and discipline it took to build that career. Most of the time we only hear and see the end result. Many have been deceived and disillusioned to think that they can have fame and fortune with little or no effort.

In these days in which we live, the world seems to have a powerful influence over the lives of many believers. For this reason, many members of the Body of Christ are looking for that book, conference, or seminar that will be a short-cut to spiritual maturity. When it comes to our spiritual lives and having *boldness* of faith, we want instant results with little or no effort put into it. As a pastor, I would have to say that to have boldness in the faith, there must be three key ingredients.

Time: Just as physical growth takes years, spiritual growth also takes time. As we come to spiritual maturity we become more and more confident to speak out for the Lord. Focusing on ourselves causes us to fear man and be reluctant to speak out. It takes time to learn to take our eyes off ourselves and to focus on Him.

Discipline: It also takes discipline to sit down with the Word of God and study to acquire a knowledge of the Scriptures. We don't mean just reading the Bible devotionally, for it is said that we retain only about 20 percent of what we read. But, if we read and study the Scriptures, we retain about 60 percent. The better equipped you are in the Word of God, the more comfortable you will be to share the truth rightly divided.

Consistency: If we are to gain the respect of others in order to more effectively minister the gospel, we must be consistent with the truth. In short, don't sound an uncertain trumpet; be able to substantiate what you teach with the Blessed Book. Not only should we speak the truth in love consistently, we must also live the truth. Our lives are the only Bibles some men will ever see. That's why the Apostle Paul warns us to, "put away lying, [and] speak every man truth with his neighbour: for we are members one of another" (Eph. 4:25). True boldness in the faith does not come naturally, it is something we grow into as we increase in the knowledge of Him who has called us into the glorious light.

THE GOSPEL OF SALVATION

Dear sinner friend, have you trusted Christ as your personal Savior? The Word of God teaches, "The wages of sin is death!" Thus when Christ stepped across the stars into this world of sin and woe, death was powerless over Him. Christ knew no sin. He was the sinless, spotless Lamb of God; therefore death could not lay its icy grip upon the shoulder of our Lord.

Tell me then, how is it that at the end of His earthly journey He is suffering and dying in shame and disgrace? You see, Christ wasn't dying for His sins, for He knew no sin. He was dying for *your sins* and *my sins* upon that cruel tree. Our sins and iniquities were laid upon Him that He might redeem us back to God through His precious blood.

Now God turns to a lost and dying world with the good news of Calvary. Simply believe that Christ died for your sins *personally*, was buried, and rose again the third day, and God will wonderfully save you from the wrath to come according to the riches of His grace. We beg you to remember the chilling voice of those that perished in the days of Noah, *"believe, before it's too late!"*

YOU'VE GOT MAIL

"But that ye also may know my affairs, and how I do, Tychicus, a beloved brother and faithful minister in the Lord, shall make known to you all things: whom I have sent unto you for the same purpose, that ye might know our affairs, and that he might comfort your hearts" (Eph. 6:21,22).

Tychicus was one of Paul's faithful companions. He was a brother, beloved, to whom the apostle dictated this epistle due to failing eyesight.[4] In addition to being given the responsibility of hand delivering this letter, Tychicus was to give a report regarding the *affairs* of the apostle to those at Ephesus. These saints would have naturally been concerned about the aging apostle with regard to his imprisonment at Rome. Namely, were his needs being met?

Undoubtedly, Tychicus also shared that the apostle wasn't disheartened, nor were they to be discouraged over his incarceration, for the gospel was going forth into an uncharted territory. Since the Book of Philippians was written about the same time, Tychicus probably made known to them what the apostle was writing to the saints at Philippi. "But I would ye should understand, brethren, that the things which happened unto me have fallen out rather unto the *furtherance* of the gospel; so that my bonds in Christ are manifest in all the palace, and in all other places" (Phil. 1:12,13).

The apostle closes the epistle with the following benediction: "Peace be to the brethren, and love with faith, from God the Father and the Lord Jesus Christ." (Eph. 6:23). "Peace be to the brethren" could have only been said to believers. The world knows not our Savior; therefore, it will never know the peace we enjoy in Christ. The doctrines of redemption, forgiveness, peace, and deliverance from the

381

wrath to come stand as towering timbers upon which we may build our lives.

Clearly, it is impossible to exhaust the matchless grace of God. However, those who seek the truth shall find favor with the Lord. Brethren, may God give us a full assurance of understanding that we are *blessed with all spiritual blessings in heavenly places*.

"Grace be with all them that love our Lord Jesus Christ in sincerity. Amen!"

Introduction

1. C. I. Scofield, *The Old Scofield Reference Bible*, Oxford University Press, New York, New York, 1909, 1917, 1937, 1945, pg. 1252.

Chapter 1

1. For a more comprehensive study of the phrase "Lord's day" and "day of the Lord," see the author's book, *The Triumph of His Grace*, pgs. 24-26.

2. James Ussher (1581-1656): The dates ascribed are based on Ussher's dating system.

3. James S. Hewett (Ed.), *Illustrations Unlimited*, Tyndale House Publishers, Inc., Wheaton, IL, 1988, pg. 218.

4. Arno C. Gaebelein, *The Annotated Bible,* Vol. III, *Matthew to Ephesians,* Loizeaux Brothers, 1970, pgs. 234,235.

Chapter 2

1. IBM *World Book 1998 Multimedia Encyclopedia* under "canonization."

2. W. E. Vine, *Expository Dictionary of New Testament Words,* Fleming H. Revell Company, Old Tappan, NJ, 1966, pg. 226.

3. For a more comprehensive study on this subject, please see the author's book, *The Triumph of His Grace,* Chapter 3, pgs. 56,57.

Chapter 3

1. *Merriam-Webster's Collegiate Dictionary,* Electronic Edition, Version 1.2.

2. For a more comprehensive study of this subject, please consult Pastor C. R. Stam's work, *Divine Election and Human Responsibility*.

3. See *Strong's Concordance* #2602 and W. E. Vine's *Expository Dictionary of New Testament Words,* pg. 128.

4. For a more comprehensive study of the dispensation of the fullness of time, please see the author's book, *Exploring the Unsearchable Riches of Christ,* pgs. 65-70.

Chapter 4

1. Selected.

2. We do not subscribe to the heretical teaching that Christ took on the nature of Satan; therefore, He lost His Deity, which caused God the Father to desert Him.

3. Dennis J. DeHaan (Comp.), *Windows on the Word*, Baker Book House, Grand Rapids, MI, 1984, pgs. 37,38.

Chapter 5

1. J. Dwight Pentecost, *Things Which Become Sound Doctrine,* Fleming H. Revell Company, Grand Rapids, MI, 1955, pgs. 9,10.

2. James Nichols, *The Works of James Arminius, D. D.*, Volume 1, Derby, Miller and Orton, Buffalo, NY, 1853, pgs. 325-327.

3. Charles Hodge, *Commentary on the Epistle to Ephesians,* Fleming H. Revell Company, Old Tappan, NJ, pg. 119.

4. George Santayana, 1964.

5. Visit: <www.stolaf.edu/people/kchanson/templewarning.html> for additional information and to view a picture of "The Jerusalem Temple Warning Inscription."

Chapter 6

1. Charles Finney was a well-known evangelist at the turn of the century.

2. Bibliography: Vernon A. Schutz, *Three Bible Churches*, Grace Publications, Inc., Grand Rapids, MI, 1974.

3. W. Somerset Maugham.

4. Selected.

5. It should be remembered that Acts Chapter 9 marks the conversion of Paul, which begins the transition period from God's Prophetic Program to the Mystery. The Book of Hebrews on the other hand appears to be an epistle of *confirmation*, therefore, it may well form a bridge back to prophecy.

6. The reader should bear in mind that there is *approximately* a 10 percent variation between the *Majority Text* and the so-called *Textus Receptus*. Most fail to understand that the King James translators (1611) did not use the *Textus Receptus*, commonly called the *Received Text*. Elzevir completed this text in 1624 well after the translators had finished their task. We do concur, however, that the *Stephen's Text* (1550) which they did use as the basis of their translation work is very closely related.

Chapter 7

1. Billy Graham, *The Holy Spirit*, Word Books Publisher, Waco, TX, 1978, pg. 81.

Chapter 8

1. Kenneth S. Wuest, *Word Studies in the Greek New Testament*, Vol. I, Wm. B. Eerdmans Publishing Company, Grand Rapids, MI, 1983, pgs. 93,94.

2. For a more comprehensive study of the sevenfold unity of the Spirit, please consult the author's book, *Exploring the Unsearchable Riches of Christ,* pgs. 91-162.

3. Selected.

4. Since we do not have an English equivalent for the Greek word *Hades*, the translators chose to translate it "hell," hoping to convey at least a partial sense of the original meaning. However, this is confusing at best. We would have been better served if they had *transliterated* the term, as they did with the word "baptism." *Hades* is *not* the literal "hell" of the Bible. Any concordance will point out that two *different* Greek words are used to distinguish between these two realms. Although *Hades* is a place of suffering, the torment presently experienced there by unbelievers should never be confused with the eternal judgment that looms over them in the Lake of Fire.

5. There has been some discussion since the turn of the century as to whether or not the sense of the original language here is "pastors and teachers" or "pastor/teachers." Although the latter is true, we lean toward the former that these are two separate gifts. There seems to be plenty of Scriptural support for this position.

6. J. Oswald Sanders, *Spiritual Leadership*, Moody Press, Chicago, IL, 1994, pg. 18.

Chapter 9

1. Of course, this is true of those who have merely made a profession, but never really placed their faith in Christ.

2. Bibliography: Jay E. Adams, *The Christian Counselor's Manual*, Zondervan Publishing House, Grand Rapids, MI, 1973.

3. We believe that the phrases "old man" and "old nature," like "new man" and "new nature" are synonymous.

4. Ken Lawson, *The MGF Messenger*, Vol. 5, No. 3, Midwest Grace Fellowship, Kansas City, MO, 1995, pg. 7. Pastor Ken Lawson is presently the President of the *Midwest Grace Fellowship.*

Chapter 10

1. Selected.

2. Dennis J. DeHaan (Comp.), *Windows on the Word*, Baker Book House, Grand Rapids, MI, 1984, pgs. 97,98.

3. For a more comprehensive study regarding the Kingdom of God, please see the Author's book, *The Triumph of His Grace*, Chapter 11, pgs. 192-196.

4. Dennis J. DeHaan (Comp.), *Windows on the Word*, Baker Book House, Grand Rapids, MI, 1984, pgs. 170,171.

5. A. T. Robertson, *Word Pictures in the New Testament,* Vol. IV, *Epistles of Paul,* Broadman Press, Nashville, TN, 1931, pg. 544.

6. Harold K. Moulton (Ed.), *The Analytical Greek Lexicon Revised,* Zondervan Publishing House, Grand Rapids, MI, 1979, pg. 329.

Chapter 11

1. Bibliography: Robert Lewis and William Hendricks, *Rocking the Roles*, NavPress, Colorado Springs, CO, 1991.

2. Edward T. Hiscox, *The Star Book for Ministers,* Judson Press, Valley Forge, PA, pg. 207.

3. William Ross Wallace.

4. Approximately 35 million abortions have been performed in this country since the Roe vs. Wade Supreme Court decision.

5. **DISTAFF:** "A part of the spindle used in spinning wool (Prov. 31:19). The obscure Hebrew word may refer to a small disk at the bottom of the spindle used to make the wheel spin faster."

6. See Pastor Stam's *Commentary on Romans* for a more comprehensive study—pgs. 352,353.

Chapter 12

1. Catacomb: "A subterranean cemetery of galleries with recesses for tombs."

2. Pastor J. C. O'Hair. Mr. O'Hair was the pastor of the *North Shore Church* in Chicago, Illinois before his homegoing in 1958.

Chapter 13

1. Paul Lee Tan, *Encyclopedia of 7700 Illustrations*, Assurance Publishers, Rockville, MD, 1979, pg. 461.

2. Dennis J. DeHaan (Comp.), *Windows on the Word*, Baker Book House, Grand Rapids, MI, 1984, pg. 134.

Chapter 14

1. Since we wrestle not against flesh and blood, but against spiritual wickedness in heavenly places, demonic possession is uncommon today; in fact, it is rare.

Chapter 15

1. F. C. Jennings, *Satan: His Person, Work, Place and Destiny,* Publication Office "Our Hope", New York City, NY, pgs. 148,149.

2. Probably this would be equivalent to a High School education today—perhaps beyond!

Chapter 16

1. Of course, some will appeal to the thief on the Cross: He wasn't baptized! True, but if he could have come down from that tree, he would have been immediately baptized according to the law.

2. The interpretation to Samson's riddle is found in Judges 14:12-18.

3. Dennis J. DeHaan (Comp.), *Windows on the Word*, Baker Book House, Grand Rapids, MI, 1984, pg. 162.

4. Ibid., pg. 23.

Revelation (Cont'd)

The Berean Searchlight

The *Berean Searchlight* is the outgrowth of a small church bulletin containing brief weekly Bible lessons by Pastor C. R. Stam in 1940. Its publication has become the largest and most important function of the *Berean Bible Society,* reaching monthly into every state of the Union and more than 60 foreign countries.

The *Searchlight* includes in its mailing list thousands of ministers, missionaries and other Christian workers. Also, it is on display in the libraries of hundreds of Christian Colleges and Bible Institutes. The purpose of the *Berean Searchlight* is to help believers understand and enjoy the Bible, through an understanding of the Word, rightly divided.

Send for our free Bible Study Magazine
and
a full Price List of our Literature

BEREAN BIBLE SOCIETY
PO Box 756
Germantown, WI 53022-0756
(Metro Milwaukee)

Cassette Tape Recordings

By Paul M. Sadler

For Furthering Your Understanding of the Word, Rightly Divided

1. *Heaven:* This album contains four cassette tapes which describe the glories of the heavenlies.

2. *Prayer, Dispensationally Considered:* This three cassette album focuses on the prayer life of the believer in the present administration of Grace.

3. *Pretribulational Rapture of the Church:* This album contains four cassette tapes that are designed to help the child of God prepare for coming events.

4. *Understanding Dispensationalism:* This six cassette album presents all of the dispensations in clear, understandable language.

5. *Hard Sayings of St. Paul:* This two cassette album deals with some of the more difficult passages found in Paul's epistles.

6. *Dispensational Position of John's Writings:* This eight cassette album primarily focuses on where the writings of the Apostle John fit into the overall scheme of things.

7. *Revelation, A Dispensational Introduction:* This album contains three cassette tapes that are devoted to clearing up the confusion that often surrounds the early chapters of the Book of Revelation.

For a *free* Tape Catalog, simple write to:

BEREAN BIBLE SOCIETY
PO Box 756
Germantown, WI 53022
(Metro Milwaukee)

Exploring the Unsearchable Riches of Christ

The Key That Unlocks The Sacred Secret

By

Paul M. Sadler

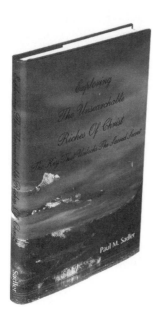

This volume takes a fresh new look at what we mean by the phrase "rightly dividing the Word of truth." The reader will find of interest that one whole chapter is devoted to *how* the ages and dispensations harmonize. *Exploring the Unsearchable Riches of Christ* guides the reader step by step through the two programs of God and includes many helpful charts, dispensational graphs and a Scripture index.

A comprehensive study in dispensational truth!

CLOTHBOUND   GOLD STAMPED   190 PAGES

Order your copy today!

BEREAN BIBLE SOCIETY
PO Box 756
Germantown, WI 53022
(Metro Milwaukee)

The Triumph of His Grace

Preparing Ourselves for the Rapture

By

Paul M. Sadler

This volume is a comprehensive study on the doctrine of the pretribulational Rapture of the Church. Midtribulationism, Pre-wrath, Posttribulationism, and the Partial Rapture theories are also thoroughly examined under the microscope of the Word, rightly divided. *The Triumph of His Grace* contains *charts, outlines, time lines,* and *numerous comparisons* to help the reader understand that the Body of Christ will be "delivered from the wrath to come."

225 PAGES

(Includes Scripture Index)

CLOTHBOUND   GOLD STAMPED

To order your copy of *The Triumph of His Grace,* simply write to:

BEREAN BIBLE SOCIETY
PO Box 756
Germantown, WI 53022
(Metro Milwaukee)

THINGS THAT DIFFER

The Fundamentals of Dispensationalism

By

Cornelius R. Stam

This volume demonstrates how the dispensational method of Bible study is the method God approves, and the only one by which the Bible makes sense. It shows the perfect harmony between the changeless principles of God and His changing dispensations. This book points out the distinctions between Prophecy and the Mystery, the kingdom of heaven and the Body of Christ, the ministries of Peter and Paul, the Rapture of believers and the revelation of Christ, the various gospels, etc. It also establishes which is our "great commission," deals with miraculous signs and water baptism, answers extreme dispensationalists, and explains the dispensational position of the Lord's Supper. *Things That Differ* provides Bible lovers with many hours of delightful Bible study and supplies pastors, Sunday School teachers, and Christian workers with ideas and subjects for hundreds of illuminating Bible messages.

(Includes Scripture Index)

CLOTHBOUND   GOLD STAMPED   293 PAGES

BEREAN BIBLE SOCIETY
PO Box 756
Germantown, WI 53022
(Metro Milwaukee)

NOTES

NOTES

NOTES